Clean and Free

A Biblical Counselor's Guide for

Understanding and Counseling

Addictive Behaviors

Ronald J. Morse, PhD

ISBN 978-1-0980-4671-2 (paperback)
ISBN 978-1-0980-4672-9 (digital)

Christian Faith Publishing, Inc.
832 Park Avenue
Meadville, PA 16335
www.christianfaithpublishing.com

Printed in the United States of America

Contents

Foreword

This book is the third revision of a work that was copyrighted way back in 1998. The original, entitled *Clean Addiction Recovery Ministry*, was an eight-session counseling ministry for inmates in the Monroe County Jail, in Rochester New York. I was, at that time, a ministry volunteer in the jail, and the chaplain asked me to develop a recovery program that could be used there. As time went on, it sort of took off and I travelled around the state giving seminars to churches and other groups on how they may use the ministry for themselves.

The first revision, written in 2001, was an expanded version of the work to be an explanation of addictive behaviors for biblical counselors, which included both part one, the eight sessions that deal with overcoming personal addiction, and part two, the restoring of a husband and father to the family and to God's design. This version has been the textbook for the ministry. So for the last twenty years or so, I have had this going but never really considered publication. Since then, the ministry has grown and there have been a number of changes, additions, rewordings, and eliminations. I remember my creative writing professor many years ago saying, "You never really write; you rewrite and rewrite."

At any rate, this is written for people who are biblical counselors or for those who are interested in understanding what addictive behaviors are, how they are manifested, and how they can be corrected. I have not used a lot of twenty-dollar words and tried to make it simple and understandable for practically anyone. The understanding or definition of addictive behaviors is clearly illustrated in the Bible, from its cause in the great fall, to the horrific consequences and the way to overcome them. Addictive behaviors are not only common to the human experience; they *are* the human experience.

I can guarantee that many people, who consider themselves fairly well-managed and in control, would not agree with the idea that they were born addicts, but that is what I believe the Scriptures tell us. It is Jesus Christ that came into this world to give us spiritual life and freedom from the idolatry of the self.

It is my hope that you will look at this with an open heart and an open mind.

Dr. Ron Morse
Aiken, South Carolina
November 2019

Acknowledgments

I must first acknowledge with all sincerity and humility, my Lord and Savior Jesus Christ, who has, by His grace and immeasurable love, saved me from a life of sin and opened my eyes and heart to His Word, and in whom I owe all things pertaining to life and happiness. It is by His grace that I have survived in this world, after years of rebellion, choosing not to retain the lie and blessings of the knowledge of Christ that I received in childhood, but in His good timing and pleasure recaptured my heart and has since directed my path. It is by His goodwill that I joyfully serve Him as a minister of the gospel and will continue to serve as He so mercifully permits, until He takes me from this mortal frame to be with Him forever in His Kingdom.

I also wish to acknowledge my beautiful wife, Cynthia, who has been ever with me, encouraging me and blessing me with her love, patient perseverance, and companionship.

Introduction

There is a crisis in America. The crisis is one of addictive behaviors. The crisis of addiction is mostly focused on the use of drugs and alcohol, but though they are in the forefront, they are not the cause of this crisis. The use of intoxicating substances is only one of the symptoms of a much deeper societal problem. In the decades of the 1960s and 1970s, there was an increase in the use of drugs for recreation or therapy that was unheard of. The popularization of the use of drugs like LSD and marijuana, followed by experimentation with PCP, peyote, psilocybin, and amanita mushrooms, particularly in the baby boomer generation and that subculture, later increased in the use of cocaine and the cheaper derivative *crack* or cocaine base. Pharmaceutical use of therapies for anxiety, depression, and chronic pain literally exploded in this new age of discovery. Powerful drugs for the treatment of these and other maladies emerged, and the development of Benzodiazepines and selective serotonin reuptake inhibitors (SSRI's) along with the promise that *help for whatever ailed you* was only a prescription away, helped the generation of a pill-popper society and a drug-related culture. The rock band The Rolling Stones produced songs in the 1960s like "Mother's Little Helper" and "19th Nervous Breakdown," which were distinctly directed at these new therapies and applied a sharply acute sarcasm of a real growing problem. In their song "Mother's Little Helper" the "little yellow pill" is Valium. In some respect, the pharmaceutical companies have sold us a bill of goods, in their marketing of drugs. The claim is that all of our problems can be simply solved by a new pill. I believe it was the DuPont chemical company's one-time slogan, "*Better living through chemistry.*" With tongue firmly planted in cheek, that is what we are promised every day on TV with some new drug. We have become a truly drug-centered society.

Today, the war is against a new trend in the pharmaceutical industry—pain management. The crisis in the overdose and misuse of opioids, particularly drugs like *Oxycontin* and *Fentanyl,* have created a national emergency that, through the increasing number of deaths related to the misuse of these drugs, has gotten the attention of the US Congress. The problem that is consistent with opioids is that they are exceedingly powerful, and when people have been prescribed these medications are no longer able to access them legally, turn to the streets, where the cheaper and more attainable heroin still reigns as the king of drugs. One of the first states to bring this into focus was New Hampshire, where the number of deaths from heroin and opioid overdose reached epidemic proportions in 2015.

In our attempts to find remedy and recovery from these epidemics, the emergence of treatment facilities, drug treatment courts, private hospitals, and dozens of other addiction recovery programs have occurred. Although millions of dollars are spent and months of therapies, the success rates of these programs is remarkably low. I remember, when I was counseling in Rochester, New York, and worked with judge Roy Wheatley King in the Rochester Drug Treatment Court, he told me, "I know who will make it and who won't." In those he said that would make it, the numbers were very low, despite the much-touted 65 percent success rate of the program. The reason for his rather prophetic judgment will be discussed a little later in this writing.

Recently, claims that addiction is a disease has been the driving force behind many of the programs that include medical treatment. Scientific studies have shown the effects of drugs on the pleasure centers of the brain and the resultant chemical changes in the brain, which causes a physical need for the continuing introduction of the substance. This change does not occur naturally, but only when that part of the brain is bombarded with the chemical that effects that change. What I mean is that a person is not born an alcoholic or dependent on heroin. You have to introduce those toxins into the body to produce the chemical effect and the following discomfort of withdrawal that produces a compulsive behavior to relieve the agony of the withdrawal. It is the "hair of the dog" and a "fix." For this reason, many have come to the conclusion that addiction is the compulsive behavior associated with the drug. Chemical dependency is not a disease, nor is it addiction. Addiction itself is not a disease, but a behavior that can *cause* disease. For example, if you drink a quart of bourbon every day, it will eventually cause disease of the liver and pancreas. A person that smokes four packs of cigarettes every day and eat tons of deep fried foods is at a much greater risk of heart disease, cancer, or emphysema, than someone who does not. Most heart disease can be prevented by a lifestyle that encourages healthy choices.

It is vitally important for us to understand the root cause of addiction if we are going to provide help for those who are suffering and for their families. As I said before, drugs and alcohol are not the cause of addiction but are symptoms of a deeper societal problem. Though they are in the forefront, addictive behaviors extend to hundreds of other areas of normal life, like food, work, money, sex, relationships, sports, recreation, education, religion, *and I could go on for hours*. There is a root of addictive behavior that is behind all of these differing expressions of the behavior. As a biblical counselor, I believe that the answer to all of this is clearly laid out for us in the Scriptures. Now, the Bible does not speak about heroin or crack cocaine, but it does speak about the human condition. It is the human condition that is at the root of addictive behaviors.

What I will attempt in the writing of this book is to uncover the root condition that can be defined as addiction and the remedy for it. Addiction is a societal malady that is as old as humanity itself, and none of us are immune to it, and it has in these last days become a vastly varied and malicious problem in America. Not all will agree with what I have to say. In fact, many will be greatly offended by the confrontational nature of the book. That is okay. That is a part of the problem! The great English journalist Malcom Muggeridge said, "The depravity of man is at once the most empirically verifiable reality but at the same time the most intellectually resisted fact."

The explanation of the root and nature of addiction will have this effect. I pray that you would read this with an open mind and an open heart, and that the truth of Christ may take hold of us all. To God be the glory!

Part 1

What Is Addiction?

Before we can get an understanding of addiction, we should probably come to understand what it is not. Addiction is not a disease; it is a behavior. It is also not a "moral failure," as we, as a society, defines what is moral and what is not. The question of morality only comes into view when the addictive behavior is associated with that which is harmful, illegal, or not accepted as part of our civilized society. The moral question typically arises with the use of alcohol or drugs, or when a behavior like gambling takes away from a person's responsibility to himself and others. Drunkards, as they used to be referred, have always been the objects of social disdain. Their lack of control over their use of alcohol has ever been regarded as weakness and immorality. It is the same with drug use, which leads to other behaviors not typically accepted as part of our social environment. Drug use often leads to crime, usually beginning with stealing money or valuable objects from family and friends. It may then lead to larceny, burglary, or even violent armed robbery. The habit needs to be filled; however, it can. These are examples of what we normally consider addiction is. We single these behaviors out because they are damaging. But there are hundreds of ways that people may be "addicted" sometimes without even knowing it. If the behaviors are not harmful to themselves or someone else, they are viewed as merely habits or peculiarities. Think about those who work themselves to death or those who overeat, or chase money, or relationships. Any activity that is pursued to attempt to fill a void in a person's life can be thought of as addiction, as it is currently understood. Addiction is not what we think it is, and it is more commonly associated with the human condition than we know or would like to admit. We are, in fact, addicted by nature. How is this so? What does it mean to be addicted?

Addiction is as common to human behavior as breathing. It is in our very nature to be addicted. *It is so because it is what we are created to do.*

Now that is a rather provocative statement. It should be obvious from it that there is a specific worldview implied. In our attempts at understanding the human condition, more particularly addictive behavior and the epidemic of that behavior we see in our world today, worldview is very important. Worldview is basically how we view the world around life, death, meaning, behavior, and destiny, according to a particular belief. The worldviews that are of import today and of our understanding for addictive behaviors and how they are defined are founded upon two different beliefs. Those beliefs are of the origin of life. There are only two possibilities in this argument and why there are only two worldviews. The first is that life is a special creation by God, and the second is that life originated by chance without the direct creation of a superior being. In other words, life either appeared on purpose or by accident. There is no other way of looking at it, and you can't logically have neither or both. That is the amazing thing about true logic; it is contradictory. Something either *is* or it *isn't*.

The Importance of Worldview

Our worldview can determine how we act and understand both our own nature and part in civilization and society. From our perspective of trying to understand and correct addictive behaviors, it is important to look at the two worldviews and their impact in our culture. Please bear with me as I go into the depths of these worldviews, as they will later make sense in our quest.

The Worldview of Special Creation

Over the last few thousand years, the consensus worldview was that man was created by God and that we are accountable to that higher authority. There is in man a desperate need to know who we are and where we came from. After years of searching for scraps of fossilized bone in the barren region of the Olduvai Gorge, Dr. Richard Leakey was asked why he did it. He said, "Because I want to know who I am and where I came from." Rick Warren, in his most popular book *The Purpose Driven Life,* asks a similar question, "Who am I, and why am I here?" That book is advertised to date the best-selling nonfiction book of all time (excepting of course the Bible itself). The reason it is so popular is that people are driven to answer those questions.

The famous Christian apologist, Dr. Ravi Zacharias, said, "There are four questions that must be answered: Origin, Meaning, Morality and Destiny."[1] These questions and the belief system that attempts to answer them is what becomes worldview. The answers to these four essential questions also help us to understand our four basic needs (which we will observe later). For the time being, we will leave the last three questions out of this part, as they all rely and follow the impact of the first question, "Where do we come from?"

In the western culture, since the spread of Christianity, the Bible is the accepted source for the explanation of that worldview. The Scriptures are remarkable in that they not only present the origin of all things, but also do so in an historical context. The history of mankind in the world, the explanation for our human condition, and the reason it is so, is unapologetically brought forth in the Bible. The Bible presents the understanding of the existence of God as assumed for the very first words. There is no question or explanation of where God came from or why He exists. It is presented as though it was already an understood fact in the human conscience. The Bible also presents humanity in all of its flaws and faults. It pulls no punches. The historical record of the Bible is extraordinary and has been proven irreproachable. The truth of its application in human life, its wisdom, beauty, and guide as a source for morality and wisdom transcends language, culture, and time. It is a book about God and His relationship with humanity. In respect to Dr. Zacharias's question on origin, the Bible introduces the origin of life and mankind with authority. We are here by the direct action of God for His purpose

---

[1]   Zacharias, Ravi. 2006. RZIM.org

and pleasure. Because of that premise, we can understand that we are also accountable to our Creator for our lives. He created man for a purpose, and the purpose of God gives life meaning.

God is glorified in worship, and worship is key to our understanding of addiction.

The Worldview of Secularism (Evolution)

In the middle of the nineteenth century a challenge to the creationist worldview arose, as was made notable by Charles Darwin. His theory purports that all life evolved over eons of time, from simple forms into the millions of forms of life we see today. To be fair for poor Charles, he was limited in his observations by the technology of his time, and the incredible complexity of life in its most basic components was unknown to him. Still, at the time of his adventure on the HMS Beagle, the world was changing. The emerging industrial machinery that began our technological advancements coincided with the new theory and seemed to add credence to his mechanical theory of the emergence of life. In the beginning of the twentieth century, technology began to explode with the invention of the internal combustion engine, which made automobiles and aircraft possible. The first and second world wars fueled these advancements into the electronic and nuclear age. This was not just a mechanical age, but also the age of "science." Darwin's theory of the "Origin of the Species and the Descent of Man" was made by a naturalist who observed the difference in the beaks and habits of finches, as well as other strange creatures, on the Galapagos Islands. The conclusions drawn from his observations were that all life arose from a single source and that different species branched off as they evolved and adapted along their own lines. Before the discovery of DNA, the theory of evolution was accepted as sound science. But even Darwin admitted that his theory was on shaky ground and depended upon the fossil record to justify it, or not. Lacking the fossil record of what would have had to be millions of transitional forms from one species to another, the fossils tell a different story. In spite of the true scientific data that makes the idea that life originated from nonliving matter mathematically impossible, the introduction of the theory of evolution is still regarded as science and taught in schools and academia as such.

At the time of the turning of the nineteenth century into the twentieth, there also arose two new ideas, which I believe were the result of Darwin's theory. The first was the political rise of socialism and communism, and the other was the art of psychology. Fostered by this new, godless theory of origin, brilliant men who rejected the idea of a God began to try to search for natural, mechanical understandings of the problems of the human mind and the explanation for the human condition or *why we do what we do.* Sigmund Freud, considered the pioneer of modern psychology, was a devout atheist, who hated religious beliefs and assaulted them in his works. In his book *The Future of an Illusion* in 1927, Freud wrote, "Religion is comparable to a childhood neurosis." His book *Civilization and Its Discontents* was published in 1930, and in which he wrote:

> The whole thing is patently infantile, so foreign to reality, that to anyone with a friendly attitude to humanity it is painful to think that the great majority of mortals will never be able to rise above this view of life. It is still more humiliating to discover how a large number of people living today, who cannot but see that this religion is not tenable, nevertheless try to defend it piece by piece in a series of pitiful rearguard actions.[2]

Psychology, in its birth, claims to be the science of studying the mind. But in its founding fathers there follows a pattern of rejection of religious ideology. Freud embraced Darwinism as true science and found it to be particularly useful in his hatred of religion.

Carl Gustav Jung followed in his mentor's footsteps as they developed psychoanalysis. He too was an atheist. In fact, all of the great contributors of psychology as a practice were either atheist or

---

[2] Cherry, Kendra. *Freud on Religion.* Psychology about.com. 2014.

agnostic. Skinner, Rogers, Adler, and even Maslow, all rejected the idea of a personal God. It is strange that the most universal phenomenon in human history is that man is irrepressibly religious, and the men who tried to understand the human condition rejected that.

It is not strange, if you accept only a mechanical view of the origin of life, that the understanding that life has more mystery and is greater than we can behold is rejected. In Paul's letter to the Corinthians he wrote:

> These things which we also speak, not in words which man's wisdom teaches but which the Holy Spirit teaches, comparing spiritual things with spiritual. But the natural man does not receive the things of the Spirit of God, for they are foolishness to him; nor can he know them because they are spiritually discerned. (1 Corinthians 2:13–14 NKJV)

Those who reject the understanding of God cannot know the things of God, because they can only be known when that person is spiritually "reborn." If you reject the gospel of Jesus Christ, you are blind to the things of God and they are foolishness to you. Now, there are many who hold to the worldview of creation and profess to have a belief in God (which is natural as it is in the heart of every person) but are not true believers. Though they hold to the religious worldview, they are still merely natural men. Those who are genuine believers cannot hold the secular worldview because it denies the existence of God. There is a difference between a person who is not a true believer and a person who denies the existence of God—what is called atheism. A more in-depth examination of this will be later.

Keil and Delitzsch, in their marvelous commentary on Psalm 14:1, "The fool hath said in his heart, there is no God," on the word fool, explain that as:

A free spirit of this class is reckoned according to the Scriptures among the empty, hollow, and devoid of mind. It is not merely practical atheism that is intended by this maxim. The heart according to Scripture language is not only the seat of volition, but also of thought. The fool is not content with acting as though there were no God, but directly denies that these is a God, i.e. a personal God.[3]

The word *fool* they also define as someone who is benighted, in moral and spiritual darkness. That is pretty strong language, but very applicable for our understanding of addictive behaviors. The person who rejects God as an atheist is the extreme, but sadly, it is said that perhaps as much as 75 percent of those who profess to be Christians, who sit in church every week, give generously to the church, and may even be involved in some ministry of the church, are not genuine believers. Though they do not fit in the same category as those who outwardly reject God, the thought of God is far from them in their practice of daily life. This type of worship, if you can call it that, is that God is not the true object of worship, but rather a means by which a person may find comfort, community, fellowship, and service. They might also find that in any of the numerous social clubs in America. In that regard, many people use religion in association with their own addictive behaviors. An explanation is coming, I promise!

Darwin's theory was also popular in the political world, as Karl Marx (who dedicated Darwin's book) developed communism and socialism. These political entities thrive in the worldview that believes life was born by mere chance and that there is no special purpose in man. Some of history's most notorious criminals were adherents to this worldview. Stalin and Mao Tse Tung between then killed between sixty and eighty million of their own people in a period of less than a quarter of a century. Hitler effectively threw an entire

---

[3] Keil & Delitzsch. *Commentary on the Old Testament. Vol. 5. Pg 126.* 1996. Hendrickson, Peabody.

world into war and was responsible for destroying over ten million people, six million of them Jews, in less than ten years. He systematically decimated over 80 percent of the European Jewish population.

As I said, the two worldviews are opposite each other and cannot coexist with each other. They logically cannot be neither or both. True logic is contrary: it is or it isn't. In these two worldviews, the belief system that defines them is whether God or chance created life. There can be no other view. It either happened on purpose or by accident.

In the early twentieth century, some theologians, alarmed at the growing popularity of the new "science" of evolution, attempted to reconcile it with the Bible through "theistic evolution," which was brought forth by Scofield and other scholars. They tried to put forth that God created life and left it to evolve over the millions of years. Neither evolutionists nor creationists embraced this and rightly so.

The importance of the emerging worldview of non-creation and its implications has much to do with the degree of addictive behaviors today. Sadly, there are those who hold the worldview of special design or the *religious* one and are still ensnared by addictive behaviors. Remember, I said that addiction is what we were created to do and is common in both worldviews.

The Importance of a Christian Worldview in Understanding Addiction

The differing worldviews can create vastly different patterns of behavior, and it is remarkable that in this increasingly secularized society those differences become more and more indistinguishable by society as a whole. However, to those who hold the worldview of creation by an Intelligent Designer, or God, the seemingly subtle changes in societal behavior are stark and troubling. The emergence of a crueler, self-centered, and materialistic society is the consequence of the rejection of the worldview of creation by design. A worldview that is based upon the idea that life and the origin and development of humankind was purely by chance through materialistic means, must by necessity question whether life has purpose or meaning beyond its natural role of individual conscience and need for a peaceful coexistence. Without the understanding that we are created for a purpose and that we are accountable to our Creator for our behavior and destiny, effectively strips away all basis for what has been regarded as truth, responsibility, punishment, and reward. For that matter, the ideas of conscience and peaceful coexistence, having their origin in the (let's call it the religious) worldview, have no other basis of origin or meaning. Essentially linked in this chain is the question of morality. Apart from the Judeo-Christian standard for morality, which is given by God in the Ten Commandments, there is not any natural source for morality. Without the limitations on behavior presented from the religious worldview, the individual can justify any and all behavior, no matter how crude, barbaric, or abhorrent. Without the constraints of the moral code there is no basis for any of the laws that hold society together. If there is no subjection to a higher accountability for our actions, what is the justification for any restraint apart from personal and individual desires?

Now certainly, there arises the argument that many primitive societies, prior to the giving of the Law of Moses on Mt. Sinai, have held many of the same principles and developed their own systems of justice and society. They also developed their own systems of religious worship too, even if the identity of the object of their worship was of their own making, it was still an authority greater than them and they subjected themselves to it. As the human family increased in the world, tribes and later nations have all instituted their own rules and rites for mutual preservation. There are, among the widely dispersed people groups in the world, similar rules or constraints regarding murder, theft, and other behaviors that do not contribute to the wellbeing of their individual societies. The laws of God have been practically placed within the hearts of men, whether or not the ultimate source of those laws is known. It is not unreasonable to suggest that this seemingly natural understanding of what is acceptable behavior all emanated from a single source. Along with that, there is the understanding that there is a higher authority from which these constraints originated, and that, no matter how differing the standards are between cultures, the belief in an unseen, spiritual intelligence is common among them all. The knowledge of God, of His existence and authority, is innately placed within the hearts of all mankind.

The greatest evidence for this is the fact that man, regardless of culture, language, or exposure to other groups, is by nature religious. There are currently over five thousand distinct religions in the world, all centered on this belief—whether the god of their focused worship is one, many, or directed toward objects that exist in nature—that there is more to life than what we see. There is something greater. There is a spiritual world, of which we know nothing about. The most common and universal beliefs all attempt to answer a simple question: "What happens to us after we die?" This belief, coupled with the understanding that there is a higher spiritual entity to which we must account, is the very basis for all religions. The morality of man and the great mystery of death drive the search for meaning and attempts to not only answer that great question, but how this spiritual authority may be appeased or served, to give assurance of a life after death. It is curious that along with the knowledge of a spiritual authority, there is also the universal belief that there is existence beyond the death of the flesh. Solomon wrote, "He has made everything beautiful in its time. Also, he has put eternity into man's heart, yet so that he cannot find out what God has done from the beginning to the end" (Ecclesiastes 3:11).

This is, without exception, the most prevalent question in the mind of mankind from the very beginning. There is no culture, or race, or tribe of people that does not have that strange concept of life beyond the death of the flesh. It is a universal understanding in mankind.

Striking the Root

The understanding of addiction is the understanding of man's religious tendencies and what makes us human. Remember, I said we were created to be "addicted." How so?

The American Standard Dictionary defines addict as: 1) tr. v. *To devote or give oneself habitually or compulsively.* 2) *To cause to become compulsively and physiologically dependent on a habit forming substance.* n. *A devoted believer or follower.*

The same source defines the word worship as: 1) n. *The reverent love and allegiance accorded to a deity, idol, or sacred object; a set of ceremonies, prayers, or other forms by which this love is expressed.* 2) *Ardent, humble devotion.* 3) v. *To honor and love as a deity, to love or pursue devotedly.*

The similarity in these definitions is the synonymous terms such as love, devotion, pursuit, and may I add one myself—*sacrifice*.

Addiction is worship. It is the natural state of man, the inherent need to be fulfilled, to find meaning and satisfy the most archaic need in human existence. We *need* to worship.

Now we know that worship is beneficial to society in general. It is a fact that people who are in the hospital and believe that they will get better through prayer, and have others pray for them, do get better at a faster rate than others. The order and governance of a peaceful society has everything to do with worship. John Adams said, "This government is established for a moral and religious people, and is wholly unsuitable for the governing of any other."

George Washington, in his farewell address, warned us that, "Of all the dispositions and habits which lead to political prosperity, religion and morality are indispensable supports. In vain would that man claim the tribute of patriotism, who should labor to subvert these great pillars of human happiness, these firmest props of the duties of men and citizens. Whatever may be conceded to the influence of refined education on minds of peculiar structure, reason and experience both forbid us to expect that national morality can prevail in exclusion of religious principle."

There is the question then that if addiction is worship, how is it that worship, in the sense of religious belief and practice, is particularly beneficial to society, the family, and to the health and wellbeing of the individual, but addiction is considered to be that which is harmful and destructive?

To answer that takes a bit of doing. First, what we consider worship, which is the religious version of that, along with the cultural norms associated with religious worship and how it has shaped our culture, laws, and societal conduct, may not be all that is different from the addiction that plagues this same society. Both are synonymous but with different results.

The answer is then that addiction, as we must understand, is worship, but that it is *wrongful* worship. The determinate factor as to whether worship is right or wrongful is the object of that worship. Addiction and addictive behaviors are not only common in the human experience—they *are* the human experience!

In order for us to fully understand what this means, we must leave the unbelieving world aside to consider the proper object of worship.

Mankind was created for a purpose—to glorify God. Frankly, there is no other reason for anyone to exist in this world apart from that. This is the only reason we are here, if you accept the idea that we are all created especially by God and that there are no accidental births. We can get that from the Scriptures:

> For you formed my inward parts; you knitted me
> together in my mother's womb. I praise you, for
> I am fearfully and wonderfully made. Wonderful
> are your works, my soul knows it very well. My
> frame was not hidden from you, when I was being
> made in secret, intricately woven in the depths of

the earth. Your eyes saw my unformed substance; in your book were written, every one of them, the days that were formed for me, when as yet there was none of them. (Psalm 139:13–16 ESV)

Before I formed you in the womb I knew you, and before you were born I consecrated you; I appointed you a prophet to the nations. (Jeremiah 1:5 ESV)

Every human being born in this world is a special creation of God for His purpose and pleasure. No matter where you are from, or what you look like, or what language you speak, you have been made by God in this time and this place for His glory.

Man was created for one purpose: to glorify God. God is glorified in worship. If that is our highest purpose, it must also be our greatest need. There is nothing else in human existence that can define the purpose of life and the meaning of life more than that. Man must, by the nature and purpose of his reason for existence, worship. This worship, of course, is to be directed to the Creator of the universe, who alone is worthy to be worshipped, and created man for that purpose.

So what went wrong? How did we, created to worship, get twisted around into false worship? Why are there so many religions in the world and why are they so different? Not only that, but what has happened to mankind in that we are plagued with wrongful worship?

We must find that answer in the Bible. The Bible tells us that we are created in the image of God, as it is written in the first book.

"Then God said, 'Let us make man in our image, after our likeness'" (Genesis 1:26).

Well, what does that mean? What is meant by the *image* or *likeness* of God? Certainly, we must consider that God is an intelligent being, with self-awareness, creativity, and displays emotions. That is all true, and we are also in that likeness. But what is the essence of the Creator God? What is His *nature*?

We learn that the greatest tenet of the Christian faith is that God is one God, in three distinct persons. He is triune. That is His nature, His essence. It is impossible to properly explain what that means; it is above us. We are carnal, finite beings, trapped in a physical world that we cannot escape or experience anything outside of it. God is not confined to a physical universe or the limitations imposed upon it. We are not omniscient—our intellect is limited. Isaiah wrote, "For my thoughts are not your thoughts, neither are your ways my ways, declares the LORD. For as the heavens are higher than the earth, so are my ways higher than your ways and my thoughts than your thoughts" (Isaiah 55:8–9 ESV).

The evidence for the triune Godhead is found in creation itself. Everything in nature is triune. For example, the smallest elemental structure in our physical universe is the atom. The hydrogen atom is the simplest of all, but in its essential structure it has one proton, one neutron, and one electron. It is a single atom but comprised of three individual particles. Every element that follows is simply a multiple of the three basic particles, with oxygen having eight of each and carbon twelve, etc. The physical universe itself is triune, being one universe comprised of space, matter, and time. They are intrinsically bound together into a singular form.

Mankind is also triune in his nature, in the likeness of God.

God	Man
F (Father)	Flesh
S (Son)	Soul
Sp (Holy Spirit)	Spirit

Our flesh is the earth suit we walk around in. It is the organic dwelling place for our soul and spirit. It grows and ages, is frail and mortal, and eventually becomes too worn out to remain inhabited. Like an old pair of shoes, we must at last discard it and step out.

Our soul is our living, sentient self. It is our personality and our life that inhabits this earth suit and is intrinsically bound to it. It is certainly a part of who we are, but not all. The flesh and soul are what makes you *you*.

Lastly, we were created with a spirit, because God is a spiritual being. The spirit connects us to our Creator.

This is how we were originally created. We were in perfect communion with God, connected to Him through our spirit to His, and were innocent and holy. Mankind, created in the likeness of God, has freewill. It is this freewill that got us into trouble.

The Bible gives a historical and philosophical accounting for the nature of mankind, from their first innocent appearance in this world until, well, *presently.* The most remarkable feature of the Scriptures is that they do not make apology for the actions of man, but rather expose them. In this, the Bible is absolutely unique in all of the religious writings of the ages because it shows mankind in all of its faults. Mankind, though created originally perfect, by his own nature is a terrible creature. No other animal on earth makes war on its neighbors or devises instruments to perform this action with increasing effect. No other creature covets, or steals, or lies to another to gain something in return. No man is alone in all of these. The nature of man is not basically "good" regardless of how we may wish to think of ourselves. If that were true, the law would not be necessary. We do not need laws prohibiting murder if it is not in our nature to do so. The same can be said for any other actions that are deemed morally abhorrent to society.

I remember my youngest daughter, when she was maybe not quite three years old, and there was on the kitchen table a plate of freshly baked cookies. I strictly told her not to touch them, because they were for after dinner. I was gone from her presence for less than three minutes to return to find that several cookies were missing. There she stood, with cookie all over her face, and I asked, "Did you eat those cookies?" To which she replied without hesitation, "No." Now I had not instructed her in the fine art of denial or deception, it just came out naturally. Another time, we were at the store and she was just little, about the same age as the cookie incident. She was walking in the aisles of the store, and I was just watching her; she was so cute. Suddenly she stopped, staring at something on one of the shelves. I was curious as to what she was doing. Then, in a moment, she looked one way, then the other, and then when the coast was clear began stuffing fruit rollups down the front of her pants! My god! I was shocked! She is a thief! This is just the nature of man. Where did this come from?

This nature, the Bible explains in beautifully poetic language, came about when the first man and woman disobeyed the direct command of God not to eat of the fruit of the tree in the middle of the garden—the tree of the knowledge of good and evil. Up to this point, man was innocent. Now I don't believe there was anything magical or special about the fruit of this particular tree, it was merely forbidden. The story shows that man, given freewill by God to act independently with responsibility, failed. The knowledge of good and evil came the moment they ate of the fruit. The realization that they had disobeyed that which was directed them not to do gave them this knowledge. Obedience was good; disobedience evil. From that point the nature of man clearly goes downhill. The separation that all men have, over history, tries to restore by their own will occurred because imperfection was introduced into the world, and God, who is perfect, will not permit imperfection to stand before Him. Well, those are His rules, not ours, which is good by the way. The Bible tells us, "And the LORD God commanded the man, saying, 'Of every tree of the garden you may freely eat; but of the tree of the knowledge of good and evil you shall not eat, for the day that you eat of it you shall surely die'" (Genesis 2:16–17).

The death that is spoken of is separation from God, the spiritual death. Now certainly Adam and Eve did eventually die physically, but not on that day. Their death was of the spirit that connected man to his heavenly Father. That death of the spirit became the inheritance for all of their descendants forever. If you have a human father, the curse placed upon Adam is also upon you. We are unclean before a holy God and cannot stand before Him. This is perhaps the most terrible thing to accept. We will not be judged at the end of our life, on some great cosmic scale, where our good deeds and bad deeds will be weighed, and hopefully, the good outweighs the bad and God says, "Okay, come on in!" No, friend, we have already been judged, found guilty, and sentenced to be separated from God forever. That is the natural state of man. The spirit that once connected us to God has been severed, and there is nothing that we can do to reattach it. We cannot make a dead thing come back to life, no matter how hard we desire it or try. We, who are imperfect, cannot make ourselves perfect. As Job said, "Who can bring a clean thing out of an unclean? Not one" (Job 14:4 KJV).

The spirit that connected us to God is dead. We can neither discern nor know the things of the spirit of God for they are spiritually discerned. If we are spiritually dead to God, we cannot know Him. How can we know this? The epistle of Paul to the Ephesians helps us to understand this. I particularly like the way it is worded in the New Living Translation:

> Once you were dead, doomed forever because of your many sins. You used to live just like the rest of the world, full of sin, obeying Satan, the mighty prince of the power of the air. He is the spirit at work in the hearts of those who refuse to obey God. All of us used to live that way, following the passions and desires of our evil nature. We were born with an evil nature, and we were under God's anger just like everyone else. (Ephesians 2:1–3 NLT)

The question that a person would ask is, "What do you mean 'I was dead!' What part of me was dead? My body is and always has been alive, and I can certainly walk and talk and think and act freely. What do you mean I was dead?"

The only answer to that is that the spirit, which connected us to God, is dead. We are like three cylinder engines firing on only two cylinders. We know that there is something missing, but we cannot discern what it is because it has always been missing, from our birth.

It is like a person who is born without eyes. All of his life, what he experienced with his other senses of taste, touch, smell, and hearing, would be considered all there was to experience. Having never seen, he would never know what it is to have eyes or to see. Not until someone, who clearly has eyes, says to him, "Isn't the sky a beautiful blue today?" To him, the color blue, or any other color, would be completely unknown and unknowable to him. He might think the other person was speaking gibberish. It would be foolishness to him. However, if a number of people began to tell him that there was more to experience than he knew, he would either reject it or begin to wonder if there was truly something more to experience that he could not nor ever had experienced. This would leave a gnawing doubt and perhaps a desire to experience something he never had. Spiritually, we were all "born without eyes." All that we could experience in this world is not all there is to experience. Because we are spiritually dead, we could never know what it is to be connected to and have a relationship with the God who made us.

We can never know God, but we have the knowledge that there is a God encoded within us. We *know* there is a God, but we can't know Him, because He is spirit. To be left in this condition would be considered cruel, but God did not intend for us to be left this way. He sent a Savior into the world to give us eyes to see.

The natural man cannot know the things of God, for they are spiritually discerned. Now, couple that with the greatest need, the need to worship, and that is the root of addiction. Until we are spiritually reborn, we can't worship as we were intended to worship. A gaping hole is in our innermost being that we don't know how to fill. We are incomplete. Because our greatest need is not met, and we have no understanding how or even the ability to remedy it, our worship is turned inward and we seek to find ways to obtain fulfillment and wholeness in the things that we can experience and know. Unfortunately, there is nothing in this world that can fulfill that need, because only a relationship with God can do it and make us complete. All of our worldly pursuits are attempts to fill that hole with things that cannot achieve it. We go to drugs, alcohol, food, sex, relationships, work, money, sports, activity, arts, and a million other ways we seek to find out who we are, where we belong, and what will give us fulfillment, love, and peace.

Why Are Addictive Behaviors so Prevalent Now in This Generation?

This, particularly in the western cultures, is a sociological phenomenon that continues to grow. After the Great Depression and the Second World War, a generation of people that came out of that horrific struggle began to find prosperity in this land and others. With this newfound prosperity came a drive toward materialism, and with that, a desire to take life a little less seriously. The emergence of a powerful middle-class fueled suburban expansion. "Keeping up with the Joneses" and a desire to have more and better things took hold of American life. More time was spent in leisure activities, and there was a surge in "family building" that lasted through the decades of the 1950s and 1960s. Those who suffered and were deprived of so much during the 1930s and 1940s wanted more for their own children, and the baby boomers did not lack for anything. At this same time, the religious and moral character of the west declined. Citizens began questioning the role of Christianity in the nation, and the *separation of church and state* was redefined in our nation's courts. So much of the common faith of our forefathers was stripped from public life, out of our schools and government, that sociologists declared this as the "Post Christian Era." The cost for this has been enormous. Once you remove the supreme authority for what is right and wrong, what is moral and immoral, you have no basis to judge any actions that were previously abhorrent to society. An example of that is gay marriage. Prior to this generation, the idea that two men or two women could be legally married was ridiculous. When this issue was taken to the Supreme Court, they could not judge it to be a moral question because the authority for that moral stand has been stricken from society. We kicked God out. Man has become the source for determining what is right and wrong. If we no longer subject ourselves to God's laws, or what may also be called *natural laws,* we will be either subject to someone else's law, or be a law to ourselves, with whatever the individual determines what is right and wrong, what is true and false. The rejection of God's law, or natural law, and the authority of God, leaves only someone else's law, which produces tyranny, or your own law, which produces anarchy. It is in this environment that man, who has an innate need to worship, and that worship is not directed toward God, turns it inward to the self. Even in the first century, the apostle Paul warned of this.

> But understand this, that in the last days there will come times of difficulty. For people will be lovers of self, lovers of money, proud, arrogant, abusive, disobedient to their parents, ungrateful, unholy, heartless, unappeasable, slanderous, without self-control, brutal, not loving good, treacherous, reckless, swollen with conceit, lovers of pleasure rather than lovers of God, having the appearance of godliness but denying its power. (2 Timothy 3:1–5 ESV)

I know that practically every generation since he wrote this has pointed the finger at the next generation with utmost sincerity, and as a confirmation of the "last days." My parents pointed at us with the same judgment, and we have as well. The sad thing is that it is mostly true, and each generation in turn gets worse. In this "post-Christian" era, it has become remarkably so. This is the reason for the crisis that we face today. We have generations of a society that is "all about me."

It's All about Me

One of the more interesting problems associated with addictive behaviors is the confusion of chemical dependency with addiction. As I mentioned before, addiction is worship and not chemical dependency. A person is not *addicted* to heroin, but *chemically dependent* to it. There is a difference. The addiction is to the self, and the substance is the altar where the self is worshipped. In the case of certain substances, they not only relieve pain, both physical and psychological, or create a sense of euphoria, but also alter the delicate balance of the chemistry of the body and brain. The introduction of these substances for the reason of pleasure or recreation, repeated, creates a change in chemistry that, when it is no longer available, makes a great deal of discomfort. Anyone who has struggled with opioids can attest to that. It is very hard to come off of them. The process by which the body works to get back to its normal state can be painful. People coming off of these powerful drugs can be physically sick, vomiting, shaking, sweating, and even flopping around like a fish out of water. The nerves and muscles react violently to this sudden change. However, once the chemistry is back to normal and the effects of the substance are gone, the struggle ends. You are no longer bound to it. It is the same with alcohol, tobacco, and hundreds of other substances that we willingly invade our bodies with. It is so hard to quit smoking. The effect of nicotine deprivation can make us nervous, grouchy, and very uncomfortable. Even caffeine, which for so many of us is a morning ritual, if missed, produces a splitting headache. A single cup of coffee will alleviate that headache in a jiffy.

What about other addictive behaviors? What about relation-ships, or the lust for money, or work, or other activities? They are not substances that alter the chemistry of the body. They can excite the pleasure centers of the brain, and we like that. But we are not physi-cally bound to them, like heroin or caffeine.

All of these behaviors are pursued in an attempt to fill a void, a need, that otherwise cannot be filled. This void, of course, is the spiritual void—our need to be connected to the living God. Because we are spiritually dead in our natural state, it is impossible to make this connection. Man has, through the ages, made every attempt to breach this gap, this longing to be connected to God. That is what religion is: man's attempt to reconnect with God. The root of the word religion is the Latin word *lige*, which means "connect." It is where the word ligament comes from. *Re-lige* means to reconnect. That is what religions desperately try to do. Unfortunately, man's attempts at reconnection all fail. They must. Man does not make the rules by which God must accept him. God is God, and He makes the rules. The idea that through some practice or ritual, or behavior, or whatever will qualify us to acceptability with God is error. Cain, the son of Adam, introduced the first attempt at religion into the world.

> In the course of time Cain brought to the LORD an offering of the fruit of the ground. And Abel also brought of the firstborn of his flock and of their fat portions. And the LORD had regard for Abel and his offering, but for Cain and his offering he had no regard. So Cain was very angry, and his face fell. The LORD said to Cain, "Why are you angry, and why has your face fallen? If you do well, will you not be accepted? And if you do not do well, sin is crouching at the door." (Genesis 4:3–7a ESV)

The LORD said to Cain, "If you do well." Doing well was what Abel did. He offered a life. This would be atonement for sin through a burnt offering before the LORD. It is apparent that Adam instructed his children regarding their sin and the penalty. When Adam and Eve were driven out of the garden of Eden, they were no longer naked but covered with animal skins. The animals did not have zippers. They were the first things in creation to die. The covering of their sin was accomplished in the death of the animals, with the skins literally covering their bodies. It is interesting to note that the word in the KJV that is translated as "naked" is the Hebrew word *orum.* The word means literally "to be exposed" or to be "shamefully exposed." It also means naked and guilty by the way. When Adam and Eve were created, they were "naked" and exposed to God, but they had no shame, because they were innocent. After they ate of the forbidden fruit they tried to hide themselves because they were exposed in shame. I find it amusing that they supposedly "made aprons" out of leaves. Their shame was not in their sexuality; they knew they were different and unique. They saw every other kind of animal in the world of two sexes. The LORD commanded them to be fruitful and multiply before they ate the fruit, so I am quite certain they understood what He meant. No, when they had sinned against God and were "exposed," they, like children would, hid under leafy bushes to hide from God's gaze. When God called Adam out, he told the LORD that he was afraid because he was naked. God said, "Who told you that you were naked?" Like a parent questioning a child when it is completely obvious Daddy knows the truth, God made Adam account for himself. It is after this, that God covered them with the skins and drove them out of the garden. It is also reasonable to believe that Adam conveyed this story to his sons. Abel was obedient and offered to God what He demanded—a life. The gravity of sin is to be understood this way. Cain offered what he thought the LORD would accept, without regard to the proper requirement of God. He wanted to do it *his* way, rather than what God required. Now Cain could have gone to his brother, traded his goods for a lamb, and offer to God what was right. But he did not do well. It is wonderful how God spoke to him, asking him why he was angry. God offered Cain another chance to do right, but he refused. What happened after that is a testimonial of man's fallen nature. He murdered his brother. I can imagine Cain, in his bitter anger, saying to his heart, "You want a blood offering, I will give you one!" The word in Hebrew that is translated in the King James as "slew" is the word *hawrag*. It is an ugly sounding word for an ugly act. It is only used in the Torah in one other place, and that is in the preparing of the lamb for sacrifice. It was the priestly act of slitting the lamb's neck and draining out the blood. The first man born into this world murdered his younger brother in a most horrific way, because he couldn't get his own way.

The early part of the book of Genesis can teach us some really amazing things about human nature. In the beginning, when man was created in the world, he was innocent and perfect. He was spiritually alive and connected to the God who made him. It was the same with the woman that God brought to Adam. The reason for their fall was not merely the act of disobedience by eating the forbidden fruit, but for the temptation behind the act.

> So when the woman saw that the tree was good for food, and that it was a delight to the eyes, and that the tree was to be *desired to make one wise*, she took of its fruit and ate, and she also gave some to her husband, who was with her, and he ate. (Genesis 2:6 ESV; italics added)

The words in italics are it. The serpent tempted Eve to eat of the fruit because it would make her like God. The temptation was not so much the knowledge of good and evil, but that it would make them like God and become gods themselves. This desire to be equal with the Most High God was also shared with Satan, which was the reason for his fall. Since then, the desire of man is to be in charge, to be his own god. The history of mankind is one of conflict, oppression, and dominance. It is about power and glory.

The baby boomers grew out of their "hippie" clothes and began sporting their "yuppie" suits. The "young urban professionals" were poster children for a society that was "looking out for number one." It was a time of greed and one-ups-manship. It was no longer just keeping up with the Joneses, but outdoing them. Money and power was what it was all about. The previous generation, "the greatest generation" as it was known, who sacrificed so much and vowed to never go through want again, spawned a generation of self-consumed materialists. One of the funniest shows on TV during the 1990s was *Seinfeld,* a show about nothing but the interaction of six totally self-consumed people. We laughed at the absurdity of it, but it also stung a little. It has been often said that "art imitates life," and this show was a good example of it.

We have become inundated with self-help, self-survival, self-aid, self-employment, and scores of other "self" related things. Our greatest interest is to take care of me, to make sure that I get everything that I want, and feel I deserve. Nothing much else matters.

We are driven by a great need, to be complete again—to be spiritually alive and connected to God. The need to be whole, complete, and fulfilled, is created by our spiritual poverty, and because we cannot fulfill that spiritual need, nor even discern how to fulfill it, we turn to the things of this world to find that fulfillment. The idol of our worship is the self—the worst form of idolatry. It is all about me. The substances, behaviors, and objects we turn to in hopes of finding fulfillment are the altars where we go to worship ourselves.

Altars of Worship

As I mentioned before, addictive behaviors are common in every person born in this world, whether they are directed to drug use, gambling, relationships, work, money, sports, activities, food, or whatever. Also, we have noted that addiction is worship, so addictive behaviors are actually *worshipful* behaviors. The object of that worship is the self, though it would be strongly denied by most. Man has always had a blind eye to his own depravity and failures. We have "more excuses than Carter has pills!" as my mother used to say. Man will always seek to justify his own behaviors and judge himself as being better than what is true. The idol of our worship is the self, and all of the worshipful behaviors associated with that are merely the altars where we go to worship ourselves.

As you may imagine, there are multitudes of ways, or altars, by which this worship is practiced. Any behavior that is motivated by a need to fill that void, to find meaning or fulfillment, pleasure or self-satisfaction, is an altar of this worship.

For the time being we will not look at the obvious, destructive behaviors that can easily be associated with the egocentricity of self-worship. Let's start with some hard ones to swallow.

The Altar of Religion

There are over five thousand distinct religions in the world today. The "classical" religions make up the greatest adherers, but there are hundreds of sects, schisms, and cults that, springing from them, form distinctions of their own. The classical religions are Christianity, Buddhism, Islam, Hinduism, and Judaism, in order of the number of adherents. Of these, Judaism, Christianity, and Islam are monotheistic, meaning belief in one God. Hinduism, much like the ancient pagan religions and mythologies of Greece, Rome, and the Nordic and Celtic pantheons, has many gods. Buddhism is an offshoot of Hinduism, which is similar in some tenets but rejects the pantheon of gods. In each of these religions are sects and denominations, each holding their own special rules for practice and adherence. The newest and quickly growing religion is atheism, the favorite of such influences as communism, socialism, antinomianism, and anarchy. Without laboring through all of the five thousand religions, we will stick to the classics and discover some troubling things about the adherers of them and why they have such a strong influence.

There is perhaps enough information that has been gathered over the millennia that points to all religions emanating from the same source. One example of this is the shared story of the flood, which, barring some minor inconsistencies, are quite similar. There are seventeen different variations of the story as told by as many cultures and peoples that had no contact with each other in the ancient world. Though there are differences, the idea that at one time a flood devastated the world and one man with a boat saved the animals runs consistently in each narrative. It is one of the most universally shared stories in the world. Another, related to it, is the time of the dead. The origins of Halloween in Europe and America, the Day of the Dead in Mexico, and many other ancient celebrations all depict a time when there was a great tragedy, and many people died. Even the Persian month of November is *Mordad* or the *time of the dead*. It is strange that at the same time every year, in so many cultures, removed from each other, that there is a remembrance for the dead. The Celts in Britain held a ceremony on the first of November, where the people mourned and a ceremonial sort of shrine was burned. A new one would be built, signifying the renewal of the earth after the tragedy, and the ritual around it so somber, that, in the ritual of carrying the materials to rebuild the shrine, if you dropped something it cost your life.

The Bible gives a rather detailed account of the flood, with a genealogy of the people involved from the first man Adam to Noah. Prior to the invention of the written word, histories of people were passed down in an oral tradition from one generation to the other, and the Bible is no exception. Genesis tells the story of the flood, with the names of the survivors and their continuing history. It tells how the tribes of men separated from each other, the introduction of new languages, and where they travelled. An interesting book, *After the Flood* by Bill Cooper, claims that he can trace the ancestry of some of Europe's royal houses back to Noah through direct genealogies. If so, it is plausible that all of today's many peoples are directly descended from three individuals: Shem, Ham, and Japheth—the sons of Noah. If all of the races and tribes of the world did so, then it is equally plausible to believe that the same stories would have been passed down from generation to generation, giving an explanation for the universal flood sagas and such. From these oral histories, the emergence of the varied religions must have also taken root. Religion is the most uniquely universal phenomenon of human history.

Also unique is that almost entirely every religion in the world is based upon the idea that man, through the obedience of rituals, sacrifices, laws, doctrines or superstitions, can appease his God or gods and win the acceptance of said deity into their heavenly presence. The other uniquely human part of this is that man, through his religious fervor, can merit the reward of eternal blessing. This means that man cannot only earn his right into the glories of eternity, but that the deity he worships is obliged to reward such merit. This is the works-based religion that justifies man in spite of his nature or wrongful actions.

This works-based practice is so common that many believe that when they leave this world, there is some great, cosmic scale upon which is balanced all good and bed behaviors, and that the good (without exception) outweighs the bad, and that merits acceptance. God is obliged to honor the good over the bad and reward us with eternal life. This works-based justification is found even in many who profess Christianity. In this way of thinking then, *man* determines what God must deem as acceptable, giving man authority even over his chosen deity. This is not a true worship of God, but of man, and it is a great deceit.

In the classical religions of Hinduism and Buddhism are the tenets of Karma and Samsara. It is rather complicated, but they are connected to each other. Karma is what happens to you in this life because of actions done in a previous life, plus, what you do in this life will affect your position in the next. Samsara is the belief in reincarnation, which is that there is an unending cycle of birth-death-re-birth, until total awareness is achieved, where the soul (in Hinduism) is welcomed into the realm of the gods, or Nirvana. In Buddhism, the cycle of reincarnation ends when total awareness is achieved and the soul is released into nothingness, or what is known as nihilism. This, of course, depends on which sect of Buddhism you adhere to. There is no god in Buddhism. Karma is the system of works that determines where in the endless cycle you are. In Hinduism, this creates the caste system, whereby if you are poor, destitute, or sick, or crippled, it is because of karma. You are in that state because that is what you have put on yourself from the deeds of your previous life. Also, if you are born into a good family, with money, opportunity, and the like, it is also because of karma. A person is always conscious of their karmic state and would do nothing to potentially cause it to slide backward into a more miserable new life. It creates a dispassion for suffering and is, in my opinion, a totally hopeless belief system.

In Islam, the five pillars must be perfectly adhered to in order to appease an angry god (Allah). The five pillars are: 1) testimony of faith (There is only one God and Muhammad is his prophet.); 2) prayer (must be done five times daily toward Mecca); 3) giving (contributing to the needs of the poor); 4) fasting during the month of Ramadan; 5) pilgrimage to Mecca (the Haj is required once in a person's lifetime). The pilgrimage involves going to the Kabal, where inside is the "Moon stone." Pilgrims march or dance around the Kabal seven times, then go to a nearby wadi and throw stones at the devil. This practice and the Kabal long predate Islam. Prior to that, images of pagan gods were in the Kabal, until Muhammad, who worshipped the moon god, changed it. The only way a person can appease Allah and go to heaven is to fulfill the five pillars. In some, more radical teachings of Islam, self-sacrifice in the cause of the faith, which is to die in the process of killing infidels, assures a place in heaven—sometimes with the reward of seventy virgins as wives. This is not what is considered "mainstream" Islam.

In Judaism, it is the observance of the Laws of Moses, which must be perfectly adhered to. There are more than the Ten Commandments in Judaism—there are 613. Many of the laws laid out in Judaism are ceremonial, intended for the priest's service to God. There are three division in the Law: the moral code, what is better known as the Ten Commandments; the ceremonial code, which is for the priest's service in the tabernacle (later temple); and the civil code, which is for daily conduct of the people. The laws were a burden too heavy for any man to bear, and many of them were forgotten. When the temple was destroyed in AD 70 and the Israelites scattered all over the world, the ceremonial codes of the priesthood, for a great part, disappeared as well. What took its place were traditions. The traditions passed down from generation to generation, though not the law strictly, became the religion of the Jews. Judaism, like most other of the classical religions, is also segmented into groups differing in the interpretation of orthodoxy and observances.

In Christianity, with the emergence of the Roman Church in the fourth century, traditions and church law became more important than the Scriptures, which were mysterious to those outside of the most learned. The Bible was rare and very costly to copy. In the Roman Church, the Latin Vulgate was the version used, and any other was prohibited. Also, the interpretation of the Scriptures was at that time an allegory, which made it impossible to understand. The Dark Ages introduced many false teachings into the church. In the first two centuries of her history, the Gnostics were a plague to the apostolic faith. Later, in an effort to bring more people under the arms of the church, pagan influences and abuses crept in. The doctrine of salvation by grace was replaced with the doctrine that salvation came through the church. The doctrine of *excathedra* explained that the church and baptism in the church was the means to salvation. In other words, you had to be in the church to be saved. It is interesting that the Bible clearly teaches just the opposite—that you had to be saved to be in the church. The church had become the instrument for salvation, and outside of the church you could not be saved.

What had been the apostolic, biblical faith appeared to have been lost in the traditions and edicts of the powerful Roman Church. The common folk could never obtain a precious copy of the Holy Scriptures, nor did they understand Latin. Over time, the church became a strong political force in the world, seeking to control the great populations of the wild lands and gather them into the fold of the church. Though the Roman Church was not the only Christian influence or sect in existence at that time, it was the most powerful. All who opposed the church's particular brand of faith were brutally persecuted, burned, or hung. When the church became the instrument for salvation, many abuses and false doctrines—doctrines of a works-based religion, like baptism in the church for salvation, the mass, Mariolatry, the worship of saints and graven images, transubstantiation, purgatory, indulgences, and infant baptism—emerged. The Reformation changed much of that, returning the Scriptures to their proper place of authority and reverence. Martin Luther, following in the footsteps of Wycliffe, translated the Hebrew and Greek texts into the common language of the German people. This presented a new problem: how to interpret what was written. Luther insisted that each word should stand in its own natural meaning, and that the Bible was written for common man and not just for the elite. Luther wrote on this: "*Unum, simplicem, germanum, et certin sensum literalum*" (One, simple, germane and of a certain sense literal interpretation). The Reformation was fueled by the invention of the printing press, the translation of the Bible into the common languages, and a return to a literal interpretation of the Scriptures. Still, the yearning for people to *earn* salvation through works survives to this day because it is man's nature. The Bible clearly teaches otherwise, and Christianity to this day is the only religion that rebukes this natural tendency of man,

The Bible speaks very bluntly about the human condition and the problem of justification by works.

"None is righteous, no, not one; no one understands; no one seeks for God. All have turned aside; together they have become worthless; no one does good, not even one" (Romans 3:10b–12).

In this verse and many others, the Bible convicts all people under sin. Sin is the result of man's fallen nature and a blemish of uncleanness or imperfection before a holy God. The just penalty for sin is separation from God forever, death, both spiritual and physical, as stated previously. This imperfection cannot be undone by any human effort, as is written in Job: "Who can bring a clean thing out of an unclean? Not one" (Job 14:4).

God, not man, can only remedy the hopeless state of man. The penalty for sin is death, and without the shedding of blood there is no remittance. This is God's law, not man's. In the Law of Moses, the Jews were made to understand the calamity of their sin and were permitted to offer a substitute, a lamb, to *cover* their unintentional sins. It was a picture of the Lamb of God, the Lord Jesus Christ, who is full God and fully man, who would offer Himself to pay for the sins of the world. The Jews knew that the violent and bloody sacrifices they made were insufficient to pay for their sin and feared the judgment of God. The great tenet of the Christian faith is that Christ is the promised Messiah, who would, through His death, make full payment for the sin of all who would only believe. This is not a work, but a belief in God's promise that justifies.

As long as a person views religion as a means by which through acts of obedience, good works, efforts, charity, or sacrifices, his God must or even will accept him, it is a vain religion. The religion becomes only an altar where he worships himself. This includes *all* of the classical religions: Hinduism, Sikhism, Buddhism, Islam, Judaism, and even most of what is practiced as Christianity.

George Barna, who keeps track of these sorts of things, estimates that less than 20 percent of self-identifying Christians are fully committed to their spiritual development. That is a staggering statistic![4] Jesus's parable of the sower, found in the Gospel of Matthew, speaks of seed that is received by four types of soil. The soil, He later explains, is the heart of those who receive the word with "gladness." The difficult part is that only one of the four who received the word bore fruit. Does this coincide with what Barna's work concludes? In

---

[4] Barna, George. *Maximum Faith.* 2011. Metaformation. Redding.

my humble opinion, I believe so. So what does this mean? Could this imply that perhaps 75 percent of those good folks who go to church every Sunday, sing in the choir, maybe even teach Sunday school, are not true Christians? Perhaps. This would be a tough thing to preach on and would cause a lot of resistance among those we could call *marginal Christians.*

In their eyes, they profess to be genuine and would be very angry with anyone who would dispute that. For many, however, maybe their knowledge of the faith is only "head knowledge." They know the stories, believe that Jesus is the Savior of the world, but have never fully embraced what it means to be "born again." The church is a great comfort, a source of fellowship and belonging, and a place to learn how to treat each other, but they fall short of saving faith. How many "faithful" Christians worship God on Sunday but come Monday, He is far from them in thought and deed? The cares of this world and the search for pleasure, rest, and retirement drive their every thought and action until they go back to church on Sunday and redeem themselves from a self-seeking week. Ouch! There is a huge distinction between people that *add* Jesus to their life and those who have Jesus *as* their life.

A great example of this is what they believe the Christmas season is all about. For many in the church, it is a time for family, for giving, for sharing, and for loving each other. Those are all wonderful things to be sure, but that is not what Christmas is about at all. It has nothing to do with decorations or presents, about goodwill toward men. It is about God making peace with men who have declared war on God, who live their lives fulfilling every desire of their own hearts. God has extended His goodwill toward men, that while we were yet His enemies, He gave His Son to die for us. That is what it is about.

This is a rather harsh judgment, but consider please those who profess to be Christians, *where is the fruit of their faith?* How many professors of the faith actually dare to share their faith with others? Jesus told a parable of the unjust steward who was given a great treasure, but he was afraid of his master, so he buried it in his backyard. When his master returned from his journey, he dug it up and returned every coin of it to him. His master was furious, because he did not invest the treasure he was given to increase it, so that he could present it doubled or more to his master. In the end he was bound hand and foot and cast into the outer darkness. The great treasure we have been given is the gospel, and we are not to keep it buried in our own hearts but to invest it into the world around us, sharing it with all who will hear it. It is peculiar that there are people in the church that are always very critical of either how the pastor preaches, or what the music is like, or the colors of the carpet and drapes, but never give of themselves to build the ministry. It is commonly complained in churches that 95 percent of the work is done by 5 percent of the congregation. I don't know how many times I have counseled people who have left their church because they claimed they "weren't being fed." That is so dishonest. If you go to church because you like the particular style of music, or that it is entertaining, or simply because you seek to be emotionally uplifted, and do little or nothing to encourage or serve in the church, or because you go to church to be inspired, forgiven, or seen, chances are good that church is there only to serve you and fulfill your needs. It is one of many altars where we go to worship ourselves. It is about what *I* want; it is all about *me*.

The Altar of Relationships

We are social animals. Relationships with people, particularly those that are romantic, the kind that lead to marriage and family, are a necessary part of our lives. It fulfills one of the four basic needs (we will get into them specifically later), which is to love and be loved, to belong and have companionship. Since the very beginning of time, God intended for us to have deeply committed relationships. The first chapters of the Bible tell us that God created all things. He created the heavens and the earth, the seas and land, and all that is on it. In all of the things that were made, He declared them to be "good." Now God cannot make anything bad—in fact everything made was perfect—so the "good" does not mean in a qualitative sense but that it was in perfect accordance with His will. The first thing that is not good is that the man should be alone.

"And the LORD God said, 'It is not good that man should be alone; I will make him a helper comparable to him'" (Genesis 2:18).

Immediately after that God brought all of the animals to Adam so that he could name them. For each animal there was a male and a female, which caused him to wonder, "Where is my counterpart?" God intended to bring a partner for the man, but the man had to understand his need for one and desire for one. When God presents the woman to him, he says, "This is now bone of *my* bone, and flesh of *my* flesh; she shall be called Woman, because she was taken out of Man" (Genesis 2:23).

This was a partner for him, perfect for him. It was not a monkey, or a bird, or a dog—it was human like him and comparable to him yet different.

"Therefore a man shall leave his father and mother and be joined to his wife, and they shall become one flesh. And they were both naked, the man and the wife, and were not ashamed" (Genesis 2:24–25).

The need for relationships is beautifully established in these verses, placed into the heart of man by God, and fulfilled by the woman. They were not alone, but together. They complimented each other—what the one had the other needed, and what the other had, the other needed. It was perfect. Nothing has changed since then.

I have married many couples over the last few years, and I have always found it amusing as we went through premarital counseling that the woman always hopes that her husband will change, and the man always hopes that she won't, and they are always disappointed! Well, maybe not so, but isn't that life and the joy and struggle of relationships?

Relationships extend far beyond the marriage of man and woman. There are families, and clans, tribes, villages, and nations. The social order of man grew out of necessity, for survival, and apart from the desire to bump off a competing tribe, and how that has never left us (even after world wars) has been a wonderful thing. Cultures and languages, governments and order, have created a beautiful mosaic of human life in this world. Relationships are nearly as essential to human existence as worship.

The problems in relationships happen because of the self. How many have heard the exhortative warning to leave someone because "he is just using you?" People get into relationships for selfish reasons, and the wants of the self can cause terrible problems. If a person is not a believer and his worship is not directed at the true and living God, then the self rules. Two people, both ruled by self, can compromise for the sake of love and need. This is what holds them together—the willingness to compromise some of what they want for the greater thing that they want or need. Elizabeth Elliot, a renowned author and speaker, once said, "It is a miracle that two people can live together for two weeks without killing each other." That was meant to be humorous and to point out the struggle we all have in relationships. The struggle is never with the other, but with the self.

For some people, the need to fill the empty place in their soul that was meant for God can be filled with a human relationship. This is no different than seeking to fill it with drugs, pleasures, religion, or whatever. It is an altar to worship the self, seeking to fill the spiritual need with a carnal thing. This is what relationship dependency is—the need to find meaning and fulfillment in another person. There are many problems with this. The first is that the desperate need to be filled cannot be done by anyone. The expectations of that hunger are too great for anyone to fulfill. When a person is relationship dependent enters into a relationship, it is with the impossible hope that *this* one will be "the one" that will do it and be everything that person dreams and imagines them to be. After a while, the person begins to realize that this is *not* the one and begins to become disillusioned, disappointed, and unfulfilled. This creates an unhappiness, which can turn bitter. The person begins looking for the *real* one, seeking another someone who may fulfill their expectations. In this process, in order to get rid of the failing one, the relationship-dependent person will actually sabotage the relationship to cause it to dissolve and do it in such a way as to make it appear to be the other person's fault, and thereby alleviating the guilt of hurting the other and the pain of breaking up. This is devastating for both parties.

I remember one case of a man who I knew that went from one relationship to another, with women that he worked with. He was very charming and able to seduce these women into a relationship with him. As time went on and children were born, the relationships dissolved because they weren't *the one,* one right after the other. Eventually, the man was paying so much court ordered child support for the children he left in his selfish need that it was more than he was earning. He hit a brick wall that he could not escape or get over, so he killed himself.

Another case was a woman, who claimed to be a Christian, and sought after a Christian partner because she had the idea that a godly man would be able to fulfill her need. She went from man to man, church to church, leaving a wake of broken hearts. When confronted with this behavior, she would simply go to another church or another town. Rather than face the truth about her own condition and find remedy, she found no fault in herself and indignantly denied any wrongdoing. She was her own god and felt justified in all that she did. It was so sad to see a life destined for loneliness and ruin, bitterness and pain. All because the altar where she worshipped herself was in relationships.

There are some instances where the relationship is part of a more complex problem. Relationships provide security, stability, and resources. For a person who is a drug abuser or alcoholic, the relationship is a sort of "base of operations" from which they pursue their irresponsible behaviors. The home, family, work, friends, and others become objects or resource to the abuser and nothing else. They are things to be used. In my classes on this I use a simple diagram that illustrates this.

The large circle in the middle is my universe and I am in the center of it. Around it are several smaller circles: w=wife, k=kids, f=family, fr=friends, j=job, and c=church.

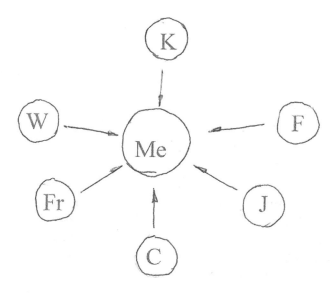

When it is all about me (I am god and there is none else), I can do whatever I want to fulfill my needs. When I want my wife to be with me, I bring her in; when I don't, I push her away. The same goes with all of my relationships. Unfortunately, when a person only takes from others and does not give back, it is not relationship, but the important people in his life only become the means to get what he wants when he wants it. This may go on for a while, but eventually people take a rather sore idea of being used and depart from that situation. First to go is the job, then church. Friends don't usually last too long if they are only being used. Sooner or later the wife will have had enough and take the kids with her. That leaves the family. Sadly, so many people who are so self-oriented cannot understand it when their mom and dad say, "Son, we love you, but you have to go."

When a particular resource is needed or wanted, they are employed. When they are not needed, they are ignored. The self is the center of that universe, and all else are only satellites that orbit the self. For those who are in a relationship with the abuser, in order to appease, or attempt to control, excuse, or tolerate the behavior for the sake of the relationship can enter into codependency. That is, that their need for the relationship to continue causes them to make the abuser's life easier. They will cover their tracks, make excuses, work extra hours to pay bills, and withdraw from confrontation. As much as the abuser is dependent on his or her altar of worship, the other persons in his world become equally dependent, offering them the ability to continue to worship as they please.

This happens often in families where the husband is the main source of income and yet is dependent on drugs or alcohol. Or in families where a child is engrossed in abuse and the mom and dad, meaning to do well, and help the child, only permit him or her to continue unabated in their selfish pursuit. They hate to see their child fail and do whatever they can, sort of confrontation, to not allow them to fail. They are just as much of the problem as the abuser.

I know a family whose son is a chronic drug abuser, and it causes him to lose jobs and has landed him in jail a few times. The mom and dad talk tough, but all the while, they have taken out second and third mortgages on their home to pay for little Nimrod's legal fees, to keep them from the agony of having their little darling go to jail. Now the son does not care enough for the family to alter his own desires and pursuits, but will, for a short time, behave himself, because the cost of losing his lifeline would be too steep. We will get into this in more detail later.

The Altar of Money

It is commonly said, *money is the root of all evil.* This is actually not correct. It is a misquote from the Bible. The quote is from the apostle Paul in his letter to Timothy. The correct quote is "For the *love* of money is a root of all kinds of evil, for which some have strayed from the faith in their greediness, and pierced themselves through with many sorrows" (1 Timothy 6:10 NKJV).

Money is a necessary thing in the world we live in today. It has been a common instrument for exchange for thousands of years. It is believed that the ancient city of Sardis, in what is now modern Turkey, was where coins were first minted. The use of money (which was typically made from four prized metals: gold, silver, copper, and bronze) as an exchange for goods and services was part of the advancing of civilization. Before the introduction of coins or lumps of metal, people traded what they did in exchange for food, clothing, weapons, tools, or other necessities. Bartering was only good if what you had people wanted or needed. A common means of exchange solved that problem. You could trade gold for anything and sell what you had or did for the same. The world changed and grew. Today, money is made of paper, and the government of the country that prints it backs its value. It was a lot easier to carry than a heavy bag of gold and silver coins. In recent times, the United States ceased to mint coins of larger denominations. Silver dollars and half dollars are things of the past. In fact, a small plastic card has nearly replaced currency altogether. Cash is being used much less in purchases today. People now purchase goods online, on their computer, and use a credit or debit card to pay. This is the thing of the future. I imagine at some point, the minting of cash will become obsolete. For the time being, however, paper money is printed in the millions of dollars every day.

However the money is handled, whether in cash, credit, or simply electronic transfers, it is a necessary part of life. People work for wages, invest into businesses, and risk investing into the stock market, all to get more. Depending upon where you live, the amount of money you *need* to live can vary. I was transferred in my job from New York to South Carolina. I was paid the same salary, and yet because the cost of living in South Carolina is much less than New York, it was like getting a substantial raise. It was a good move. The more money you have, the better you can live and the more stuff you can buy. It is funny that no matter how much money you can make, you find ways to spend it all. I know some people that make tons more money than I do and are strapped financially, because they spend it as fast as they can get it. Oh sure, they can buy fancier cars, bigger houses, and what not, but that only is a contributing factor to their somewhat less than frugal behavior. Money is not only a means of exchange, but also a symbol of status within the community that you live. This status is flaunted by the make and model car you drive, the neighborhood you live in, and the size and shape of the house you live in. The sin of coveting blossoms in this atmosphere, like flowers in the spring. The expression "keeping up with the Joneses" arose in the booming economy after World War II. In America in the 1950s and 1960s, the status of having *more* than the neighbors around you showed them that you were more important, that your life was more significant than theirs. After growing up during the terrible depression of the 1930s and the enormous sacrifices during the Second World War, people felt that they should have more. It was a time of working hard to get all that you could. The American dream became one of luxury and recreation, and the generation that suffered so much pursued this dream with all of their strength and determination. Soon it wasn't enough to have just one car; you had to have two. Then it wasn't enough to have a nice home, but you needed a vacation cottage. The demand to have more became too much for one income, and both the husband and wife had jobs to increase their income. Two incomes were needed to fuel that fire.

Today, the ultimate goal for the American dream is retirement. "How soon can I retire, and how well can I live?" People are not focused on what they have or how they can help others as much as that incredible drive to become rich enough to lay back and take it easy for the rest of life. There are dozens of advertisements for investment companies and strategies to reach that dream. It seems the only thing we live for and strive for. "Can I get rich enough so that I don't have to work for a living? Can I make enough money so I can retire and enjoy life more?"

Now, the struggle is not just to survive in the elder years, but "How early can I retire?" Parents are telling their sons and daughters that they need to go to college, a good college, and get a degree in something that will make the most amount of money—an amount that will enable you to not only live well, but retire as early as possible, so that they can enjoy life more. That is a lot of pressure, and so many kids today are falling into that greedy trap.

Status and comfort are not the only things that can be acquired with wealth. Power and money are joined together like the bones in your arm. The money bone is connected to the power bone. Throughout history people with wealth were also with influence. They used their wealth to buy influence and power, as a means to acquire more of each. In our system of government today, it seems that money and connections can buy power and influence. Power and wealth begets more power, and certainly more wealth, and a deep hunger for it. In the communist countries, like the old Soviet Union, power was the means to get money. In that system, money was hard to come by. Gaining political power through the party was the means by which money was acquired. So either money buying power or power acquiring wealth, the connections were the same and the ends as well. The problem with the accumulation of wealth and power is that they corrupt.

Power corrupts, and absolute power corrupts absolutely.

This is the famous quote by Lord Acton to Bishop Creighton in 1887. It was true then, and it is true now.

There is nothing wrong with money. It is merely an object. But the desire to accumulate wealth to the point it becomes a need or an obsession makes it only an altar where we worship the self. When the quest to obtain wealth causes you to sacrifice in other areas of life, you might have a problem. If you profess to be a Christian but are striving to accumulate enough wealth to accomplish the dream of independence and luxury, of retirement and ease, you might want to question your faith and your motive.

Randy Alcorn, in his book *The Treasure Principle,* writes:

> In stark contrast, Jesus spoke of a rich man who spent all his wealth on himself. He planned to tear down his barns and build larger ones, storing up for himself so he could retire early and take it easy.
>
> But God called the man a fool, saying, "This very night your life will be demanded from you. Then who will get what you have prepared for yourself" (Luke 12:20).
>
> The greatest indictment against him—and the proof of his spiritual condition—is that he

was rich toward himself, but not rich toward God.[5]

The desire to accumulate wealth is all about me. It is the sign of an inward-facing heart. I have a saying: "The inward-facing heart is never filled: the outward-facing heart is never emptied."

It is a matter of worship. The altar of money is a sign of idolatry, the worship of me.

The Altar of Social Media

Okay, this is one of the most bizarre things I have come across, and it is relatively new to an ever-growing generation. Social media outlets on electronic devices, mostly smartphones, have become the new rage in meeting people, discussing relevant issues, share stories and comedic events, and of course, post personal experiences to invoke a reaction. Particularly in the generation call "millennials" the use of these outlets are a means by which a person discerns their value in this electronic community. Young people are obsessed with "posting" personal information or events, only to wait anxiously for how many "likes" they get. By this, they determine their status, value, and relevance in their generational society. Some are so anxiety filled and emotionally distraught over the results, or lack of them, that they even commit suicide. The suicide rate in people in this age group is growing at an alarming rate. The grip is so powerful on people that it has replaced good old-fashioned face-to-face encounters with real conversations and accountability. No one talks to each other anymore unless it is through the filter of that little electronic box. In some ways, it is safer for them. They do not have to risk actual contact and the consequences of that experience. The phone is their shield, and their hiding place. It is very strange to see two people sitting at a table together, with both of their heads bowed into the world of their palm held magic box, totally absorbed into that private

[5] Alcorn, Randy. *The Treasure Principle.* pp. *10, 11.* 2011. Colorado Springs. Multnomah Books.

little window where they are sending texted messages to each other. This has become a dangerous altar for self-worship, as a lost generation seeks its identity through electronic gossip and completely disengaged from the world around them. Applications and mobile sites like Facebook, Twitter, Snapchat, and others have become the arbiters of social standing and worth.

The Altar of Substance Abuse

This is the most prevalent of the symptoms of the plague that is upon us—the problem of substance abuse. This is not a new problem; it has been going on since forever. The term substance abuse can be applied to any number of substances. It could be intoxicating ones like drugs or alcohol, or healthy ones like protein shakes, and yes, even food. It could be fast cars or houses. Any *substance* that is used in hopes of finding fulfillment as a replacement for God can be an altar of self-worship. Generally, when we think of substances, they are the kind that are ingested or introduced into the body some way. There is any number of different substances that we ingest daily that can be abused for the purpose of getting high, or have more energy, or simply to comfort us. There are pills for everything you can imagine that help with depression or anxiety, weight loss, or for whatever ails you. There are thousands of "dietary supplements" that are marketed today that promise all manner of benefits, which may be otherwise acquired through a healthy diet and exercise. These all have good purposes but can be abused when they are taken in excess or beyond their prescribed use. The substances that we abuse can be naturally made within our own bodies, like adrenalin. When the body is under stress, or fear, it pumps adrenalin through the endocrine system. The hormone increases blood flow to the muscles, causes the heart to pump harder, and increases arousal (because of fear). There are people that take pleasure in this heightened arousal and fear and become what are called "adrenalin junkies." They enjoy engaging in activities that are physically demanding and produce fear, like skydiving, or base-jumping, driving way too fast, or other "extreme" sports.

Substances that are necessary for our survival are food. In the Southern United States, where I live, there are a group of foods that are called "comfort foods." These are great, delicious things that make you feel great but probably shouldn't be a part of the daily diet. They have a tendency to be fatty, or sweet, or heavy. They sure are good though! As one of my friends in South Carolina says, "So good it'll make you wanna slap your momma!" I am not sure what that means. There are people that eat to comfort themselves from a negative emotional experience. Take for example, a young lady who has been stood up on a date, and she eats a large amount of ice cream to comfort herself. That is not in itself a problem, but simply a way to cope with an emotional letdown. However, if the coping mechanism becomes a habit, where every little stress or excuse leads to Baskin Robbins, there is a problem.

I think at this point you get the idea. It's important now to look at the more damaging substances that are habitually turned to as an altar of self-worship—the intoxicating and mood-altering substances that are the big issue today.

To begin with, let's look at the word *intoxication*. The root of the word is simple—*toxic*. It means to poison you, in so many words. Intoxicating substances have been the bane of society as far back as Sumeria, Egypt, and Babylon. In fact, the Bible speaks of this, in particular, the problem with alcohol. The very first mention of this is right after the flood. Noah, after leaving the ark to a new world, became a vinedresser, and he became drunk on wine.

"And Noah began to be a farmer, and he planted a vineyard. Then he drank of the wine and was drunk, and became uncovered in his tent" (Genesis 9:20–21 NKJV).

Alcohol and embarrassment have always gone together, like soup and sandwich. In biblical times, there were only two forms of intoxicating beverages: wine, which was the fermented juice of grapes or fruit, and strong drink, which was beer. The Babylonians invented beer, and the process of making an alcoholic drink from wheat or barley became popular. The Bible warns about the sting of the viper that comes from too much wine. There are also thirty-nine verses mentioning "strong drink." I imagine the alcoholic content of the beer was greater than the wine, which gave it the honor of being so called. Of the thirty-nine verses regarding strong drink, thirty-eight of them are warnings. The Bible does not condemn the drinking of wine or beer, but strongly maintains that to do so is playing with fire.

> Wine is a mocker, strong drink is a brawler, and whoever is led astray by it is not wise. (Proverbs 20:1)

> He who loves pleasure will be a poor man; he who loves wine and oil will not be rich. (Proverbs 21:17)

> Do not mix with winebibbers, or with gluttonous eaters of meat; for the drunkard and the glutton will come to poverty, and drowsiness will clothe a man with rags. (Proverbs 23:20)

> "Who has woe? Who has sorrow? Who has contentions? Who has complaints? Who has wounds without cause? Who has redness of eyes?" Those who linger long at the wine, those who go in search of mixed wine. Do not look on the wine when it is red, when it sparkles in the cup, when it swirls around smoothly; at the last it bites like a serpent, and stings like a viper. Your eyes will see strange things, and your heart will utter perverse things. Yes, you will be like one who lies down in the midst of the sea, or like one who lies at the top of the mast, saying; "They have struck me, but I was not hurt; they have beaten me, but I did not feel it. When shall I awake, that I may seek another drink?" (Proverbs 23:29–35)

I like that last one the best. It really gets to the core of the matter. It is important to consider that the distillation of liquors did not come into history until the Middle Ages. There are some contentions regarding that, as some claim it may have been done in the early fourth century in Arabia (*alcohol* is an Arabic word). However, the introduction of liquors was a large step in a bad direction.

The effects of the early use of wine on civilization were dramatic. Someone once said that the downfall of every civilization in the world could be directly attributed to alcohol. The powerful nation state of Rome fell because of it. As Rome became greater and slaves did the labors (80 percent of the Roman empire were slaves), it left time for leisure and the seeking of pleasures. Bacchus, the god of wine, was celebrated with drunken orgies and vomitoriums, where people ate and drank until they were sick. The drunkenness causes a lapse in religious principles, which in turn led to governmental corruption and social decay. Public entertainment in the form of gladiatorial spectacles became more and more outrageous and violent. The crowd was controlled by these events (rather like our Super Bowl) until they became boring. The shocking events in the Colosseum grew less shocking to a public that demanded more, for entertainment sake. Rome became weak because of it and could no longer support her world conquest and military might. The armies were divided, after long wars in Germania, Gaul, and Britain. The empire was too big, too spread out. It was not long before the Goths, who found the Romans to be effeminate, weak, and lazy, made their move and sacked the once most powerful city in the world. What a difference from the mighty power that ruled and brought law and civilization to the known world with an iron boot!

Alcoholic beverages are the most dangerous legal drugs in the world today. Americans have embraced them into the very essence of our culture. If you don't think so, watch a football game on TV. Nearly every advertisement is for beer or some popular alcoholic liquor. Though the companies become wealthy and the nation takes a ton of money in taxes on liquor, more money I spent of trying to help families that have been destroyed by it, or on people whose lives have been consumed by it. Hospitals, treatment facilities, flophouses, shelters, and rehabs are a heavy price. More crimes are committed under the influence of alcohol than any other. Drunk drivers cause more traffic accident deaths that any other reason. Yet it is socially acceptable, even encouraged. It has destroyed more families than any other substance, behavior, or problem. Now, the drug marijuana is gaining social acceptance as well.

Marijuana, from the plant *Cannabis Sativa* in the west and *Cannabis Indica* in the east, has been around for a long time. The Arabs cooked it down to create hashish, which they gave to wicked men so that they would be able to be bold enough to murder. The word assassin comes from *hashishan* (one who eats hashish). In the 1950s, the use of marijuana in cigarettes began to emerge, mostly in small, isolated groups like musicians, though it was used long before then—even in the '20s and '30s. In the 1960s smoking "pot" was the rage, and an entire generation celebrated this new and powerful intoxicant. It was glorified in music and art and was the cool thing to do. The chemical intoxicant in marijuana is tetrahydracannibinol or THC. Marijuana use was strongly condemned in America's "war on drugs" during the 1970s, but it continued to grow in use and popularity. Today, it is quickly becoming mainstream, with many claiming that it is no more dangerous than alcohol. Well, that is saying a lot. Many states now have either decriminalized the use and possession of marijuana or have legalized it for recreational use. Pot shops have sprung up in Colorado, Oregon, Washington, and California, with the states hoping to reap billions of dollars in tax revenues as they try to regulate the sale and distribution. Today, the THC content of street ready pot is twenty to twenty-five times what it was in the 1960s. The debilitating effects of prolonged use are just now being discovered. It has been learned that THC, especially when used by people under the age of twenty-three, when the prefrontal lobe of the brain is fully developed, that loss of memory, focus, and motivation occurs, which can be a permanent injury. Long-term use can produce episodes of nervous disorder, seizures, and even schizophrenia. We used to laugh at those "scare tactics" that we heard back in the 1960s, but the science is getting better, and we aren't laughing anymore. Add to that the idea that you are inhaling deeply the smoke of a burning dead plant and all that goes with that, such as lung cancer, emphysema, COPD (chronic obstructive pulmonary disease), bronchitis, and heart disease.

So why are people attracted to intoxicants? What is it about them that is so desirable? The answer is simply that they alter the way that you feel. They can produce euphoria or a soothing sort of numbness that relaxes you. People drink alcohol and take drugs for the effect. It is, in a way, a substitute for true spirituality. Intoxication can be related to as near a spiritual experience as can be found in this cursed world. It satisfies a longing for the self to be pleased, to have a mind- or mood-altering experience that really feels good. People do not take drugs for any other reason than to feel good. Period. The problem with these intoxicating substances is that they are both inherently dangerous and they do not satisfy the need that the user hopes for. They are unhealthy. Marijuana supporters claim that it is no more dangerous than alcohol, which is legal. That is not very assuring and still not a good enough reason to legalize it. What is commonly experienced is that the effects of drugs like pot become stale after continued use. Alcohol does the same, as the body builds a tolerance to its effects. This is the argument for claiming that they are "gateway" drugs. Alcohol, because of its availability and afford-ability, is the primary gateway drug. Marijuana is another of these gateway drugs because it is not as dangerous as many others. Those who desire to legalize it hotly dispute this point. The more danger-ous and illegal drugs like cocaine, crack, methamphetamine, and heroin are experimented with, the "high" of pot or booze gets old. Pharmaceuticals, especially antidepressants and antianxiety drugs, are obtained illegally for recreational use, and pain-control drugs like Fentanyl and Oxycodone are highly sought for escape, stress relief, and pain control. Opioid use has become a national disaster, where people who are legitimately prescribed these medications become dependent on them, and when they are no longer able to receive them legally turn to the street. Chemical dependency is an issue we will discuss in depth a little later, a terrible trap that so many fall into. Regardless of the substance or its effect on the body, the ultimate rea-son for abuse is that the intoxicating effect is an altar of self-worship.

The Only Acceptable Addiction

We have found that addiction is not a disease, but can lead to disease. It is a behavior, and that behavior is worship. It is not even a voluntary behavior, but one in which we are programmed to do. We were born with the need to worship because it is what we were created to do. We have already seen that addiction is not only worship, but that it is wrongful worship directed at someone other than what was intended—to worship the living God. We have also seen that in the two differing worldviews that the one that rejects the idea of God, following the evolutionary model, *must* direct that worship to someone other than God and is by nature the addiction of false or self-worship. We have also seen that those who hold to the Special Divine Creation worldview are just as susceptible to the false worship as the other worldview. We have seen examples of the many altars in which people worship themselves, some without even being aware of it as self-worship. However, in the creation worldview, there are those who are true believers, having been born anew in the Spirit, and worship God in spirit and in truth.

The Bible teaches us that we are lost in this world, having been separated from the communion with God by our sin nature. We are sheep that have gone astray from our Shepherd and are wandering in the dangerous wood. Jesus said that His purpose on earth was to find us and bring us back to fellowship with God.

"For the Son of man is come to seek and to save that which was lost" (Luke 19:10).

Our separation from God had doomed us to live apart from the knowledge of who we are, why we are here, and to be without hope in the world. But God, who is rich in mercy, has sent us His Son, that we may be reconciled to God in life and fellowship.

The irony in our natural state is that we are created for one pur-pose—to worship God—but because we are spiritually dead in our natural state it is impossible for us to do so. There is a gulf between God and us that we cannot cross, despite our most fervent desires or zealous adherence to ritual. So how do we cross that gulf? How do we become spiritually alive so that we can stop worshipping the false god and idol or our life?

First and foremost, we must believe that God is real. The Bible teaches us that God has placed the knowledge of His existence upon the heart of every person so that we all are without excuse. There are no real atheists in the world, just people that for whatever reason deny their own understanding. We have already observed the foolish nature of one who denies the natural understanding of the existence of God in his heart. In Hebrews it reads, "But without faith it is impossible to please him: for he that comes to God must believe that he is, and that he is a rewarder of them that diligently seek him" (Hebrews 11:6).

That is the easy part. God has already given us the understand-ing in our hearts that He exists. But, is believing in God enough for us to break the false worship that plagues us? No, it is not. The apos-tle James wrote, "You believe that there is one God; you do well: the devils also believe, and tremble" (James 2:19).

In this, James tells us that demons believe in God, but there is no salvation for them. They know this, and they tremble, knowing the judgment that awaits them. The natural man does not have the spiritual discernment to tremble.

The power to break our false worship can only come when we have a restored relationship with God and the life-changing experi-ence that comes with that. In order for us to have a restored relation-ship with God we must come to Him on *His* terms and not ours. We, by our own nature, have in effect declared war on God, and we can-not make the peace. God has made a peace offering for us that we can either accept or reject. Acceptance of this offering is the only hope for peace and to break the chains of addiction. There are three things that must be accomplished in order for this life-changing relation-ship to be established. These are the terms of God for our surrender.

1. *We must accept the unthinkable about ourselves.* The Bible tells us that we are not going to be judged when we leave this life. We will not have a chance to stand before God and have our good deeds and bad deeds placed on a grand, cosmic scale, and hopefully have the good outweigh the bad and be accepted by our merit. The Bible clearly teaches that we have already been judged and found to be guilty. We, having the imperfection and stain of sin, cannot meet God's requirement of holiness or perfection. We are unclean before Him. There is no deed great enough or any amount of works that can be done that can alter or erase that judgment. Once imperfection is found, who can go back in time and undo it? We may have told only one lie in our entire life and, once committed, cannot go back and erase it. Done is done. The penalty for our imperfection is separation from God, and there is nothing we can do about it. We are all hell-bound sinners and can do nothing to stop it. That is an unthinkable situation. Who, in their right mind, would want to believe that? I don't know a single person that would want to believe that they were on their way to eternal torment and had no power to dissuade God in His judgment. Mankind always seeks a way to justify himself. We all want to think that we are on relatively good terms with the Creator of the universe. We all want to think that He will love us and let us come to heaven no matter what. We get this false impression that God is like some great old grandfatherly type, who will wink at our sin and give us what we want. That is a falsehood. The truth is that the Bible is right when it says, "There is no one righteous, not any; all have sinned and fall short of the glory of God" (Romans 3:23).

Whether we want to believe that or not, we know in the depths of our hearts it is true. It is not difficult to admit that we are not perfect. The work of the Holy Spirit in the hearing of the Word is to convict us of our sin. It is the spirit of God that puts that into our hearts so that we would repent and turn to Him for mercy.

John wrote, "For God did not send his Son into the world to condemn the world, but in order that the world might be saved through him. Whoever believes in him is not condemned, but whoever does not believe is condemned already" (John 3:17–18 ESV).

2. *We must believe the impossible.* We must believe that Jesus Christ is more than just a good man, or religious leader, or prophet. We must believe that He is the living God incarnate, who took upon Himself humanity for the sole purpose of going to the cross for our sin. We must believe that He has the power to forgive sins and to reconcile us to God by His own blood. We must believe that He, having laid down His life, had the authority to do so, and to take it back up again and that He is raised from the dead. Again, the work of the Holy Spirit is also to "instruct in all righteousness." The Bible emphatically claims that Jesus is God in human flesh and that He was crucified for the sin of the world and was raised from the dead after three days in a tomb. The testimonies of the apostles who witnessed this is undeniable. Twelve men gave their lives, most horrifically, because of the confession of the risen Christ. No one would give their life in such a way for a profession that they knew was not true. They saw Him, and touched Him, and spoke with Him after His passion. The apostle Paul wrote on this: "But now is Christ risen from the dead, and become the firstfruits of them that slept" (1 Corinthians 15:20).

3. *We must trust in God, who we have never known.* The greatest decision of a person's life is to trust their eternal life to a God they have never known. Before receiving Christ as Savior, we are dead in spirit and are not able to perceive anything about the true and living God. We have absolutely nothing to base our trust on except what the Bible teaches us, tells us about God, and the internal prompting

in our hearts by His Spirit. Paul wrote, "But the natural man receives not the things of the Spirit of God: for they are foolishness to him: neither can he know them, because they are spiritually discerned" (1 Corinthians 2:14).

The Bible also teaches us that when we trust Jesus Christ with our eternal life, He enlivens our once dead spirit and we are made complete. Our spirit being made alive enables us to worship God in spirit and in truth and frees us from the darkness and hopelessness of our self-worship.

That is the only acceptable addiction.

So in this modern, post-Christian world, where moral relativism and political correctness, where truth and righteousness are only what you perceive them to be, and "what is true for you may not be true for me," and all religions are a path to God, that statement is alarming and offensive. How can anyone say that there is only one way and one truth and one God? How can anyone say that my life is not my own and it is not all about me? How can you say that your religion is better than the other 4,999 and that even in your religion that most people are not really believers?

I am glad you asked.

There is a word in Greek that Peter uses when he says that we are to be always ready to give a defense for the hope that is in us, to anyone who asks. The word for defense is (apo-**log**-ee-ah), which is from two words: "apo" which means "from," and "logos" which means "words." It is where we get the English word *apology.* Apologetics is the defense of the faith and the Scriptures, using the words of the Bible itself. Our defense of the faith comes from the words. There is another defense of the faith, and that is of human experience. These two together, the words of the Bible and the human experience of true believers, provide a powerful defense for the faith in the one true religion of the world.

For this section, I will refer to my dissertation on the Bible and the Human Condition, chapters two and three.

RONALD J. MORSE, PHD

The Christian Experience

It is of paramount importance to discuss the unique experience of true Christianity. When I say "true" Christianity it is the fundamental, aboriginal, apostolic experience that signifies genuine discipleship. Over the centuries, the accepted faith has been altered, maligned, and misunderstood in its application and from its foundational tenet. What is generally held by what we would call fundamentalist or evangelical Christians is perhaps at its root and teaching what is as close to the apostolic era experience as is extant today. It is not my intention to point fingers or make accusations or comparisons from one group or sect to another, and it is impossible to judge whether the adherents to one particular so-called form of Christianity or denomination are right or wrong, lost or saved. Those distinctions were sharply made during the Reformation, and more lately, through the liberalization of church doctrine to accommodate societal changes. Clearly, not all who claim to be Christians are truly believers. One of the more strange phenomena of the Christian faith is that not everyone gets it. Christianity is not merely a mental exercise, or a means to social engagement, or a life of rules and structures that make many people feel secure and comfortable. It is a unique transformation that occurs when a person genuinely believes, not just intellectually, but trusting in that belief enough to make it an action of the will. This action is called faith. It is common that people, enamored by the story of Jesus and having a sincere understanding of the concept of redemption, are drawn to Christianity for its

68

many merits and long history of good works. It is a peaceful, loving, and accepting order of human behavior that is immensely attractive. For some, there is the comfort and safety of the strict, hyper-conservative church that makes them feel warm and welcomed. For others, it is the idea that they won't be rejected—that no one will judge or malign them. For many, it is a part of their culture, and all of the trappings and rites of a particular denomination gives them a feeling of family and belonging.

These are all good things, and to be sure, they are all a part of what it is to be Christian. However, for many, if not most, the essential experience of truly being "born again" does not occur. Billy Graham claimed that as many as 75 percent of those who attend Bible-believing, Bible-teaching churches are probably not truly saved. In a more recent poll, less than one in five self-identifying Christians claim to be invested in their own spiritual "development." How these things are judged or discerned is beyond me, but the fact that many who claim to be Christian and live their lives unaltered by the confession is troubling.

Throughout its history, the Christian church has been fraught with abuses, savagery, usurpations, political manipulations, wars, and too much else to shamefully admit. The church was responsible for the inquisition, when hundreds of true Christians and Jews fell prey to an authoritarian and frankly unbiblical leadership. Those who engaged in such horrific practices were only Christian by loose association with a tradition.

Jesus taught in the parables of the Kingdom of Heaven, as found in the gospels of Matthew and Luke, that not all who claim to believe are true; particularly, the parables of the sower (Matthew 13:1–9) and the wheat and tares (Matthew 13:24–30).[6]

It is important, in this brief digression to discern what "true" Christianity is and what is not. For the purpose of the rest of this writing, the term Christianity will be understood as the true faith that is evidenced by the presence of the work of the Holy Spirit in a transformed life. The importance of this is in that the ability to break the chains of addictive behavior, that deeply ingrained self-worship, is found only when we surrender the ownership of our lives to Christ. This is what Jesus meant when He said we must "take up our cross." When He said that to His disciples they knew exactly what He meant. People were publicly crucified at that time. The cross was a terrible place of execution. No one survived it. To take up your cross meant to them that their life, as it was, was over. Paul wrote, "I am crucified with Christ; it is no longer I who live, but Christ lives in me; and the life which I now live in the flesh I live by faith in the Son of God, who loved me and gave Himself for me" (Galatians 2:20).

True Christianity is not self-deprivation, as some believe. It is not about giving up things or denying yourself food, clothing, or shelter. It doesn't mean I have to give up dancing or going to the movies, for crying out loud. That is more in the line of Greek stoics, who denied all earthly pleasures in an attempt to defeat sin.

True Christianity is not self-degradation either, as others believe. It does not mean that we are worthless and totally unworthy of God's love and salvation. That is false pride.

True Christianity is the denial of self-deification. It is the understanding that my life is not my own. I am bought with a price, and the life I live is for and about the Son of God. In the long run, at the end

---

[6] Morse, Ronald J., *The Bible and the Human Condition*. 2015. Louisiana Baptist University, Shreveport.

of all things, nothing else matters. Christ is real. His death was real, and His resurrection is real. He will return to judge the world and to take His own out of it. What on earth could matter more than that?

Four Essential Needs

In 1943, Abraham Maslow published his "Hierarchy of Human Needs." His theory was that human beings needed to develop psychologically through stages to achieve the highest state—self-actualization or self-transcendence. His theory is built on a pyramid, with the lower foundations being psychological, safety, love, and finally self-actualization. Each of his needs were built into a hierarchy, where more elevated or sophisticated needs could be sought only after the more basic ones were achieved. It has been shown, however, that the hierarchy does not exist in many cases. Poor Abraham also missed the most fundamental need because he was an atheist. Our most fundamental need is not safety, or love, or family, but to be connected with our God. His highest goal was *self-transcendence,* where the selfish interests are abandoned. It was a noble goal, but without Christ, it cannot be achieved: but *in* Christ, is already there.

The proof of this is that a person can be deprived of food, shelter, and safety. He can be cut off from family, friends, or any human contact, and still be filled with an inexplicable joy. The history of those men who knew Jesus Christ is indeed a strange one. Twelve men who suffered many dangers, rejections, and for all but one, terrible deaths, were still impassioned with their message of hope and filled with the joy of their knowledge of Jesus Christ no matter how high the cost.

The prophets of old in the Bible also suffered. A witch chased Elijah, Isaiah was sawn in half with a wooden saw, and Jeremiah was scorned and imprisoned. Daniel was thrown into a lion's den. Their human needs were all subsequent to the most vital—the need to be connected to God.

There are four basic needs for a person to be fulfilled and healthy. They are not hierarchal, as Maslow put it, but coexistent; not in a pyramid, but more like a pizza. I don't mean to be flippant,

71

but the idea is that each of these needs is essential and separate, but joined together to make a whole. In the case of addictive behaviors, and more particularly in the treatment of them, it is important to understand how these needs are affected by the behavior and degenerate over time. Though the needs are coexistent, I have placed them in a specific order—the order in which they degenerate in the continued life of a person who is caught in the worship of self. Though there are four needs, they correspond to the idea that we are triune, with the first part correlating to the *spirit*, the second and third to the *soul* or our conscious self-awareness and being, and the fourth our *fleshly* body.

Years ago, as I was counseling a young man who was struggling in his marriage relationship, I tried to make him understand that as a husband and the leader of the marriage and family, it was his responsibility to meet the needs of his wife—her spiritual need, her emotional need, her psychological need, and her physical need. It was from this that the four essential needs came to light. What I intended to teach this young man was that it was his responsibility to take care of his wife. He is to be the spiritual leader of his household—to pray for and with his wife, to be active in church and Bible study. He is responsible to see that her emotional need of being loved and cherished was being fulfilled and to make her happy. He is responsible to support and encourage her psychological, intellectual growth, and interests; and he is responsible to take care of all of her physical needs and to learn what makes her feel happy, loved, and secure.

The first and greatest of these needs is the spiritual need. God created man for a purpose, and that is to worship Him and have fellowship with Him. In fact, there is no other reason for anyone to be in this world than that. God made every one of us specifically for that purpose. The Bible explains that God has created everything and that He has placed within our own hearts the knowledge of His existence. Paul wrote, "For since the creation of the world His invisible attributes are clearly seen, being understood by the things that are made, even His eternal power and Godhead, so that they are without excuse" (Romans 1:20).

Solomon wrote that we know that life continues eternally, but we do not know the mystery of what God does.

"He has made everything appropriate in its time. He has also set eternity in their heart, yet so that man will not find out the work which God has done from the beginning even to the end" (Ecclesiastes 3:11).

It is interesting that in every race, culture, and people of the earth, the same question drives them: *What happens to me after I die?* This innate knowledge that the death of the flesh is not the end but that life goes on eternally somewhere is the most common understanding in human kind. It is this great mystery, along with the natural knowledge of the existence of a greater, spiritual power, which brought the need for man to bring religion into the world.

Why we worship is because that is what God created us to do. We were created to worship the true and living God for His pleasure and purpose. Worship is a need, just as eating, sleeping, and companionship are needs. In Genesis, we learn that humans are the end creation. The amazing order of creation is sequential in that all things that are made were done so that man may be sustained and that we may see the revelation of God in nature. God made the heavens and the earth. The earth was a rock, with an atmosphere above it, for life to breathe. The earth was empty and covered with water, and God made the dry land appear. Then He made grass and trees and plants that bore seed, so that man would have things to eat. Then came the birds to bear the seed across the earth to replenish it and the beasts of the earth. Lastly, when the support system was complete, God made man and woman.

There are no accidents in God's plan. Every person born into this world is by the direct creative design of God. It doesn't matter who you are or what you look like, God made you exactly who you are and what you are in this time and at this place for His purpose and glory. We all have a special purpose, and it is our responsibility to find out what that is.

I ask those who attend our addiction recovery classes a few, simple questions: Did you choose your parents before you were born? Did you choose whether you were going to be a boy or a girl? Tall or short? Black, brown, white, or green? How about your gifts, talents, and abilities? Or how about how many teeth you have, or toes, or fingers? How about where you were born, or when, or why?

We really don't have a lot to say about ourselves. It is amazing that people take pride in something that they didn't have anything to do with. Paul wrote, "But indeed, O man, who are you to reply against God? Will the thing formed say to him who formed it, 'Why have you made me like this?'" (Romans 5:20 NKJV).

God made you exactly who and what you are for His purpose and His pleasure in this time and in this place. That is an awesome thought. We belong to Him, and it is our responsibility to find out what He made us to do.

So if our greatest purpose is to worship God, then it must naturally translate to our greatest need. As I mentioned before, we can be deprived of safety, food, water, and companionship, and still be complete if our relationship with God is established. The understanding that this is our greatest need is evident in the religious tendencies of mankind across time and geography, culture and language. Where Maslow states that self-actualization is a lofty goal, it is the most primal, basic need in human life and society. We must have the answer to the great question in life and an explanation for the natural understanding that there is a spiritual world and that there is a God who rules the things of this world. John wrote in the Revelation, "You are worthy, O Lord, to receive glory and honor and power: for You have created all things, and for Your pleasure they are and were created" (Revelation 4:11).

God made all things for His pleasure and His purpose; it is the only reason we are alive. The Westminster Confession of Faith says, "The chief end of man is to glorify God and enjoy Him forever."[7]

God has placed upon the heart of man the knowledge that He "is." Every religion is man's attempt to reconnect with the mysterious spirit God that he knows is there. Alas, religions all fail, because

---

[7] *The Westminster Confession of Faith and Catechisms.* pg 153. ©2005, 2007. Lawrenceville. Orthodox Presbyterian Church, Christian Education and Publications.

they are man's way to reach God, not His. There are over five thousand distinct religions in the world today. Someone has to be wrong because they certainly cannot be all right. The resurrection of Christ assures us that who He said He was and how we might be reconciled to God is true. Jesus said, "I am the way, the truth, and the life; no one comes to the Father but by me" (John 14:6).

This was not the making of man, but of God, as it says the He is the "Lamb slain before the foundation of the world." It is God's plan to reach man, not man's plan to reach God.

Without the spiritual need being properly met, that is, by a true worshipful relationship with God through Jesus Christ, as a "born-again" believer, the foundation for all of the other needs being met is compromised. I will explain that in the next chapter.

The second need of our lives is the *emotional need*. This is the understanding that we, created in the image of God, have emotions that are the natural reactions to our surroundings and situations. God is an intellectual being and has revealed to us in His Word that He too has emotions. God can be pleased, angry, delighted, jealous, or wrathful. These entire He has bequeathed to us as the image of His being. So, like God, we are happy, sad, or angry. We have some emotions that are part of our experience on the earth that God does not have. One of these is fear. Fear and anger, in human experience, are defense mechanisms to protect us from harm. We can also be anxious, guilty, or ashamed. Guilt and shame are the products of our disobedience to God and a part of our fallen sinful nature. We were not originally created with these. However, all of these distinct expressions are automatic reactions to situations or attitudes. When someone surprises us with a gift, we are delighted. When someone attacks or insults us, we respond with anger. When we are uncertain of a future outcome, we become fearful, or when we are in danger, we are fearful. When we commit an act that is harmful to others and are confronted with it, we feel shame. We can also be jealous or shocked. These emotional outbursts are immediate and, though they cause a course of thought and action, are quickly disbursed, fading away as a mist. This is how the brain, in this particular way, works.

For example, when we sense an immediate threat of danger, our brain sends signals to the endocrine system, which pumps adrenalin into the body. The heart begins to beat faster, pumping blood and oxygen into our muscles, the lungs work faster, and we begin to sweat—which both cools us and makes us slippery and hard to grasp. Our blood recedes from our limbs into our core to keep us alive, and should injury occur to the limbs, we won't bleed out. The stimulating effect of the adrenalin and other substances creates a fight-or-flight response. We will either fight real hard, with super strength, or run away faster than we could before. This is an automatic reaction that we cannot control. Once the danger passes, the body returns to normal. It is the same with all emotional reactions. If you hear a real funny joke, you may laugh out loud—it is an automatic reaction—but you don't continue to laugh all day like an idiot. Once the initial response passes and the brain receives new information (which it does hundreds of times per second), the effect fades. Only when we deliberately hang on to these events and continue to refresh those feelings, do they linger. There are some people who can be angry for a very long time. That is not an emotional reaction but a chosen state of mind. We will get into that later. It is healthy for a person to feel emotions, in the wide range of emotions that we enjoy. It is good to be angry when we should, sad or happy when it is appropriate to do so. This is part of what makes us human.

The third need is our *psychological need*. Our psychological need is our ability to understand our self-worth or value, which gives meaning and purpose to life itself. It is a condition that comes from an intellectual assessment of life based on experiences such as failure or success. Unfortunately, many people assess their value and worth based upon false models that the world provides. Some of these are physical appearance, social and economic standing, education, or intellectual capability. These false models detract from the true value and meaning of a person's life, which can only be found in Christ. We must not base our value on a false TV type model or by that which society dictates as success, but what the meaning of life is based upon the Word of God and what He declares for us.

The fourth need is the *physical need.* This is our need to be healthy and strong and to live in a manner that is not destructive to our physical health. In the case of people who are struggling with the incredibly destructive abuses of bad habits like drug abuse, alcohol, overeating, or dangerous actions, the physical need is focused on resisting the temptations to fall back upon that altar of worship that we know is destructive and following the path that God lays out for us to follow.

The Downward Spiral

When the first, the most primary need, the spiritual need, is not met—that is, the need to be connected to God in a personal, living relationship with Him through Christ—it diminishes our ability to effectively understand and manage our other needs. Without spiritual life, there is a gaping hole in our being that hungers to be filled, and because we cannot discern or truly sense what that is, having never experienced spiritual life, we can only seek to fill it with things that we do know and can experience. Our search for fulfillment is a powerful, driving force that ever seeks to find meaning, relevance, and belonging. We cannot find it through our other, more carnal needs, and yet, because they are the only ones we can experience outside of Christ, they are where we go. It is our spiritual need, that once fulfilled, cascades into our other needs and gives us a better understanding of how to fulfill them. Each and all of our other needs, whether it is emotional, psychological, or physical, is dependent upon the spiritual need to be fully enjoyed and experienced. Perhaps that is what Jesus meant when He said, "The thief comes only to steal and kill and destroy. I came that they may have life and have it abundantly" (John 10:10 ESV).

I rather like the Good News translation of this verse as well: "The thief comes only in order to steal, kill, and destroy. I have come in order that you might have life—life in all its fullness."

Jesus came to give us life—spiritual life. He came to restore what we lost in the garden of Eden, when Adam and Eve disobeyed God and the curse of spiritual death came to mankind. Only in Christ can our once dead spirit become reborn so that we may be connected to the living God. Paul wrote, "And you were dead in the trespasses and sins in which you once walked, following the course of this world, following the prince of the power of the air, the spirit that is now at work in the sons of disobedience…But God, being rich in mercy, because of the great love with which he loved us, even when we were dead in our trespasses, made us alive together with Christ" (Ephesians 2:1, 2, 4–5a ESV).

Our spiritual life being restored, we are given life to the fullest in abundance. I believe this means that once that greatest need is fulfilled, it fills all of our other needs as well. We were blind to the things of God, but in Christ have been given "eyes" to see what is true, what is real, and what pertains to life in all of its many aspects.

In the case of addictive behaviors, when the first need is not met, the resultant effect causes a degeneration of the other needs, in the likeness of a downward spiral. This downward spiral is particularly most visible when the altar of self-worship is drugs and intoxicants. The reason that the needs are placed in the order in which I have shown, is because that is the order in which they degenerate. Let me give an illustration.

A person, let's call him "Barney," chooses drugs as the means by which he seeks to worship himself and satisfy that emptiness and longing that is in him. This is a typical story of the progression of abuse and decay that occurs.

Barney is married and has two young children. He works in construction and does all he can to get by. His wife, Betty, stays at home now because she lost her job. Barney feels that there should be more to life than what he is getting. He needs something more. He feels he deserves it, but he doesn't know what it is. After a long, hard week, Barney gets his paycheck and decides he is going to have a little "Barney time." After all, it is *his* paycheck, that *he* worked so hard to get, and he should be allowed to have a little *me* time. Barney isn't thinking about his responsibility to his wife and family, he is only thinking about Barney. Aren't we all a little guilty of this?

Barney meets up with a friend who says, "Hey, Barn, you have got to try some of this." After a couple of beers and some laughs, Barney takes the dare and goes with his friend, who takes him to the local crack house. Here he meets Tito, who offers Barney a free bag. Barney hits the crack pipe and wham! This is a rush of feeling that he has never experienced before, and though it is a little scary, he likes it. Soon, the effect of this powerful drug wears off though and Barney is left hungering for more. The next bag is not free. This continues until, after more time than he expected, Barney is broke. His pay has been spent, and both his friend and Tito have gone. Barney decides he better go home.

He goes through the door and there is his wife, Betty, hysterical and in tears. She asks him, "Where have you been? You didn't come home after work. You have been gone two days! I thought you were dead, I didn't know what happened to you! You look awful, and you stink! Where is your paycheck? There is no food in the house and the kids are hungry!"

Barney feels terrible, but he can't honestly tell Betty what he has done. Somehow, they make it through the next week, and Barney does what he is supposed to do. This goes on for a while, and things get back to "normal." However, the lure of that powerful experience tugs at Barney and he decides that he is due for another round of "me time."

Now, he has real difficulty staying on course. He keeps going back to his new pal, Tito, and his situation gets progressively worse. The repeated, self-absorbed behavior takes a toll on his family, and there are no lies that he can tell that will cover up what is going on. Barney no longer feels happy or sad. He has lost control of that. All of his emotions are tangled up in repeated bouts of fear, anger, guilt, and shame, until that is all that he feels.

This is the degeneration of his emotional need.

Time goes on, and now Barney has lost his wife, his job, and kids. He lives where he can and steals from others to get enough money to feed his lust for crack cocaine. It is really beginning to take a toll on him, and after getting arrested for petty crimes, landing him in jail a few times, he begins to think that his life has no purpose or meaning. Everything is out of control, and everything he touches gets ruined. He even begins to think that maybe it would be better if he was dead.

This is the degeneration of his psychological need.

Now, Barney lives under a bridge, in a bad part of the city. He no longer cares if his clothes match or are clean. He doesn't care if his teeth fall out or that all of his few possessions fit in a stolen shopping cart that he pushes around all day, searching for empty cans—at least enough to redeem toward another "bag." Eventually Barney gets sick and succumbs.

This is the final degeneration of his last need, his physical need.

Barney has travelled down a long spiral to his eventual death, and it is an incredibly sad thing.

That illustration may seem to be extreme but is more common than you can know. Though most people do not experience that dramatic a spiral, no matter what their "altar of worship" is, no matter whether it is drugs, or food, or sex, or relationships, or gambling, or money, or work, or sport, or whatever, if that first and most essential need is not met, life spirals down. There is nothing in this world that can satisfy the human longing for fulfillment, to be whole and to be connected to God. Sadly, every day, countless numbers of people wander through life without the assurance of Christ, and after years of searching and frustration pass into eternity outside of the knowledge of Christ and the forgiveness of God. Here is another:

Spiritual

Emotional

Psychological

Physical

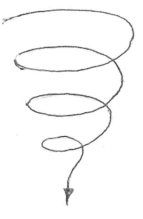

The downward spiral begins when the spiritual need is not being properly met. It is one of the saddest things to see.

The Road to Recovery

The road to recovery is a counseling perspective and plan that addresses each of the four needs, starting at the very bottom of the spiral, at the physical need, and working our way back to the top. Essentially, the first need, the spiritual need, must be dealt with in order for this to work, because without Christ, we can do nothing. Our spiritual life and connection to God enables us to stop the decay of self-worship and find understanding and healing for all of our other needs.

Once, of course, that primary need is met then the process begins at the bottom of the spiral. Over the course of counseling people through this program, not everyone has reached the absolute bottom of the spiral, to the point where they have given up and are struggling just to survive. Some individuals coming into counseling may be at the very beginning of the struggle and dealing with only the emotional upheaval that their behaviors have brought into view. Some, having been through the many episodes of lies, anger, and have suffered the loss of family and friends, haven't yet come to the point where they conclude that their life is without meaning. Then, there are those who have come to that dangerous crossroad, where their complete loss of control over their life and the loss of everything of value and relationships question whether their life is worth anything at all. And then there are those who are in desperate struggle and are at that bottom level. It doesn't matter just how far down they are in the spiral, seeing that every one of the needs must be dealt with and addressed in turn for complete recovery.

So we start with the addressing of the physical need. Our physical need deals with such things as chemical dependency, habitual behaviors, triggers, and temptations. From there we move to the psychological need, which is our need to understand the purpose and meaning of life. After that, we explore the complicated issues of emotions, particularly the more negative emotions of fear, anger, guilt, and shame, and how they affect our lives. With this there is a little more focus on anger and anger management. Lastly, we deal with issues of spiritual growth, discipleship, and service.

When a person completes the first phase of counseling, which is eight counseling sessions, and having been truly born again in a relationship with Christ, they have all of the tools necessary to walk in newness of life and to walk away from the altars where they worshipped themselves.

I remember a guy, who had come to faith in Christ, and having gone through the sessions and doing very well, came to me and said, "I want to go home to my family and be the husband and father God wants me to be." So I said, "Great! Go get 'em, tiger."

A few days later he came back, visibly upset, and I asked him what the matter was. He told me, "I went home and told my wife that I was better and I wanted to get back together. She threw an ashtray at my head and yelled, 'Get out of here you [can't print this] and don't come back!' Now what do I do?"

Well, I considered this for some time and eventually came up with phase two, which deals with family restoration—bringing the offending person into the proper godly leadership role his or her family needs. Phase two deals with biblical instruction in pragmatic, daily life. Issues of responsibility, trust, betrayal, submission, control, and finances are presented, as well as the issues of reentering a family situation where the once offending person returns as a Christian, perhaps to a Christian family or to a family that does not know Christ. It is necessary for a person, hopeful on regaining the trust and leadership of his or her family, to appreciate and take responsibility for the damage that they may have caused. Sometimes, this just won't work. Sometimes, there is too much hurt, or there has been divorce and the ex-spouse has moved on. Issues of forgiveness and spite play a large part in this.

So for the remainder of this exercise, the counseling sessions as they are presented and have been taught and refined over the last twenty years or so will constitute the bulk of the remnants of this book. I hope you will find them interesting.

Working Out the Knots

As I said before, the process of recovery deals with each of the four essential needs of a healthy life, and the needs are placed in a specific order. The reason for this is because in typical cases of addictive behaviors, there is a degeneration of those needs from the first and most essential (the spiritual need), to the emotional need, then the psychological need, and finally the physical need. The process of recovery must go to the very bottom of the pile, to the physical need, and work back up the spiral through and addressing each need in turn.

So we must begin with the physical need.

The physical need, in the process of recovery, deals with addressing the habits and lifestyle that exemplifies addictive behavior. In this regard, Alcoholics Anonymous has, along with many other programs, identified three elements or triggers for addictive behavior. They are people, places, and things. Because addiction is worship that seeks service in the material world, at the altars of our own choosing, these three elements are applicable, for they are all material. The intent here is to identify the triggers and to avoid them. If your friends are all drug users or alcoholics or whatever, you must find new friends. If the places you frequent provide an accessible or supportive means to your behaviors, then you must go to different places. If there are things or activities that promote or cause you to think of those behaviors, you must remove them. Now this does not mean that you must go to some mountaintop cave and live like a hermit. That form of stoicism does not protect you, but may in fact become another altar of self-worship.

There was a movie called *Cold Turkey* that was about an entire town that was challenged to quit smoking for a period of time in order to win a large corporation's building and investing in that community. The promise was a lot of new jobs and prosperity to an otherwise poor town. In the movie, Tom Poston played the town drunk, who was a wealthy bachelor, and said he could not possibly quit smoking because he was a drinker and the "smoke bone is connected to the drink bone." His habit and dependence on tobacco was so closely related to, and part of, his everyday activity that he could not remove it. This is part of the physical need.

It is absolutely important to understand that chemical dependency on a substance introduced into the body or the overstimulation of natural chemicals within the body is not addiction. People do not become addicted to heroin. They become physically and psychologically dependent on it, but that is different. A person who never uses heroin will never be dependent on it. The same goes with nicotine, or alcohol, or any other of the powerful substances that are available for use today. The body is a wonderful, biological machine, capable of repairing itself and, with proper maintenance, will sufficiently perform for the tasks we require of it. Like water, the body seeks its own level. This means that the body is constantly working to remain at a status of optimal condition and use. We know that if a person who is a smoker quits smoking, after a number of years, their health will improve and the risk of serious disease is lessened. As I mentioned earlier, addiction is not disease, but can cause disease. If you drink a quart of applejack every day, eventually you will get very sick. Your stomach, liver, pancreas, and brain will be seriously damaged. If you smoke four packs of cigarettes per day, you will eventually get lung cancer, throat cancer, emphysema, high blood pressure, heart disease, and other maladies. However, if you stop before too much damage has been done, you can improve significantly. We are wonderfully and fearfully made, amazingly complex organisms that have the ability to heal.

There have been many studies and research in the areas of the brain that are affected by substance abuse. The limbic system, which regulates emotions, pleasure and sexual arousal, hormones, and other regulatory functions, can be overstimulated by the introduction of certain chemicals. Alcohol, nicotine, and other drugs activate changes in the amygdala and the hypothalamus, which can produce reactionary responses when the substances are not there. This produces cravings, physical and emotional discomfort, and is key in the development of dependence. I believe that continued overstimulation of the limbic system can also cause a dulling of the system's ability to properly regulate emotions, which may cause emotional deregulation, which is also found in certain mental health problems like PTSD, bipolar disorder, and others.[8] This "desensitization" can cause sexual dysfunction in a person who frequently bombards his brain with pornographic images.

We will take a closer look at the amygdala and the limbic system when we deal with the emotional need.

Apart from the physical difficulties of chemical dependency (though difficult, can be overcome) there are also the associated problems with habitual behavior and temptation.

Anyone who has ever tried to quit smoking quickly realizes that it is much more than just the cravings and physical discomfort that it brings. The "habit" of smoking is a wide range of behaviors that are automatically in sync with actually smoking itself. For example, there are events and situations that are triggers for smoking. They can be: answering the phone, waiting for a bus, finishing a meal, or just waking up in the morning. Coffee breaks, work breaks, conversations, stressful situations, or situations that require a lot of thinking, are all triggers that fire up that conditioned response to fire up a cigarette. So in this case, both the physical dependency and the conditioned response make it very hard to overcome. However, conditional responses can be "reconditioned" to a more favorable behavior. It takes time, determination, and in some cases, help.

This brings us to the third part of the physical need, which is temptation. So what is temptation?

The American Heritage Dictionary defines "tempt" as 1) to entice (someone) to commit an unwise or immoral act, esp. by a promise of reward; 2) to be inviting or attractive to; 3) to provoke or risk provoking; 4) to incline or dispose strongly.

---

8   Koob, George F. *Brain Res.* 2009. Oct. 13:1293: 61–75.

There is no one who is free from temptation, because that is part of our fallen nature. Again, the origin of this is found in the first chapters of the Bible when the serpent beguiled the woman. He did not tempt her, but deceived her. Satan does not have to tempt us. He only presents the opportunity to fall in our temptation. In the case of Eve in the garden of Eden, at the tree of the knowledge of good and evil, there are some important details to observe.

Let's look at these few verses for a moment.

> Now the serpent was more crafty that any beast of the field which the LORD God had made. And he said to the woman, "Indeed, has God said, 'You shall not eat from any tree of the garden?'" The woman said to the serpent, "From the fruit of the trees of the garden we may eat; but from the fruit of the tree which is in the middle of the garden, God has said, 'You shall not eat from it or touch it, or you will die.'" The serpent said to the woman, "You surely will not die! For God knows that in the day you eat from it your eyes will be opened, and you will be like God, knowing good and evil." When the woman saw that the tree was good for food, and that it was a delight to the eyes, and that the tree was desirable to make one wise, she took from its fruit and ate; and she gave also to her husband with her, and he ate. (Genesis 3:1–6 NASB)

The serpent does not tempt Eve to eat from the tree; he gets her to doubt God's intent and veracity. Her response is interesting. She said that they may not eat or *touch* it. God did not say that. His command to Adam was "From any tree of the garden you may eat freely; but from the tree of the knowledge of good and evil you shall not eat, for in the day that you eat from it you will surely die" (Genesis 2:16b, 17 NASB).

God did not say that you couldn't touch it. That is interesting in that it is the first time that man added a law to God's law to insulate him from the danger of breaking God's commandment.

Now Eve saw that the fruit was good for food, which is the lust of the flesh, and that it was a delight to the eyes, which is the lust of the eyes, and that it was able to make one wise, which is the pride of life. The first two were enticements in the sense that people will justify disobedience with such things. That in itself is a problem that continues in the human condition. The real stickler is the third enticement, in that it would make her equal with God, and thereby becoming a god herself. The desire to be equal to God, and thus becoming our own god, is the reason for the fall of man. It was Satan's pride that lifted him up to think that he could be equal with God, and it was that pride that cast him down to the pit. He deceived the woman into falling into the same trap of pride that he did. The devil hated man from the day he was created and has ever sought to destroy God's wonderful creation. God poured out to man all of His love and mercy, a thing that must have angered Satan the most.

The things that we are so attracted to, in a particular sense, never tempt us. Temptation is a conflict that exists within each of us. The conflict is in knowing that the act in itself is something we don't want to do, but the immediate gratification, the physical rush, or whatever, the *reward* weighs heavily on us. The inner conflict of temptation is not even about the act or the substance or even the temporary reward, but it is all about control. Who has control over me? Who is the boss of me?

I remember my daughter, yup, the same one that lied about the cookies, telling me, "You're not the boss of me!" That is a very common response from children who struggle with authority—like all of us. She quickly learned that I was the boss of her, and it would be demonstrated and enforced.

In addictive behaviors, it is all about me. We are all resentful of authority to some degree and the control that responsibilities has over us. I just read recently that more than 75 percent of the working people in America hate their job and that the overwhelming reason they hate their job is because they hate their boss. We are and have always been resentful and rebellious to authority. The first-born child in this world, according to the Scriptures, demonstrated this; the man named Cain.

This goes back to what we have seen so far. The natural man, with an inward and intense need to worship, but does not have the spiritual ability to worship the God we are intended to worship, must turn that worship elsewhere. The prevailing object of that false worship is the self—we become our own gods. For all of the history of our existence in this world, that has been the conflict and the source of the conflict: man's desperate need for God and his selfish desire for autonomy without restriction. The conflict is between man and God. The Bible also tells us that there is not only our old nature that defines the conflict, but also that God will give us a new nature—a nature of obedience. Paul wrote, "Therefore if any man be in Christ, he is a new creature: old things are passed away; behold, all things are become new" (2 Corinthians 5:17).

The Bible also tells us that we must avoid those things, places, and people that cause us to stumble and gives us the consequences for those who pursue them. Those behaviors that cause harm to us are offensive to God, who only means the best for us. That which offends God is sin. The Bible teaches us that the pleasures of sin last for a season, but it eventually brings death. God warns us about many things.

The sin of drugs or alcohol:

> Who hath woe? Who hath sorrow? Who hath contentions? Who hath babblings? Who hath wounds without cause? Who hath redness of eyes? They that tarry long at the wine; they that go to seek mixed wine. At the last it biteth like a serpent, ad stingeth like an adder. (Proverbs 23:29, 30, 32)

The sin of adultery:

> And why wilt thou, my son, be ravished with a strange woman, and embrace the bosom of a stranger? For the ways of man are before the eyes of the LORD, and he pondereth all his goings. His own iniquities shall take the wicked himself, and he shall be holden with the cords of his sins. He shall die without instruction; and in the greatness of his folly, he shall go astray.
>
> Can a man take fire in his bosom, and his clothes be not burned? Can one go upon hot coals, and his feet be not burned? So he that goeth in to his neighbor's wife: whoever toucheth her shall not be innocent. But whoso committeth adultery with a woman lacketh understanding: he that doeth it destroyeth his own soul. (Proverbs 6:27–29, 32)

The sin of gambling:

> He that is greedy of gain troubleth his own house. (Proverbs 15:27)

There is also the great sin of causing others to stumble in their weakness or being enticed by others to follow into trouble.

> It is good neither to eat flesh, nor to drink wine, nor any things whereby thy brother stumbleth, or is offended, or is made weak. (Romans 14:21)
>
> My son, if sinners entice thee, consent thou not. If they say, Come with us, let us lay wait for blood, let us lurk privily for the innocent without cause: let us swallow them up alive as the grave; and whole, as those that go down into the pit: we shall find all precious substance, we shall fill

our houses with spoii: cast in they lot among us;
let us all have one purse: My son, walk not thou
in the way with them; refrain thy foot from their
path. (Proverbs 1:10–15)

So far, we have identified the problem, which is self-worship.
We understand that we are our own worst enemy and that we have
developed an entire lifestyle of bad behaviors around this self-worship. We see how the downward spiral of addictive behavior effectively destroys every area of our needs. We also realize that we cannot,
by our own power, resist the temptations of our lifestyle and must
trust in the Lord Jesus Christ for all our needs. The Lord told His
disciples, "I am the vine, you are the branches. He that abides in me,
and I in him, the same brings forth much fruit: for without me you
can do nothing" (John 15:5).

Conversely, we can be assured of victory over anything in our
lives by the power of Christ.

"I can do all things through Christ which strengthens me"
(Philippians 4:13).

Having this hope and this confidence, we can change the behaviors that have enslaved us.

The impulses we receive as part of a patterned lifestyle are powerful, as I said before. They are powerful because they are like a well-
worn path through a briar patch. It is easy, if not automatic, to follow
the path of least resistance and the impulses of our habit. If the path
we follow is the destructive sin path of addictive behavior, and realize
that it is not the path we desire to take, the impulses to follow that
track are temptations. We are desperate to cut a new path through
the thick, painful briars, but constantly aware of a smooth, well-worn
path.

For the natural man, apart from Christ, the power to have victory over temptation is not there. Without the freedom and blessing
of the Holy Spirit, the only power man has over temptation is his
own will power. Though some may be strong-willed, it is not enough
to break the chains and remove the claws that have brought so much
trouble to life. Only God can grant such power. If there is no born

again relationship with God through Christ, there is no presence of the Spirit and the idolatry of the *self* rules. However, when a person comes to Christ, the power of our sinful nature is broken and we are free to choose. It is a strange thing that when we come to Christ, we are given a new nature, a nature of obedience to God. What is stranger still is that our old nature, our sin nature, is not taken away. We are then found with two disparate natures—one of obedience in faith to God, and the other to the obedience of sin and self. Jesus said, "No one can serve two masters; for either he will hate the one and love the other, or he will be devoted to one and despise the other. You cannot serve God and wealth" (Matthew 6:24 NASB).

I like that version of that saying because "mammon" means more than just money. It means worldly gain and avarice, which the lusting after is an altar of self-worship. That is the conflict that is in our souls every day. Who is worthy to be worshipped? Who is worthy to have rule over me? That is what our temptation is.

For believers, we *do* have choice. When tempted over the issue of the ownership of me, we can choose God and say no to me. God promises us that we can have victory over temptation. Paul wrote, "No temptation has overtaken you except such as is common to man; but God is faithful, who will not allow you to be tempted beyond what you are able, but with the temptation will also make the way of escape, that you may be able to bear it" (1 Corinthians 10:13 NKJV).

This is one of the most important verses we can have in our struggle with addictive behaviors. It is God's promise to give us an escape—an escape from the same repeated, self-indulgent behaviors that cause us to fail and bring misery to our lives and our families. God's love for us is such that He desires the very best for us, and He knows better about that than we do.

Now, there are elements of this verse that need to be examined a little more closely. The first is *"No temptation has overtaken you except such as is common to man."*

There is nothing that shocks or surprises God. No matter what temptations have come your way, someone else somewhere has struggled with the same thing. They are *common* to man. We all have the same hopes, the same fears, the same problems. They are common among all men now and have been since that terrible day in the garden when Adam and Eve chose to disobey God. There is, as Solomon put it, nothing new under the sun. Sometimes we feel like we are absolutely alone and that there is no one who understands what we are going through. God assures us that it is not so; He knows all we have gone through and all that we will go through. Jesus told us, "In the world you will have tribulation; but be of good cheer, I have overcome the world" (John 16:33b).

Job said, "Yet man is born to trouble as surely as sparks fly upward" (Job 5:7 NIV).

God knows all our temptations. The second part is the promise: "But God is faithful, who will not allow you to be tempted beyond what you are able."

God knows all that we are tempted of, and for those who are His children, He will not allow them to be left alone, without help.

"But with the temptation will also make the way of escape."

This is a place where many fail. God does not take the temptation away, but offers another path. So many have come to me in the past, saying, "I tried going to church, I tried praying, but the temptation is still there, so I think God won't help. He doesn't care, and I give in." Paul continually tells us that we need to get rid of the "old man," which is our sin nature, and put on the "new man," which is in Christ. It is a decision that we must make and one that we can make if we are believers. The choice is to either follow God or our own desires. He is the escape. The choice is "who is in charge of me?" God will allow us to choose wrongly, but we will suffer the consequences. His desire is that we will say no to us and yes to Him. Another way of looking at it is like this: life is sometimes like a thick briar patch that surrounds us. It is high and dense, and there is no way through. Temptations are like the well-worn path that seems to be the only opening, the only way out. Life begins to close in around us, pressing the briars ever closer, and when we cannot take it any more we head down that well-worn path, even though it leads us to a place we don't really want to go. God does not want us to continue taking that route but wants us to blaze a new trail through the briars. He will lead us and give us the strength to cut the new path, but it won't be easy. We are likely to get scratched up quite a bit in the effort, but as we go, the old path will grow over and disappear.

Temptation is a fork in the road. One way is my way, and the other is God's. We can choose either. If we decide to go our way it is because we reject the rule of God at that moment and declare our own sovereignty. God is merciful and gracious, and He will let us fall on our face. When we choose to go our way, we know where it goes. Most of the time, it goes around in a circle and brings us right back to where we were.

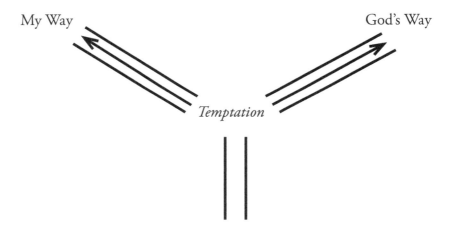

My Way   God's Way

Temptation

Temptation is the fork in the road to choose who is boss of me: me or God.

We have no idea where God's way will lead, but we do know that God is good and that He means the very best for us. My way will lead to a place we know all too well—disappointment and failure. That road also circles back around to where we were. God will permit this to happen until we learn that His way is better.

The temptations will never stop. We must choose every day to follow God and to acknowledge that He is God and we are not.

Finding Our Value

Working our way back up the downward spiral brings us to the next essential need—the psychological need. The psychological need is our need to understand that life, our life, has purpose and meaning, that it has great value. In the downward spiral, after suffering repeated failures and relapses, our emotional need is shot to pieces and it then goes down to affect the psychological need. This is a very dangerous point in the life of a person suffering from the false worship of addictive behaviors, because it is at this point that a person begins to assess that the many failures and disappointments that they experience in life, as well as the pain and suffering that they cause in the lives of those they love, make them doubt that their life is worth living.

Man has ever sought for the meaning of life and for the purpose of each individual life. Some people, throughout history, have been driven with an incessant need to make a mark in the world so that they will be long remembered after their demise. Man has always looked in esteem at those who have done heroic deeds or who have changed the course of the world with what they have contributed. Great captains of industry and invention have certainly left their mark, though after long years, their names are lost to time. It is most probable that old Bach will outlive us all. J. S. Bach, the prolific composer and one of the fathers of modern music, said, "All music should be written for the glory of God." His music lives on, as well as Beethoven and Mozart and so many others. Henry Ford, whose name is still attached to the front of all of the company's cars and trucks, made automobiles affordable for all with the invention of the assembly line. These are remarkable achievements that continue to leave a legacy of greatness throughout the world.

Others have also left their mark, but in a way that has caused great calamity and harm. Adolf Hitler, Mao Tse Tung, Karl Marx, and Joseph Stalin, have all shown the world their drive for power. The cost of their personal ambitions is counted in the more than one hundred million lives that they destroyed in the last century alone.

The frailty and quick passing of our mortal lives creates this need for legacy and, with that, the need to be valued by others. In this world, people seek to find the meaning of their lives and their value by what is seen or noted of them by others. How do we stand out in the crowd?

Our drive for legacy, purpose, and meaning, to be remembered for being in this world are byproducts of our search for identity: *Who am I, where do I belong, and what am I supposed to do?* One of the most extraordinary examples of this can be found in adolescence. High schools and middle schools are laboratories for social awareness and the desperate search for kids to find out who they are and where they fit in. In every high school in America, there are distinct tribes of young men and women, morphing into whatever group that they are drawn to and that will take them in as one of their own. There are jocks and preppies, nerds, goths, gays and straights, skaters and druggies, and others. In certain areas gangs like the Bloods and the Latin Kings, as well as biker gangs like Hell's Angels, are all part of the same tribal need to feel a part of and secure in their particular society.

As interesting as all that is, those groups and the activities and behaviors associated with them are only *what you do* and not *who you are*. Membership in a gang is something you do, not who you are. In our desperate search for meaning, we have a tendency to settle into whatever group we fit in and wrongly determine our identity and purpose through that.

In this social scrutiny of who's who and where-do-you-fit-in-the-stratum-of-acceptability, the world has its own ideas and judgments. We get these Hollywood, GQ, and Cosmopolitan views that attach value to appearance, fame, celebrity, fortune, and pleasure. If you aren't a movie star, or sports star, or fabulously wealthy, then you are of little or no value. If you don't have the right hair, or nose, or pedigree, if you don't have a PhD from Harvard or wherever, you are no more than the dirt you will be buried in. There is nothing to remember you for and no legacy that you will leave for the rest of us. In the European history, nobility defined value. To this day, in certain parts of Europe, if you are not of the *peerage,* you have no real value. Nobles had *names,* which were generally associated with a "house." Many of these names have designations in front of them to show that they are from, or of, a particular house or land. The German "Von" as well as the Dutch "Van," or the Scottish "Mac" or the French "Le," were all common designations. If you were not of the favored blood, you were called by what you did. Smith worked in metals. Cooper was a barrel maker. Farmer, or Shepherd, or Miller are names given to those who worked in those areas. This is all part of man's fallen nature—a nature that desires to lord over and dominate others. It is the reason for the curse of slavery, and subjugation, and war.

Well, what do you expect from a fallen world, full of fallen people—a world where self-worship is universally explored and celebrated?

So how do we come to find out who we are, where we belong, and what truly is the value, purpose, and meaning of life?

There are three possibilities, two of which I have just touched on. The first is that we determine our value and meaning by what we do. In this, the need to accomplish great things, whether we succeed or not, by the way, is an altar of self-worship, driven by ego. Ouch. The greatest doctor or scientist in the world, who has accomplished wonderful things, is *not* what he has learned or done. That has nothing to do with *who* he is. A person who claims he is what he does has missed the boat. By that same line, *what* you are does not determine *who* you are either. The world pigeonholes and judges by appearance, after the flesh. When I say *what you are,* I mean that which is determined by DNA, not by choice. The peculiar shade of your skin, or the interesting culture that you were raised in, or the geographical area of your birth, or the environment of your upbringing do not determine *who* you are. Those things can determine how and what you think and how you behave only.

So often, we hear about people who have made bad decisions in their life and end up committing crimes and going to prison. It is said that they are "products of their environment." Environment can certainly affect how you think and certainly how you behave, but it does not determine who you are. A great example is Dr. Ben Carson, who was born and raised in a terrible neighborhood, in abject poverty, to a family structure of a single mom. His environment did not make him who he is, though it probably contributed to his strength of character. The fact that he overcame that environment to become an accomplished neurosurgeon is remarkable, but still, he is not what he does.

We should not be too quick in determining our value or purpose. I have made a lot of mistakes in judgment over my long life, and I will more than likely continue to do so until the Lord takes me home. I do not have perfect judgment. I have made conclusions about things that I was quite certain of, but later found out to be in error. Why would I think that my conclusions about my own value are valid?

Secondly, we have the value judgment of the world and the mess that that is. The problem with that standard of value is that there is no one who can actually achieve it. Fame and fortune are both fleeting things. The great movie idols of the '20s and '30s are vanished. Their celebrity faded quickly, as new "stars" hurried to find their own fame. Time and age are the inevitable enemies of fame and fortune. In the days of the Romans, conquering generals would be paraded through the city in golden chariots, thronged by masses of grateful, cheering citizens. Behind the general would be a slave, whispering in his ear a gentle but solemn reminder that this too shall pass. Of all the things people fear, death and obscurity are, to some, the most dreadful. People want to think their life was worth something. Unfortunately, this harsh world judges only a lofty few for that honor.

The third possibility is that our value is noted and proclaimed by God, who made us. This is made clear to us in the Scriptures. John wrote that God created us all for His purpose and by His will and for His pleasure. "Worthy are You, our Lord and our God, to receive glory and honor and power; for You created all things, and because of Your will they existed, and were created" (Revelation 4:11 NASB).

It doesn't matter who you are, or what you look like, or what language you speak. You are here by the direct determined plan of God, no matter the circumstance of our birth. God made you exactly who and what you are at this time and in this place for His purpose and will. Before you were born, you did not choose your parents, or you race, or your sex, or how smart you are, or how stupid. You did not choose whether you have ten fingers or not, or toes, or blind or deaf. God chose all of those things. We had nothing to say about where or when we were born. I will touch on this again later. Jesus was born in a cave and His two parents, both descended from the house of David, lived in abject poverty. He was raised in a small town in a land occupied by foreigners in a dark time in the history of the world. Yet, though He only lived for thirty-two or thirty-three years in this world, preached for just three as an itinerant preacher, and never travelled more than one-hundred miles from where He was born, His life, death, and resurrection altered human history and continues to change the world. Neither circumstance nor environment detracts from God's great purpose in you. David was amazed by God's divine purpose and power as he sang, "You made all the delicate, inner parts of my body and knit me together in my mother's womb. Thank you for making me so complex! Your workmanship is marvelous—and how well I know it. You watched me as I was being formed in utter seclusion, I as woven together in the dark of the womb. You saw me before I was born. Every day of my life was recorded in your book, every moment was laid out before a single day had passed. How precious are your thoughts about me, O God! They are innumerable! I can't even count them; they outnumber the grains of sand! And when I wake up in the morning, you are still with me!" (Psalms 139:13–18 NLT).

Jeremiah was very young when the Lord God spoke to him.

> Then the words of the LORD came unto me, saying, "Before I formed thee in the belly I knew thee; and before thou camest forth out of the womb I sanctified thee, and I ordained the a prophet unto the nations." Then said I, "Ah,

Lord God, behold I cannot speak: for I am a child." But the LORD said unto me, "Say not, I am a child: for thou shalt go to all that I shall send thee, and whatsoever I command thee thou shalt speak." (Jeremiah 1:4–7)

Looking at this marvelous creation that you are from a purely scientific point of view, you are incredibly unique. There has never been a person exactly like you in this world, and there never will be again. That is because we have learned about the incredible role of DNA in every living thing. DNA is simply comprised of two twisting "rails" of phosphate and sugar, joined together by "rungs" of adenine, thymine, cytosine, and guanine. Though this seems simple, the arrangement of these elements create a complex "code" that determines everything about you. The amount of information in one single strand of DNA is mind-boggling. Everything that you are is in that code, including future health concerns and strengths. At conception, part of the code from the father mixes with the code of the mother and a totally new and unique individual begins to take form. I could go on for pages upon pages of how incredibly special you are with the information that we have learned about how we work, but I think you get the idea.

We have great value to God, as He made you for His purpose. Jesus said:

Look at the birds. They don't need to plant or harvest or put food in barns because your heavenly Father feeds them. And you are more valuable to him than they are. (Matthew 6:26 NLT)

Are not five sparrows sold for two cents? Yet not one of them is forgotten before God. Indeed, the very hairs of your head are all numbered. Do not fear; you are more valuable than may sparrows. (Luke 12:7 NASB)

If you look at the lives of the great heroes of the Bible, you will find that there was absolutely nothing remarkable about them. They were just ordinary men and women who God used to do remarkable things. Samuel was just a boy when the Lord God called him to be prophet and priest for Israel. Josiah was eight years old when he became king of Judah, and yet, by the time he was in his early twenties, he had cleansed Israel from idols and false gods, tearing down the high places where the groves and statues of the terrible idols were worshipped. Gideon was the least in his father's house, which was the least in his tribe, which was the least in all of Israel. Yet God used him mightily to drive back the armies of the Assyrians. Deborah was a young woman, fearless, that God used to judge Israel when there were no men that had courage. Ruth was a foreign widow from Moab, whose love for her mother-in-law led her to Israel where she won the heart of Boaz and was the grandmother of the great king, David. Moses was raised as a prince in Egypt, who ran away after killing an Egyptian soldier. He was a man of slow speech and low self-esteem, but God used him to deliver his people from the bondage of Egypt. Moses spoke with God face-to-face, as a man would speak to his friend, and God gave him the Law to separate Israel from the world. Elijah, the great prophet, was a man of like passions, just as the rest of us. Peter was a simple fisherman, quick to anger and hasty to act.

Though these, and too many more to name, were not one bit more special than you, God used them to do amazing things.

One time, a young pastor came to me for counseling. He was totally burned out. He was trying so hard to build a ministry that would be better than anything else in the world and was flat on his face. I asked him, "What the heck is the matter with you?" He responded, "I don't know, I just want to do something great for God." I said that I thought that was a noble gesture, but "What makes you think there is anything that you can do that is in the least bit acceptable to God? You struggle and strive to show God how great you are, but you don't understand that it is God who is great and He doesn't want you to do a thing for Him. He wants to do something great *through* you. Rejoice that God wants to use you for His purpose and just obey. We are mere men, and without Him, we can do nothing."

If you still question your value to God, remember that He sent His only begotten Son to die on a cruel cross for you, to redeem you from this world of sin, so that you may have life and find your purpose—that you may find the meaning of life itself.

I like to tell my students that "The carpenter builds the house, but he does not build it without tools. Also, the tools that the carpenter uses can do nothing on their own. They just sit in the toolbox waiting to be used. The saw, designed to cut wood, can do nothing of its own, but in the hand of the master carpenter, can cut wood beautifully. It is the master carpenter that uses and guides the tool, that the house may be built."

The Lord is the Master Carpenter, and we are the tools He will use to build His kingdom and His church. Not all of us are hammers, or saws, or rules, or trowels, but He has made us what we are so His toolbox may be full and that we may be used by Him for His glory.

It is important to understand that we not only have great value to God, but we are also designed for a specific purpose. He made you who and what you are for His glory, not yours. It is essential that we discover exactly what God made us to do and allow Him to use us in that way for His kingdom. A great sadness in this world is the fact that most people have no idea why they are here, and what they are supposed to do, and what God has designed them to do. Every day thousands of people leave this world with no idea what will happen to them and no knowledge of Christ. Even many, if not most, of those who claim to know Christ and trust Him as Savior ever find out what God made them to do. They are consumed with making their own way in the world, to live life according to their own plans and desires, and never know the joy of knowing and doing what God designed them to do. For those who *do* discover what God has made them to do and do it, there is no greater joy. It is a life fulfilled—happy to be used by God in His service. This doesn't mean that we are all supposed to be pastors or missionaries to some foreign land, but we are all called by God to do something. That is our joy in discovery. If you have an honest desire to be used by God for His kingdom, He will show the way.

Man has always asked, "What is the meaning of life?" It is a great mystery, which is completely unsolvable in this world. The meaning of life is directly tied to our purpose and value to God. Dr. Ravi Zacharias, one of the most noted Christian apologists of our time, says, "There are four particular questions that have to be answered: origin, meaning, morality, and destiny, and when they are put together the form a worldview. A worldview is a set of assumptions or assertions you have made through which you look at every choice and decision that ultimately comes in life to shape, especially you values and your spiritual commitments that are made in your day-to-day living."[9]

In respect to origin, the question is "Where did I come from?" The question of meaning is "Why am I here?" The question of morality is "Who determines what is right and what is wrong?" And the question of destiny is "What happens to me after I die?" For each of those questions, philosophers and religionists have searched for the answers, and the only thing that completely and satisfactorily answers them, that calms the longing of our hearts and souls, is a person—and that person is Christ.

Only Christians can understand this truth—that outside of Christ, life has no meaning. He is the author and finisher of our faith, both Creator God and completely human Savior. He is the judge of all the earth, and though He was slain on a cruel cross for the sin of the world, He is alive, raised bodily and ascended to the throne of heaven where He awaits the command of His Father to the completion of all created things. He is our Lord and Savior, Counselor, Defender, King, and hope. Discovering your purpose as God has created you to do and enjoying a living relationship with the Lord Jesus Christ give life meaning that cannot be annulled or lost. Jesus said, "If you cling to your life, you will lose it; but if you give up your life for me, you will find it" (Matthew 10:39 NLT).

---

[9]   Zacharias, Ravi. *What Is a Worldview?* rzimask.org.

I believe what the Lord was telling His disciples was that if you try to find the meaning of life in this world, you will miss the whole point of your existence, but if you seek the meaning of life through Me, you will find it. That is an incredibly provocative explanation of that verse, I know, but if you consider the context of the passage in Matthew, and that the Lord also tells them that they must deny themselves, take up their cross daily, and follow after Me, it rings true.

Now, as I said, this doesn't mean that we are all to be pastors or missionaries. You can do whatever your heart leads you to do to serve. Also, God doesn't stress about what you do to earn a living. He provides all that you need. You can be a doctor, or a plumber, or a dishwasher. That is not important.

I believe one of the great problems we have in this country today is that the world tells us that the ultimate goal for life is to make as much money as possible so that you can retire as early as you can and just enjoy life. For this reason, parents push their kids to college to get a degree so that their "earning potential" will help them achieve that goal. Too many kids are going to college with this burden hanging around their necks, amassing huge debt to acquire this degree that promises absolutely nothing. They go through life with this fear that if they don't make enough money they won't be able to get that cottage on the lake or be able to travel around the world, and that they will end up broke, in old age, spending all their money on medicine and regretting that they missed life. In a point of fact, they have missed life—the very purpose of it.

God does not make mistakes. He has made you exactly who and what you are for His purpose and pleasure. You are absolutely unique, in that you have never existed before and you will never exist in this world again. This is your shot, all that you have, to discover what life is really all about and to serve in the way that God has designed you. The average lifespan of a man or woman is approximately seventy-five years. What is that in eternity? It is a tiny punch through the endless ribbon of time.

I remember my great-aunt had a player piano. It was an ancient thing, and she had rows and piles of dusty boxes with rolls in them, each made to play a particular song through the piano. As I remember, the piano had a sort of window that opened up above the keyboard, in the upright face of the thing, where you could insert the piano roll. You would pull down on the paper and feed it into a slit in a reel that would turn by some geared mechanism, and as the paper rolled down, the machine would read the holes punched in the paper and play a corresponding note on the piano. It was remarkable and tons of fun for a kid. I like to think that our lives are like the holes punched in God's eternal ribbon of time, and that, all of them together throughout long history, make up His great symphony. Your life and mine are essential notes in this ages-long symphony, and without you it is missing a note.

Your life has enormous value to God and to the world. Because God has made you for this time and this place, you also have a responsibility to discover what He has made you to do to build His kingdom and serve others. This is what gives life meaning.

Don't miss it!

Steady as She Goes

As we continue to climb back up the spiral, we come to the next of the four essential needs, the emotional need. We are created in the image and the likeness of God, and that means that we, like God, are triune in our being. The trinity of God is different from that which He has made—He is one God, in three distinct persons. This is beyond our ability to explain, but this is the essence of who God is. As He is triune in His nature, all of creation is also triune, in its own nature. Man, created in His likeness, was also triune, having a body of flesh, a soul, and a spirit. We have already seen how the spirit was cut off from the presence of God, leaving us essentially dead to Him. We have also seen that through Christ, the spirit may be "reborn" and made alive again, reuniting our fellowship with God.

Man, in his soul, is also created in the image of God. God is an intelligent being, personal, and creative. He also is an emotional being. All of our emotions emanate from God's creative plan and design. The Bible clearly shows that God is an emotional being and that His emotions are in perfect accordance with His holy nature. God's emotions are not the same as our emotions, because our emotions are reactive. God's emotions are not, as He does not "react" to situations here as we do. He holds the universe in the palm of His hand and knows the end from the beginning. It is nearly impossible for us to understand what omniscience means, as well as omnipresence and omnipotence. We cannot transcend the mortal flesh that confines us. We are bound to this physical universe, this world, and to the perpetual stream of time that we are caught in. We are like leaves, floating down a swift stream. We can't stop or go faster or slower. We can't go back or go forward apart from the current we are streaming in. Like fleas in a matchbox, who cannot experience or know of anything outside of the box, we can't fully understand the complete nature of God. A good example of this is from the book of Exodus.

Moses heard the voice of God, who called him from a burning bush and told him to return to Egypt, where God would deliver his people. Obedient and meek, Moses went and stood before Pharaoh, witnessing the mighty hand of God working in miracles. He led the people out of Egypt, crossed the Red Sea on dry land, and came to the mountain of God, where he ascended and met with Him. From there he received the Law, to give to and govern Israel. Through all of this, Moses was obedient and terrified. He did as He was instructed, and though in the presence of God Almighty, did not know Him. Needing desperately to know God better, he pleaded with Him to show him His way. What this is, is Moses asking God to show him what He intended, why He did what He did, and what was His purpose with the people of Israel. God's response was perfect: "And He said, 'My Presence will go with you, and I will give you rest'" (Exodus 33:14 NKJV).

This is God's will for mankind and His desire to be with us and to give us rest. It doesn't get any more profound than that. Moses then asks to see His glory, to which God tells him that He will show him His goodness, but no man can look upon His face and live.

Now God is a spirit, who does not have a "face" as we understand. But our face is the identifier of who we are, it is the fullness of who we are. If a person gets arrested, they take photographs of his face, not his knees, or feet, or torso. It is the face that identifies who a person is. It is the fullness of who they are. When Moses asked to see God's glory or the fullness of who He is, God told him that no one could "see" that and live. We can't comprehend the fullness of the glory of the person of God. It would destroy us.

I suppose the reason for this little jaunt down this rabbit trail is to help us understand that though God is an emotional being, He does not express emotions in the same manner as mankind. He is greater than anything a human mind could imagine and is incomprehensible in His being, and we would be wise to remember that.

With that said, God is an emotional being and has granted to us to be emotional beings as well. But what are emotions, and why do we have them?

First, let's look at what the Bible says about God's emotions and how they are conveyed.

God loves because God is love.

> Behold, what manner of love the Father hath bestowed upon us, that we should be called the children of God. (1 John 3:1)

> Therefore doth my Father love me, because I lay down my life, that I may take it back again. (John 10:17)

> For God so loved the world, that He gave His only begotten Son, that whosoever believeth in Him should not perish, but have everlasting life. (John 3:16)

> This is my commandment, That ye love one another, as I have loved you. Greater love hath no man than this, that a man lay down his life for his friends. (John 15:12–13)

> O righteous Father, although the world has not known You, yet I have known You; and these have known that you sent Me; and I have made Your name known to them, and will make it known, so that the love with which You loved Me may be in them, and I in them. (John 17:25–26 NASB)

John gave us all of those references, and there are dozens more, but you get the point.

God also hates:

> "I have loved you," says the LORD. But you say,
> "How have you loved us?"
> "Is not Esau Jacob's brother?" declares the
> LORD. "Yet I have loved Jacob but Esau I have
> hated. I have laid waste his hill country and left
> his heritage to jackals of the desert." (Malachi
> 1:2–3 ESV)

> You shall not worship the LORD your God in
> that way; for every abomination to the LORD
> which He hates they have done to their gods; for
> they burn even their sons and daughters in the
> fire to their gods. (Deuteronomy 12:31 NKJV)

> You shall not set up a sacred pillar, which the
> LORD your God hates. (Deuteronomy 16:22
> NKJV)

> The boastful shall not stand in Your sight; You
> hate all workers of iniquity. The LORD abhors
> the bloodthirsty and deceitful man. (Psalm 5:5–
> 6b NKJV)

These six things the LORD hates, yes, seven are an abomination to Him:

> A proud look, a lying tongue, hands that shed
> innocent blood, a heart that devises wicked plans,
> feet that are swift in running to evil, a false wit-
> ness who speaks lies, and one who sows discord
> among brethren. (Proverbs 6:16–19 NKJV)

God can be pleased:

> And behold, a voice from heaven said, "This is my beloved Son, with whom I am well pleased." (Matthew 3:17 ESV)

> It pleased the Lord that Solomon had asked this. (1 Kings 3:17 ESV)

> And without faith it is impossible to please Him, for whoever would draw near to God must believe that He exists and that He rewards those who seek Him. (Hebrews 11:6 ESV)

God can also be grieved:

> The LORD was sorry that He had made man on the earth, and He was grieved in His heart. (Genesis 6:6 NASB)

> How often they rebelled against Him in the wilderness and grieved Him in the desert! (Psalm 78:40 ESV)

> And do not grieve the Holy Spirit of God, by whom you were sealed for the *day of redemption.* (Ephesians 4:30 NKJV)

God is jealous:

> Thou shalt not bow down thyself to them, nor serve them; for I the LORD thy God am a jealous God, visiting the iniquity of the fathers upon the children unto the third and fourth generation of them that hate me. (Exodus 20:5)

They provoked Him to jealousy with strange gods, with abominations provoked they Him to anger. (Deuteronomy 32:16)

God is jealous, and the LORD avenges; the LORD avenges and is furious. (Nahum 1:2a, b NKJV)

Now Judah did evil in the sight of the LORD, and they provoked Him to jealousy with their sins which they committed, more than all that their fathers had done. (1 Kings 14:22 NKJV)

God is angry and filled with wrath. There are more verses that speak of God's wrath and anger than His love. Here are just a few:

Also in Horeb you provoked the LORD to wrath, so that the LORD was angry enough with you to have destroyed you. (Deuteronomy 9:8 NKJV)

And the LORD uprooted them from their land in anger, in wrath, and in great indignation, and cast them into another land, as it is this day. (Deuteronomy 29:28)

Thus saith the LORD: "Behold, I will bring calamity on this place and on its inhabitants—all the words of the book which the king of Judah has read—because they have forsaken Me and burned incense to other gods, that they might provoke Me to anger with all the works of their hands. Therefore My wrath shall be aroused against this place and shall not be quenched." (2 Kings 22:16–17)

For we have been consumed by Your anger, and by Your wrath we are terrified. (Psalm 90:7 NKJV)

And to wait for His Son from heaven, whom He raised from the dead, even Jesus who delivers us from the wrath to come. (1 Thessalonians 1:10 NKJV)

"Fall on us and hide us from the face of Him who sits on the throne and from the wrath of the Lamb! For the great day of His wrath has come, and who is able to stand?" (Revelation 6:16b, 17)

Well, that's enough of that! Those are a more than an ample number of verses that show that God is an emotional being. His emotions and, more importantly, His expression of emotions, particularly in judgment, are perfect. The punishment always fits the crime, as they say, and as God's judgment is perfect and righteous, so are His emotions.

We, however, created in the image of God and having been blessed with emotions, are far from perfect. We are fallen creatures, with erred judgment and a skewed sense of justice and righteousness. We have many of the same emotions that our heavenly Father has, with but a few exceptions. We can feel guilt, shame, and fear; God does not. We can be happy, sad, jealous, angry, love, hate, be delighted and pleased, or in sorrow and grief. All of these things we are blessed to share, and more.

We understand that God has given us emotions, but what are they, where do they emanate from, and what causes them to erupt?

In human behavior, emotions are the natural, involuntary response to situation or experience. In most cases, we have no control over the automatic response mechanism of emotions. They just happen.

Emotions are centered in the limbic system of the brain and primarily in the amygdala, which is a small, bean-shaped organ in the lower middle part of the brain. The amygdala controls these reactions and sends signals to other parts of the system that release hormones like dopamine and adrenalin. When a person is suddenly placed in a threatening situation, the amygdala kicks in and, through that, adrenaline is pumped into the body. Our heart rate goes up, we begin to sweat, and our senses become more acute. We shift into a survival mode, where we experience the fight-or-flight response. Adrenalin in the body can cause us to run faster and longer, to fight harder and with more strength. There are many stories of people suddenly given "superpowers" and lift cars off of victims, or jump over huge obstacles. The amygdala controls emotions like fear, love, anger, and laughter. Our emotions, though God gives them, are different, in that human emotions are reactive. They are the automatic reactions to situations.

Emotional responses are typically short-lived. If a person is afraid, once the situation is over, the fear passes. The amygdala shuts off, the adrenaline stops flowing, and the body returns to its normal state. If a person becomes angry or amused, the emotion quickly dies down. If a person continues to express anger, particularly once the event has passed, it is no longer an emotional response but a state of mind. We will get into that later, as we look at anger a little more deeply.

Our emotional need is to be able to experience all of our emotions within the appropriate and reasonable understanding of how and when they work. We are to be happy when we are supposed to, to be sad, or angry, or afraid when it is necessary to do so. We are also created to be social beings—we need to love and be loved, and to act and react within the norms of what is acceptable social behavior. When we react to situations in what we would consider the "norm" for our social environment, we can say that our emotions are working properly. If your emotional responses are primarily negative, like fear, anger, or shame, they are also working properly, it is just that they are the responses to the situational conditions you are experiencing.

Obviously, from the standpoint of counseling addictive behaviors, it is necessary to deal with some of the emotions that can be damaging. Remember that emotions are the automatic responses to our actions based upon our understanding. If the predominant emotional responses in life have a tendency to be negative, such as guilt, anger, or fear, then it is most likely that we are making improper actions which are based upon wrongful perceptions of the events in our lives. Emotions can be a measuring stick by which we can govern whether our understanding of an event is correct. By understanding our emotions, we can objectively judge whether our understanding is correct or not, and seek to change it.

Before we look at specific emotional responses, it is important to know that people use emotional outbursts to manipulate the actions of others. This is particularly so in the case of addictive behavior. This is done expressively, such as fits of anger, or passively, such as causing an emotional response like guilt in the other. In either case, whether the subject manipulates another by using or *mimicking* powerful emotional expression, or by evoking a powerful response from the other, it is malicious.

Of all of the emotional responses common to human experience, the two most damaging are guilt and anger. Though both of these responses have their use, they should not be experienced with regularity or frequency. In the case of addictive behavior, these two are the most prevalent and needful for our attention.

Beginning then with guilt, the Bible speaks of guilt only in connection with condemnation. It is vital in only one respect: to bring a person to understand his fallen position before a holy God and his need for salvation. We cannot know the peril we are in or the magnificence of God's mercy without guilt. We are, as Paul wrote, "Now we know that what things soever the law saith, it saith to them who are under the law: that every mouth may be stopped, and all the world may become guilty before God" (Romans 3:19).

This is so important because we cannot be astounded at the greatness of God's mercy if we are not astounded by the depth of our own sin.

Guilt came into human life in the garden of Eden, when Adam and Eve realized that they had disobeyed God by eating the forbidden fruit. It is interesting that the word in Hebrew that is translated as "naked" also means guilty. It is the word *orum,* and it literally means to be shamefully exposed. Guilt is a terrible feeling. Guilt is always condemning. It is not to be confused with conviction, particularly the conviction of the Holy Spirit. Guilt can be distinguished from conviction in this manner: Guilt condemns the person and demands punishment. Conviction condemns the action and encourages correction.

It is the duty of the spirit of God to bring to a lost sinner's attention that they are guilty before the Judge of the Universe and that they are condemned. Through the preaching of the gospel this is manifested in the heart of the lost and leads them to the cross of Christ and salvation. It is also the duty of the Spirit to bring to a Christian's attention that they are, because of sinful activity, out of the will of God and are in need of correction.

I was joking with a friend of mine, who is also involved in counseling, and mused, "The lost in the world need Christ, and the Christians in the world need counseling." The Spirit works actively in both arenas of the lost and saved.

Outside of the prodding of the Spirit to bring a lost soul to repentance, guilt is a destructive emotion that distorts self-image and provides no hope for change. It is the predominant factor for failure in the life of a person who is self-worshipping. In this case, it is clear to the offender that they are leaving a wake of destruction in their pursuit for pleasure or fulfillment—the terrible cost for *it's all about me.* The guilt associated with these behaviors causes two distinct reactions: 1) total rejection of any justification for guilt and the removal of all who would make you feel this way, because *who are you to tell* me *what to do? How dare you make me feel this way. I can do whatever I want!;* and 2) self-reflection causes him or her to judge and condemn themselves.

They do not need the prodding of the Spirit to understand their guilt. The Spirit brings a person to the cross, where remedy for guilt may be found. The self-condemned have no such refuge. They must live with their self-imposed torment and all the while continue and pursue activities that are the failing altars of self-worship.

In addictive behaviors, when you act as though you were the very center of the universe, there is a lot of disappointment. You are not God, and you can't control either people or situations to fit your continuing desires. So it is common in these behaviors that the consequences of those actions produces emotions that fly in opposition to the way things turn out. In this way, our emotions can help us to understand that there is a problem.

The way human beings work is like a train. The engine that drives that train is what we think and believe. Every moment of every day, we are constantly bombarded with information that is obtained through our five senses. All of this information goes into our brain where it is dissected, analyzed, and sorted out thousands of times per second. The brain decides what is important and what is not, what shapes the things we know as true and forms our belief systems and what is not. It determines situational events whether they are good or bad, threatening or benign, and it does all of this in the briefest moments of time. Apart from the nonstop external stimuli from our environment, there are internal thoughts, imaginations, fantasies, desires, and memories that are constantly spinning around in our heads that too have to be sorted out and properly categorized and either acted upon or stored for future reference. Once the information gets sorted, we decide what we are going to do with it, and this is the cause for our actions and behaviors or *what we do.*

The car behind the engine is the "do" car or our behaviors. These are the physical actions that are prompted by our will, which is the decision we make with the current information being processed at that time. In some cases, the action is so closely in time with the thinking that they are almost simultaneous. In other cases, we are conditioned to act without going through the thinking process at all. In far too many instances, people act spontaneously without giving thought to the consequences of their actions. Classical conditioning is exactly what that is—a sort of shortcut through the brain that goes around the analysis part.

The "caboose" is the emotions car. As I said, emotions are the automatic natural reactions to the consequences of the decisions or actions we take, or to events around us.

When our emotional life is consistently dominated by regret, fear, anger, guilt, and shame, it is probably because we are not doing the right things. If we are not doing the right things, it is probably because we are not thinking the right way. The engine drives the train, and the cars that follow are connected to the engine. The caboose (our emotions) can help us understand if our actions and thinking are on track. If your emotions are predominantly love, satisfaction, happiness, and contentment, it is likely that you are doing and thinking the right way.

There are certain activities and substances that stimulate the pleasure center of the brain, which is also where the emotions originate, and this stimulation is powerful. Everyone likes to feel pleasure or get excited because it produces a hormonal response that makes us feel great. Long distance runners experience a surge of beta-endorphins, which produces a "runners high." People that engage in risky, if not perilous, activities like sky diving, base jumping, hang gliding, and others, do so because the survival mode kicks in with adrenalin, and they like that sensation. These are commonly called adrenalin junkies. Substances, like alcohol and drugs that produce euphoric sensations in the brain do the same thing. As a person continues to bombard their pleasure center with powerful stimuli, it can create a deadening of the body's ability to respond. It is like a person who uses heroin. At first, they may be prescribed a very low dose opioid, like Oxycodone® 5mg/325. This is mostly acetaminophen with some opioid in it. When this is taken for a substantial period of time, the analgesic effect of the drug is lessened. This isn't because the drug does not do what it is made to do, it is because the body acclimates to its effect and becomes less sensitive to it. In order for the efficacy of the drug to be maintained, a higher dose is prescribed. This can begin a chain of events, that, when the prescription runs out, the person is chemically dependent on the analgesic. A reaction to it creates a compulsive desire to get more, because it is physically very uncomfortable to be without. The person turns to the street to acquire anything he can to quench this need and may turn to heroin. As their use continues, they need to increase the amount that is administered. It is not uncommon for heroin users who spend time in jail and regain a certain functional normalcy to attempt to use the same dose of heroin they did before their incarceration and it kills them.

Men that continually view pornography will become desensitized to normal stimulation and require more outrageous acts to be stimulated. There are discussions today about children (teens) that play violent video games. They are exposed to incredibly graphic visualizations of violence that they participate in as a part of the game. The quality of the graphics in these games is incredible. They are not like Pong, or even Donkey Kong, or Mario brothers. No, these are so lifelike it becomes difficult to discern what is real and what is not. This movie quality realism of violent acts desensitizes them to actual violence. It may be that prolonged immersion into this fantasy world that appears so real produces an inability to discern what real life is and what a fantasy game is. The brain is not fully developed in teens, and the ability to make decisions, which is formed in the prefrontal lobe, is not fully developed until a person is in their early twenties. Add to that the idea that the amount of time these young people are immersed in these stressful fantasies, and that is a recipe for psychological problems. It is possible that this experience could cloud a child's ability to discern what is acceptable behavior and what is not. That is dangerous.

In the same away that the pleasure center or exciter center becomes dulled, so does the body's ability to properly react emotionally. Chronic drug users of cocaine or methamphetamine do not feel sad or happy and react to normal emotional stimuli. Their emotions, like their senses, have been dulled by the continuing introduction of chemical stimuli that the brain cannot deal with. In these addictive behaviors, the overstimulation of the brain may cause a loss of sensitivity to emotional reactions.

Emotional responses that are common in addictive behaviors are fear, anger, shame, and guilt. These are, like all of our emotions, automatic responses to the consequences of our actions that produce conflict or harm to people that we love or are responsible for. There is an old expression which says, "No man is an island." We are members of a society, with relationships and responsibilities to others. It has been said that we can affect the life of one hundred people every day. We are not God, and we are not unaccountable for our choices and actions. But we are all self-absorbed, to some degree; some more than others. It is the missing spiritual need in us that cries out to be filled that is the root of all addictive behaviors that makes it "all about me." Inevitably, this produces conflict and loss, disappointment and regret, when we can't do whatever we want at whatever the cost whenever we want.

Once the spiritual need is met and we are no longer needing to visit the altars where we worship ourselves and begin to walk in the new life that is in Christ, we begin thinking the right way—God's way. Right thinking produces right behavior, which initiates positive emotional responses. The Scriptures give us much on how we are to change the way we think and behave.

"Commit thy works unto the LORD, and thy thoughts shall be established" (Proverbs 16:3). This verse tells us that if we commit our actions, which means to *completely give over,* to the Lord, it will change the way we think. The apostle Paul advises us to think differently: "Therefore, I urge you, brethren, in view of God's mercy, to offer your bodies as living sacrifices, holy and pleasing to God—this is your spiritual act of worship. Do not conform any longer to the pattern of the world, but be transformed by the renewing of your mind. Then you will be able to test and approve what God's will is— his good, pleasing and perfect will" (Romans 12:1–2 NIV).

He also writes, "Those who live according to the sinful nature have their minds set on what that nature desires; but those who live in accordance with the Spirit have their minds set on what the Spirit desires. The mind of sinful man is death, but the mind controlled by the Spirit is life and peace" (Romans 8:5–6 NIV).

For those coming to faith in Christ, the Spirit gives a new nature, a nature of obedience. He also gives the ability to know the will of God and to understand the Scriptures. As we grow in faith and obedience, our way of thinking is transformed, coming more in line with what God desires for us. This change in thinking, *the engine that drives the train,* must affect the way we behave and also the way we feel. We must choose to follow the leading of the Spirit and to discard the old patterns of how we thought and behaved. Oddly enough, though the Lord gives us a new nature, a nature of obedience, He does not take away our *old* nature, but He frees us from the bondage and ignorance of that old nature, the "old man" as Paul put it, and gives us the liberty to live for Him by choice. That takes us back, of course, to the section of temptation called *working out the knots.*

Included in our little discussion of emotions and the part they play in a healthy life, we have to look at one of the more powerful emotional displays, and that is anger.

Anger Management

Anger is one of the most interesting of all of our emotions, because most of the time, it is exaggerated beyond the point of it actually being an emotional reaction. That is one of our stranger human characteristics. Anger, in itself, is not a bad thing. God expresses anger, and man created in His image also expresses anger. Anger can protect us from harm, or when a mother is angry with her child for disobedience, anger can cause us to reflect upon our actions and correct them. The Scriptures speak of God's anger more than His love, and God is love. God's wrath and anger, against idolatry and sexual immorality, stream through the pages of the Old Testament. Yet God's anger is slow, deliberate, and short-lived. His anger, as you recall, is not reactive, like our emotions. His anger is expressed to show His displeasure with His people and their wickedness. It is not because He isn't getting His way, nor is it petulant, or peevish.

> The LORD is merciful and gracious, slow to anger, and abounding in mercy. He will not always strive with us, nor will He keep His anger forever. (Psalm 103:8–9 NKJV)

> For His anger is but for a moment, His favor is for life; weeping may endure for a night, but joy comes in the morning. (Psalm 30:5 NKJV)

Human anger is not expressed without fault because humans are far from perfect.

Anger comes in two distinct types: righteous anger and unrighteous anger. Righteous anger is directed from perfect or proper understanding and conduct, to imperfect and unwarranted actions. God's anger at sin is the prerequisite type for righteous anger. In the human experience, righteous anger is possible, but righteous expression of that anger is indeed rare. We have difficulty making the *sentence fit the crime,* and even where anger is righteously warranted, how that anger is expressed is seldom proper. This brings us to the other type of anger, which is unrighteous anger.

Unrighteous anger is directed from improper and imperfect understanding and conduct, to whatever action inflames it, warranted or not. Unrighteous anger is also anger that is warranted but expressed improperly. Well, that cuts down the chance for righteous anger to near nil in the human experience. This should not surprise us, because after all, the scripture does say, "There is none righteous, no not one." If people aren't righteous, how can one expect their wrath to be righteously directed?

We, for obvious reasons, will not venture much into righteous anger, but shall assume for the basis of counseling from the human experience, that all anger is directed from an unrighteous source and is thereby, unrighteous.

Beginning then with this assumption, we can look at the various ways in which anger is expressed and why people respond the way they do when angered.

Anger has two basic forms of expression, which are commonly classified as "blowing up" or "clamming up." The first form of expression, blowing up, speaks of violent outbursts of rage that come on suddenly. In the Bible, this anger is described in Greek as thu-*mos*), which is where we get the prefix "thermo," as in thermos or thermodynamics. It denotes heat. In the Scriptures it is translated as wrath or anger. It is the fierce and sudden explosion of hot anger, which may come up suddenly and disappear just as suddenly. The second expression of anger, clamming up, speaks of an inward presence of mind or determined state of mind. It is not as much emotion as *thumos,* and in man's experience, more menacing. Of this type, there are four Greek words used in scripture; each presenting a different level or understanding of the anger. The first is aga-*nak*-tesis), which is translated as indignation. It is a state of annoyance, grief, indignation, and resentment. It is more a state of mind than emotion. The second is (or-*gay*), which is beyond grief and resentment. It is, as Aristotle put it, "grief with desire."[10] This is a strange state of mind, in which a person is angry because he wants or desires to maintain an angry spirit against someone or something. The third is (cho-*lah*-oh), which is translated as bitterness. Bitterness is an internal seething that becomes a continuous, vengeful state of mind. Bitterness against a person can last a lifetime. It is a deep, hateful resentment, that is malicious in thought, for it not only desires vengeance against a person for wrongs committed, but desires evil or calamity to fall upon that person. The last is (pare-or-*gis*-mos), translated as provocation. This is an amplification of *orge* and speaks of bitter malice placed into action. It is anger brought to action to provoke harm.

These types of anger may be seen sequentially in the development of a rebellious youth. I am of the opinion that, though the natural man is naturally rebellious, rebellion in youth is developed and brought upon by their parents. It may develop in this manner:

A child perceives an action by his parents as hurtful (it is possible that this perception may be totally wrong) and comes to a conclusion about the action and becomes angry. The child is chided for his outburst, because he is unable to articulate his understanding with the parent to come to a resolution. The actions continue, and the child, who cannot express his feelings without consequence, becomes inwardly resentful. The resentment becomes a mind-set of anger toward the parents (who have no clue) that develops into bitterness. Bitterness in the heart plots vengeance, and the child eventually rebels against the authority of the parents or commits hurtful acts upon him to inflict guilt and pain on the parents. This comes out in many ways. Some children gravitate toward behaviors they know will be hurtful to their parents. They may take drugs, or join a cult, or enter into an aberrant lifestyle such as homosexuality, and blame the parents for it.

---

[10] Zodhiates, Spiros. *The Complete Word Study Dictionary: New Testament.* pg 1055. ©1992 AMG.

There are many issues surrounding the rebellious child, and it is a field of study that is deep and far-reaching. It is not my intent to delve into that study or to appear flippant by this simple example of rebellious behavior. I do believe, however, that anger plays a key role in rebellion and that unchecked anger develops into rebellion.

Looking back then at the different types of anger and the means by which it is expressed, it is not entirely about the protective emotion of anger, but more of a state of mind, by which we *choose* to be angry. Why on earth would anyone do that? How does that work into the cumulative behaviors associated with *addiction*?

Part of our human nature is a sense of what is right and what is wrong. This sense is in some ways cultural, varying slightly on the societal norms of acceptable behavior. It is also an individual sense, based upon our own ideas or beliefs of what should be right or not. In the case of a person who is the center of his or her own little universe, this selfish perspective is skewed to always and only get what that person wants. We all have a sense of justice that guides us, but in human nature, our tendency is mostly self-promoting. Anger erupts when a person is threatened, offended, or simply doesn't get what he wants. The violent expression of anger is a tool that we use to rectify or nullify the threat and end it. Unfortunately, our sense of justice is not perfect and, unlike God's anger, rarely fits the crime. An example of this is often found in unique social environments like, well, jail. In the jail where I work as chaplain, men and women are housed in open bays with bunk beds arranged around a central, open area with tables and chairs—basically a recreation area. One inmate walks past another and bumps into him. The other angrily says, "Watch where you're going, jerk!" The other guy then, of course, has to say something back in order to assert his position in the societal pecking order of the pod, which is usually far more vulgar and personal. Because of our tainted sense of justice, each retort must better the previous one, as violence breeds more violence. This goes on until one pushes the other, and it goes to the next level. Then things get out of control, as the altercation becomes physical and fists start flying. Well, this sort of behavior is frowned upon, and very quickly the law enforcement staff responds. This usually ends up with both of the warring knuckleheads being *locked down*, which is in disciplinary detention, in a five by nine cell, with a severe loss of privileges.

On a grander scale, minor altercations lead to ever-increasing violence, where a single event could lead to a war between nations. This nature of unjust retribution is what brought about the bow and arrow, the spear, swords and shields, muskets, machine guns, artillery, cavalry, bombs, and eventually tanks and planes, and nuclear weapons on guided missiles. When God gave the Law to Moses, it included laws on just retribution. The "eye for an eye" law is just that. The reason God gave this to man is because man is not just in acts of violent retribution. It always increases. *"You knock out my tooth, and I will cut your head off!"* *"You cut my head off, and my family will destroy yours!"*

Aren't we grand? I recently heard a commentary on a summation of the twentieth century, in which the act of one man, a Serbian anarchist, by assassinating the Archduke Franz Ferdinand of Austria-Hungary caused the First World War. After the assassination of the archduke and his wife, Austria-Hungary declared war on Serbia. Serbia sought aid from their ally, Russia, and so Austria-Hungary enlisted the aid of Germany. Soon, France and England were sucked into the fray. The "war to end all wars" created the political environment for socialism, fascism, and communism, and eventually to the Second World War, the Cold War, Korea, and Vietnam. It is stunning to think that over one hundred fifty million people died in the twentieth century, and a single nutcase from Serbia with a pistol may well have started it. *That* is the nature of man.

Getting back to our discussion on anger, the emotional reaction that is precipitated in the limbic system is an involuntary defense mechanism. That is most typically the *thumos* type of anger that is dispelled nearly as quickly as the onset. The body does its best to get back to a normal stasis. When we are frightened or excited, the adrenalin kicks in as a defense or motivational mechanism, but it does not continuously pump into the body. When the threat is over, the adrenalin shuts off and the body goes back to normal. The other "clamming up" types of anger are caused by the need to receive personal justice for an offense or injury, and we deem what is the just resolution for the offense. This is not emotion, but a determined state of mind, where we become judge, jury, and executioner to whoever or whatever was the cause of the offense. This is not anger, but actually *pseudo-anger,* a condition whereby we deliberately keep throwing fuel on the fire to keep it stoked until our desired end is achieved.

This is to be expected in people who believe that they are god, and they can do whatever they please and are justified in whatever punishment they exact upon the offender.

This pseudo-anger is a powerful tool to make sure that whatever opposition to "what I want" is dealt with without actually having to do anything severe. This tool can be used as both a weapon and a shield. Let's look at a fictitious example:

Barney is a self-employed construction specialist. He can do roofing, siding, home repairs, painting, whatever. He is very skilled and does great work. He is hired by a couple to put a tile floor in their kitchen. He works hard and quickly gets the job done to the satisfaction of the homeowners. They pay him, and he runs off to the bank to cash the check. Now that the job is finished and he has cash in hand, he decides, because he is good and can do whatever he desires, to have a little well-deserved downtime. His favorite recreation is getting high on crack cocaine. He makes a call and arranges a meeting with his "friend" who just happens to be a dealer. His friend tells him, "Sure, I can get some, and don't worry, the first rock is on me." It isn't too long before Barney has smoked away his entire pay, and more than two days and nights have passed as he has worshipped at the altar of crack cocaine. The crack is gone, the money is gone, and surprisingly, so is his "friend." Barney feels terrible. His head is fuzzy; he hasn't slept or eaten much in two days. His thumping heart has quieted somewhat, and now he just wants to go home.

When he arrives home, his wife is crying. "Where have you been? I thought you were dead. You never called or anything! You look awful, and you *stink!* Where is your pay? The kids are hungry and there is no food in the house!"

Barney, keenly aware of his failure but unwilling to bear the responsibility of such, raises his voice to a lion's roar and tells her, "Leave me alone!" She, terrified, backs away and retreats to another room. In the meantime, he makes his way to bed, thinking that he just needs to get some sleep. Betty stays away believing that he just needs to sleep. Tomorrow will be better. She will be happy that he is back to his old self and things will be back to normal.

Barney has used his pseudo-anger as a shield, to protect him from her just assault on his behavior, and as a sword, to fend her away threateningly.

This is a rather extreme example, but sadly, not unusual in too many situations today. In our own ways, with our own struggles and failures, we all use this *acting out* as a means to manipulate, threaten, or drive away people and things that have the nerve to oppose us. It might not be quite so dramatic, but we have learned how to do it and finesse it, as a science. It becomes easy; it becomes natural.

We have looked at the different types of anger and how much of that is a determined state of mind rather than emotion. There are also different ways anger is expressed. How we express our anger is a learned behavior. Parents, siblings, and other influential people in our young lives model it for us. For example, I grew up near Utica, New York, and I had a lot of Italian friends. It was really pretty funny that it was sort of a tradition that family members yelled at each other a lot. Italians are great for raising their voices I suppose. They also use a lot of hand gestures. We take amusement out of this sort of ethnic stereotype, but it does seem to be that way. This is not inherent in their genetic makeup by any means, but a continuing pattern of behavior that is learned and passed down from generation to generation. Many, if not most, of our behavioral tendencies and the way we react to situations is learned. Emotions come and quickly fade, but how those emotions are expressed is not automatic, but learned.

Anger is a powerful emotion, and we quickly learn that its aggressive and threatening exhibition can frighten people away. It can also manipulate them and the situations around which people find themselves, in confrontation. The explosive, violent, and loud, crazy kind of anger is very intimidating. People who want to control their surroundings and the people that they are engaged with can mimic this emotion as a means of getting their own way. People that are hot-headed or rash have long practiced this behavior because it gets results.

The way we express our emotions is related to the "blowing up" and "clamming up" types of anger. In the "blowing up" type of anger, it is generally expressed as *open aggressive* anger. The anger that Barney used against his wife in our little story is an example of open aggressive anger. This is the defense mechanism of the jungle, and it comes quite easily or at least with greater ease than a physical knock-down-drag-out. It is a way of scaring off an aggressor without having to come to the actual life and death struggle.

In polite society, open aggression is a tiny bit more sophisticated than the jungle, and open aggression is a means to asserting your opinion and winning an argument. In less polite society, open aggression is the standard for most violent crimes. The police departments of any major city will all concur that the most dangerous arena is the one of domestic disputes. Many police officers that sustain injury on the job obtain their wounding in the American home. Open aggression is the "crime of passion" that is so often heard about.

People that have learned to express their anger through open aggression are likely to agree with terms and conditions like these:

"I am blunt and forceful when someone does something to frustrate me."

"As I speak my convictions my voice becomes increasingly louder."

"When someone confronts me about a problem, I am likely to offer a ready rebuttal."

"No one has to guess my opinion; I'm known for having unwavering viewpoints."

"I have a history of getting caught in bickering matches with my family."

"I have a reputation for being strong-willed."

"I tend to give advice, even when others have not asked for it."

A few years ago I saw a man wearing a T-shirt with the image of a menacing looking gorilla on the front. Below the picture there was a caption that read, "If I want your opinion, I'll beat it out of you!" All humor aside, this is sort of the general attitude of the openly aggressive.

The Bible has much to say about people that express anger in this manner:

> He that is soon angry dealeth foolishly: and a man of wicked devices is hated. (Proverbs 14:17)

> A wrathful man stirreth up strife: but he that is slow to anger appeaseth strife. (Proverbs 15:18)

> He that hath no rule over his own spirit is like a city that is broken down, and without walls. (Proverbs 25:28)

> A fool uttereth all his mind: but a wise man keepeth it in till afterwards. (Proverbs 29:11)

> An angry man stirreth up strife, and a furious man aboundeth in transgression. (Proverbs 29:22)

It is quite apparent that the book of Proverbs alone has much to say about this type of anger. What about the other kinds of anger—the "clamming up" ones? What about the *orge,* or the *aganaktesis,* or *cholao?* In what ways are these angers expressed?

There are two ways that those angers are commonly expressed. The first is resentment. Resentment is an inward form of anger that is suppressed for one reason or another. Whatever the reason, suppressing anger is unhealthy. It can affect your ability to make clear judgment and can even affect a person's health. It causes stress and stress-related problems.

People that suppress their anger in resentment are likely to agree with terms and conditions like these:

"I am very image conscious. I do not like to let others know my problems."

"Even when I feel very flustered I portray myself publicly as having it all together."

"I am rather reserved about sharing my problems of frustration."

"There are times when I wonder if my opinions or preferences are really valid."

"I have suffered with physical complaints, such as frequent headaches, stomach problems, and insomnia."

This learned expression of anger, or suppression of anger, is troublesome because it requires a person to be dishonest with himself regarding his own emotions. This dishonesty is deliberate in order to make others believe that you have attained a standard of behavior that is based upon rules of conduct that are impossible to keep, specifically, the rules of conduct concerning the display of emotions. People that adhere to such rules have been trained to think that their emotion of anger is not normal. They have a history of being invalidated when their perceptions differ from this idea. They fear powerful retaliation if convinced that their expressions will come to no good end that they succumb to a what's-the-use mentality. Their suppression of anger represents a feeling of personal defeat.

In some strict, religious circles, there are those that teach that displays of emotions, such as anger, is sin and have encompassed their lives with such restricting, legalistic views that they equate that behavior with ungodliness. This is so judgmental, and not desiring to allow any other see such ungodly behavior, those followers choose to suppress their anger.

Lastly, there is a passive-aggressive expression of anger. Passive-aggressive anger is in line perfectly with the inward seething and vengeful acts of the *orge, parorgismos,* and *cholao* types. The most notable traits of the passive-aggressor are that the anger is 1) determined—the anger of bitterness and inward seething is a deliberate, determined mind-set that desires to be and remain angry. 2) Continuing—this is not anger that is let go quickly, because it is not an emotional outpouring, but it is an attitude. It will remain until the aggressor is satisfied that the other party has been punished enough. 3) Vengeful—perhaps the worst trait is that it is vengeful. To seek vengeance upon another for an offense is wrong for one sound reason; it is rooted in pride. Vengeance is one person deciding he or she has the right and authority to make and execute judgment as they see fit. It is contemplated, purposeful, and cruel. God commands us not to entertain such thoughts or actions.

"Dearly beloved, avenge not yourselves, but rather give place unto wrath: for it is written, Vengeance is mine; I will repay, saith the Lord" (Romans 12:19).

Passive aggressors express their anger by dragging their feet, being stubborn, or being a sort of roadblock. They can smile through the entire ordeal and may even disguise their anger as humor, particularly sarcasm, racial, or ethnic slurs, or sexist slurs that are hurtful. Passive aggressors are more like the open aggressive type than the suppressed anger. The difference is that they may recognize the rage that is in them and control it somewhat. People that are passive-aggressive are likely to agree with terms and conditions like these:

"When I am frustrated, I become silent, knowing it bothers other people."

"I am prone to sulk and pout."

"When I don't want to do a project, I will procrastinate. I can be lazy."

"When someone makes me angry, I will not talk with them about it."

"When someone angers me, I will treat them badly until they say they're sorry."

Like most of our anger expressions, passive-aggression is learned—it is modeled for us at a very young age. We see that behavior and conclude in our little noggins that that looks like a good way to get what we want.

Now, it is interesting that many people are completely unaware of the peculiar way that they express anger, so when I go through this part of the recovery ministry with them, I present the terms as a sort of quiz, having them check which term applies to their own behavior. If they check five or more of the terms, it is a pretty good sign that the way they express their anger is one of the three. It can be fun, and it may also be quite embarrassing for some, to discover that the way they express anger is actually categorized. Oftentimes, there will be those who take the little quiz and discover that they express anger in more than just one way. We are not locked into one way or another. We can learn other ways to use our anger and, depending on the circumstance, can opt for any of the ways.

It is helpful to recognize these unrighteous expressions of anger so that we may address those problems that are so common with addictive behaviors. Remember, addiction is worship and it is all about me, so these deeply rooted expressions of anger flow naturally as a person uses them to manipulate others and situations. They have been rehearsed and honed over years of practice, discovering which ones work the best and in which situations. It becomes so natural that a person can switch them on and off without even thinking about it. This is all part of the fallen nature of man—the human condition.

Jeremiah describes the human condition in this way: "The heart is deceitful above all things, and desperately wicked: who can know it?" (Jeremiah 17:9).

As we strive to help people who are coming out of addictive behaviors, dealing honestly with these deep-rooted behaviors related to anger is absolutely vital, but must be done with compassion and great care. It is difficult to point a finger at someone else's behaviors when we all have the same problem. I present these as a quiz, or survey, so that people can discover for themselves how they express their anger. It is often amusing, embarrassing, and surprising, but done this way, it is also not as accusative. It is also very difficult to change behaviors that have taken a lifetime to develop. They are, however, behaviors—and behavior can be changed if the way that we think is changed. It is not possible without Christ. It is the Spirit that challenges our hearts to change and gives us the humility to understand that we have a problem and that it can be fixed. So how do we fix it?

We can and must learn to handle our expression of anger, just as we must learn to handle our other passions. The power and example comes from the Lord Jesus Christ, and we must rely upon Him as our source of strength and correction. Our improper expression of anger comes from our old nature. We are to deny that "old man," crucify him and his anger, and allow the Lord to have rule over the dominion of our heart.

Paul wrote, "Be ye angry, and sin not: let not the sun go down upon your wrath: neither give place to the devil" (Ephesians 4:26–27).

I rather like the New Living Translation of this verse: "And don't sin by letting anger gain control over you. Don't let the sun go down while you are still angry, for anger gives a mighty foothold to the Devil."

I believe, in this sense, that this is what is being conveyed:

It is normal to be angry, but do not use anger as a means to manipulate others, because that is sin. Don't hold on to anger—that is also sin, as it is a deliberate and harmful state of mind. The devil can really do his work when we behave in this manner.

There are three ways that we can express anger, hurt, and frustration without intimidation or manipulation in the power of the Spirit:

1. We can be assertive without allowing harm to come to us and be considerate of others (even our enemies).
2. We can accept the understanding that we are unable to control others or the circumstances of our life. We can *drop* our anger after realizing our limitations.
3. We can also express our hurts and offences to others without being angry. It does not damage a relationship, but can in fact, strengthen one. It is thoughtful and considerate, without name-calling or refusing to admit fault. It is well-controlled and works to resolve the situation amicably.

Every day we are bombarded with choices that we must make. We go through each day without too much struggle, making hundreds of decisions about many things. We can also choose to let anger go by understanding that many people may not agree with the way we understand or do things, and it is not always necessary to be upset about it. When the Lord was on the cross, He asked His Father to forgive those who had crucified Him, because they didn't know what they were doing. If you are in contact with other people throughout the day and interact with them, chances are excellent that there will be some offence or conflict. You can't always get or even expect to get your own way. What a shocker! We can choose our battles. A friend of mine gave me some good advice about being a pastor. He said, "You need to have a soft heart and a tough hide." I have found that it is best to have one blind eye and one deaf ear also.

Spiritual Growth

The last need that must be met in order to maintain a healthy life is the spiritual need. It is obvious at this point that a person can have no spiritual life at all outside of Christ. It is also quite obvious that when a person comes to Christ in faith and receives Him as Lord and Savior, that their spiritual journey has only just begun. The Lord Himself said that we must be "born again" spiritually into the Kingdom of God.

"Except a man be born of water, and of the Spirit, he cannot enter into the kingdom of God. That which is born of the flesh is flesh; and that which is born of the Spirit is spirit. Marvel not that I said unto thee, Ye must be born again" (John 3:5b–7).

Paul said we were babes in Christ, having been newly born into the Kingdom of God. He also confessed in his letter to the Philippians' church that he had not attained perfection but was pressing for the mark. John wrote to the church in Ephesus in his first letter and specifically addressed believers as "my little children." He also spoke to those he called "young men" and those he called "fathers." These groups are understood by many expositors to be Christians of different levels of spiritual maturity.[11]

As we continue to make our way back up the downward spiral, we have addressed the physical needs, the psychological needs, and the emotional needs. At last we can ascend to the top of the spiral and address our greatest need—our spiritual need. Once that need is properly met, we have been "born" into the Kingdom of God and

---

[11] Albert Barnes wrote that the groups were actual, physical age groups. However, McGee, Clarke, Gill, Wesley, Matthew Henry, and others hold that these groups referred to spiritual maturity.

the Spirit begins His transforming work in us. This is the process of sanctification, which is the Lord conforming us into the likeness of His Son. The Bible encourages and admonishes us to grow and mature in Him.

Peter wrote:

> You therefore, beloved, since you know this beforehand, beware lest you also fall from your own steadfastness, being led away with the error of the wicked; but grow in the grace and knowledge of our Lord and Savior Jesus Christ. To Him be the glory both now and forever. Amen. (2 Peter 3:17–18 NKJV)

> Therefore, putting aside all malice and all deceit and hypocrisy and envy and slander, like newborn babies, long for the pure milk of the word, so that by it you may grow in respect to salvation, if you have tasted the kindness of the Lord. And coming to Him as to a living stone which has been rejected by men, but is choice and precious in the sight of God, you also, as living stones, are being built up as a spiritual house for a holy priesthood, to offer up spiritual sacrifices acceptable to God through Jesus Christ. (1 Peter 2:1–5 NASB)

Paul wrote:

> For the edifying of the body of Christ, till we all come to the unity of the faith and of the knowledge of the Son of God, to a perfect man, to the measure of the stature of the fullness of Christ; that we should no long be children, tossed to and fro and carried about with every wind of doctrine, by the trickery of men, in the cunning craftiness

of deceitful plotting, but speaking the truth in love, may grow up in all things into Him who is the head—Christ—from whom the whole body, joined and knit together by what every joint supplies, according to the effective working by which every part does its share, causes growth of the body for the edifying of itself in love. (Ephesians 4:12b–16 NKJV)

It is God's intent to bring us to a new way of life and to grow us spiritually. This He will perform in us through the working of the Spirit in our "inner man." The problem that we have in this process is that we resist His working in us. God is always working to make us more like Christ, but we, in our old rebellious nature, fight Him tooth and nail. You would think that we would let Him do His work so life would be a little easier!

I grew up in a small town in central New York. It was a farm town, surrounded by dairy farms and a lot of cornfields. I think there were more cows than people! I learned a lot about farming, and for much of my life I kept gardens. Gardening is a lot like spiritual growth. There are certain tasks that must be performed by the farmer and certain tasks that must be performed by God. The task of the farmer is to produce conditions that will allow a crop to grow, and the task of God is to grow the crop.

What this means is that the farmer has absolutely no control over the actual growth of the crop—he can't bring seed to sprout; he can't make it grow a single inch. All he can do is make conditions favorable for the crop to grow. In this way, farming is perfect partnership with God. Spiritual growth is also like that. The believer produces conditions favorable for spiritual growth, and God grows the believer. We can *only* make the conditions right for growth. It is God's work in the believer that produces growth.

Paul makes this quite clear, addressing the legalists of Galatia: "This only would I learn of you, Received ye the Spirit by the works of the law, or by the hearing of faith? Are ye so foolish? Having begun in the Spirit, are ye now made perfect by the flesh?" (Galatians 2:3).

There is nothing that any man can do to grow spiritually by or through his own power. There is no outer dressing, act of obedience, fulfillment of duty, or any works of the flesh that can make him grow. This is the mind-set and philosophy of the legalist: "If I do holy things, I will become holy." The problem of course is the determination as to what is "holy." There are those that say it is unholy for women to wear pants, or for believers to go to movies, or dance, or listen to "upbeat" music. The list is endless. The philosophy of legalism actually retards spiritual growth, because it does not provide conditions for growth. It creates an attitude of having grown, when no growth is present.

The fertile ground for spiritual growth comes with the understanding of the role of the farmer, the role of God, and the willingness to allow God to do His work. The farmer plows the field, plants the seed, and exercises patience. When those first tasks are accomplished, there is nothing he can do to make the seed sprout. He waits and watches. He has done his part and must wait for God to do His part. The believer must also exercise the same patience by submitting to God.

Spiritual growth is the process God uses to change us from the wretches that we are to the glorious image of His Son. This is *conforming* us to the image of His Son. Our job is not only to allow God to change us, but to avoid resisting that change. We *are* going to be conformed by God, whether we like it or not; it is simply much easier on us if we don't fight with God every step of the way. I can't imagine that it poses any great difficulty for God to wrestle with us, nor do I think it matters much to Him if we choose to make our going more difficult. He will continue to teach us lessons, test us and retest us until we learn. It we want to stay in the nursery all of our lives, He is gracious enough to allow it. However, it is extremely difficult to fight against the determined will of God to change us for the better. We must not "kick against the goads" of change.

Going back to the farm, any farmer will tell you that planting seed and waiting for it to grow is the easy part. The hard part is taking care of the tender plant. There are three basic farming tasks that provide excellent conditions for growth:

1. Pull the weeds.
2. Give it plenty of water.
3. Give it plenty of light.

Pull the weeds. The weeds in our life are the things of this world that would choke our spiritual growth. We can't make ourselves grow spiritually, but we can delay or retard it. In the case of addictive behaviors, there are a lot of weeds. It is hard to stop going to the places that we were used to going to, doing the activities we used to do, and especially break ties with relationships. In AA they encourage their participants to change "people, places, and things," for they know that those behaviors and relationships can cause a person to trip up. They call these connection *triggers*, which have a tendency to cause a person to revert to behaviors that lead them to their previous failures—the ones they so desperately need to overcome. Whatever they may be, a habit, or activity, or personal relationship, if it is associated with the altar where one worshipped the self and away from the proper worship of God, it is a weed.

There is an old story about a young native brave who sought advice from the elder chief. He complained that there were two wolves inside of him, each fighting to be the stronger. One was a good wolf, and the other a bad one. He then asked the chief, "Which wolf would win?" The chief replied, "Which one are you feeding?"

The apostle John wrote: "Love not the world, neither the things that are in the world. If any man love the world, the love of the Father is not in him. For all that is in the world, the lust of the flesh, the lust of the eyes, and the pride of life, is not the Father, but is of the world" (1 John 2:15–16).

There is an inherent problem with *pulling the weeds* of people, places, and especially things. A person cannot be expected to shut himself away from the world; he must have *new* places to go, *new* relationships, and *new* activities. Fortunately, in the Christian world, we have the church, which is a great place to begin new friendships, go to new places, and be involved in new activities. It is vital that a person coming out of a world where he or she is the very center of their universe, and into a Christ centered life, be not left to his or her own devices. It is also vital that the person be not overwhelmed with new activities and friends. For some odd reason, some folks believe that the way to escape that addictive life is to fill every waking moment with distraction. That doesn't work that well. People need to take small steps when they are learning to walk. What does work is personal discipleship, mentoring, and accountability. These are key factors in helping a person survive such a radical transition. The new believer should be connected with one person who would be willing to befriend him and introduce him to the exciting new life that is set before him in Christ.

Give it plenty of water. A plant can't grow without water, and the water of our spiritual life is the Word of God, the Bible. Deprive a plant of water and see what happens to it! The same thing will happen if the new believer stays away from daily reading and study of the Bible.

When I was studying to answer God's call to ministry as a pastor, my pastor gave me some good advice and I pass that down to those who are training under me now. He said to me, "Take your Bible and divide into thirty equal sections and read a section every day. In one month's time, you will have read through the entire Bible. When you are finished, start again."

I devoted myself to that practice, even though it was a lot of reading each day, and I continued that for many years. I have since modified that over the ages, to dividing the Old Testament and New Testament into sixty equal sections, and read a section of each every day. That way, I not only read through the entire Bible, but I get some Old and some New daily. This read-through-the-Bible plan is apart from my study of the Scriptures; it is just a read through. But it gets the Word inside me. It is ever new and continues to refresh and correct me daily. It is the greatest education I have ever had. I have developed thirty-day, sixty-day, and ninety-day plans, and even one for a year's read-through. The teaching of the Bible is necessary to equip the saints for ministry and for the life and growth of the church. It is our sole guide to truth and practice. How shall the new believer be instructed in the things of God if he ignores the instructions?

The Bible is the water that cleanses our feet from the dust of the world. I believe it was Moody who said, "This book will keep you from sin, and sin will keep you from this book."

Paul wrote, "Even as Christ also loved the church, and gave himself for it; the he might sanctify and cleanse it with the washing of water by the word" (Ephesians 5:25b–26).

Give it light. Most plants need lots of sun to live. The process of photosynthesis is how plants are able to breathe and gain nourishment. The believer in Christ is to spend lots of time in the light as well. This means being in the presence of God. Now, God is always with us, but we don't always acknowledge His presence. That is one of our greatest failures. The other great failure is that we do not *fear* God. The third commandment given by God to Moses was "You shall not take the name of the LORD your God in vain, for the LORD will not hold him guiltless who takes his name in vain" (Exodus 20:7 NKJV).

A lot of people think that this is about cussing, which is not true. What it does mean is that we are not to treat God as if He was not real. The word *vain* means empty. We are not to take the name of the LORD as empty or not being real. Too many of us treat God as if He were a genie who only comes when we summon Him. When we are in trouble or pain, we call on the Lord for help, but when things are going okay, He is far from our thoughts.

Imagine spending a day with your best friend, and all the time he is speaking to you, you ignore him as if he wasn't there. You go to places he doesn't like, and do things that he hates, and you pay him no mind at all. What kind of friend are you? Sadly, that is the way that we treat our Savior, all too often. Solomon wrote, "Trust in the Lord with all your heart, and lean not on your own understanding. In all your ways acknowledge Him, and He will direct your paths" (Proverbs 3:5–6 NKJV).

We are to acknowledge Him, His presence, in all that we do. Do not forget that the Lord knows all and sees all and is ever present with us. He wants to be with us and give us rest. Moses, who was terrified of this God he didn't really know, wanted to know Him better. He said, "Show me Your way." This means that Moses wanted God to tell him what His "way" or his desire and intentions for the people he called out of bondage. The LORD told him, "I will be with you, and I will give you rest."

That is His way—He wants to be with us and give us rest. This is not just an acquaintance but a relationship—personal and continuous.

I was counseling a young man that was having difficulty in his marriage, who also professed to be a Christian, and had been for a number of years. In fact, he was a deacon in his church. I was disturbed by his extremely hardline view of a *scriptural life*, so I asked him to tell me about his relationship with the Lord. He wasn't sure what I meant, so I asked him to define God for me. His responses were all true, and good, and right out of the book. It was suddenly apparent what the trouble was: he knew all about God but didn't know Him. I told him that once I read a two-volume biography of Abraham Lincoln. I knew where he was born, what his childhood was like, and how he got involved in politics. I knew more about Lincoln than I did of many of my friends, but I never met the man. There is a huge difference between knowing about the man and knowing the man himself. I believe there are probably a number of people that profess Christ, know somewhat about Him, but never enjoy a close, personal relationship with Him.

The apostle James provides a simple solution for the believer that wants to deepen his relationship with God: "Draw nigh to God, and He will draw nigh to you" (James 4:8a).

Drawing near to God is, for many Christians, an elusive thing. As I said, we will call on God when we are in pain, or need, or when we worship in song. It seems difficult to have a close relationship with an invisible, inaudible God. Perhaps that is because we are not looking or listening for Him. Our relationship with God was established at the cross, and it is established by trusting a God you have never known. Faith is the act of placing all of our trust in someone or something. Our relationship is developed and grown through trust also. The Word of God gives us direction and example, commandments and choices. Trusting that those are indeed true, applying them to our lives and observing the outcome builds our faith and understanding that God is faithful.

We also draw near to God in prayer. Prayer is our communication with God. God knows every part of our heart and knows all of our needs, before we can utter a single word in prayer. It is not necessary for God to hear from our lips our petitions, but it is necessary for us to bring all of our petitions to Him in spoken prayer. Communication with God is not one way. God answers all of our prayers if asked rightly. James again hits home with our faulty prayer life.

"Ye lust, and have not: ye kill, and desire to have, and cannot obtain: ye fight and war, yet ye have not, because ye ask not. Ye ask, and receive not, because ye ask amiss, that ye may consume it upon your lusts" (James 4:2–3).

We toss our prayers to God and expect immediate gratification. We get angry with God when our wants are not filled when we want them, or we, like spoiled children, cry for the same thing over and over again, until we are sure that He will give in. We do not wait on the Lord for prayers to be answered and too often reject the answer that we get. This is not communication but command, and we have placed ourselves as commander and God as servant.

Our prayers should be brought before God with trembling knees, acknowledging His power, His glory, and His majesty. We must come clean before Him, not holding anything back as Ananias and Sapphira did. In the back of our hearts there is a little room, with a heavy door and a rusted lock. Behind that door is a tarp, and under that there is a chest, covered with heavy chains and locks. Inside that chest is a little, black safe. Inside the safe is our greatest regrets, and fears, our deepest hurts and pain. That is what we hide from the world—what we even hide from ourselves. They are too difficult for us to manage, so we keep them locked in our hearts. But that is what God wants us to bring to Him. There is nothing that He cannot heal or bear. We carry the weight of those things silently, like a huge rock that weighs a ton. God wants to free us from that baggage, but we must trust Him. We need to go into that little dark room, open that chest and safe, and empty it out and lay all of those abominable things at the foot of our Master's cross. We must also come thankfully, for the grace and mercy that has been shown to us, for the privilege of being allowed to stand before Him as His own child, and make our requests.

Most of the problems we face in our daily life, which are caused by making the wrong decisions, could be averted if we would only desire, acknowledge, and enjoy the presence of our Savior with us at all times. This is perhaps the key to having a close and personal relationship with God. Our relationship with God is walking in the Light.

When I was a kid, I had a penchant for getting into mischief. There were also bullies in the town where I lived, who loved to prey on me, and I was always afraid of bumping into one. When I went out for a walk with my father, though, I wasn't afraid of bullies. I didn't even think about doing dumb things that would get me in trouble. I was with my father. I was safe, happy, content, and strong. That is much like walking in the light.

Paul wrote, "For ye were sometimes darkness, but now are ye light in the Lord: walk as children of light" (Ephesians 5:8).

Someone once said, "Spiritual growth is seeing more of God and less of me." It is a matter of focus. If we are focused on ourselves, we will retard our spiritual growth; if we keep our eyes on Jesus, we will open the doors of our hearts for Him to grow us.

*****

This is the end of the first part of our exercise. It is written so that all of the principles for an individual to walk free and clean in this world are here. If they are followed, success will come.

The first part is focused on the individual, with a biblical understanding of what addiction truly is. Understanding that is the key to everything. So many people who work so hard at this problem come so close to the answer, but just miss it. Addiction is worship—the false worship of the self. It is easily missed, perhaps it is because that in its essence, it is so accusative and does not paint a pretty picture of human nature. Man is always seeking to justify himself, to deny the thought that we truly are as lost and wicked as God declares. Desperately wicked, as Jeremiah put it.

The downward spiral of the four essential needs of a healthy life is also easily seen in addictive behaviors, as we vainly pursue our selfish goals, and it is common in all such behaviors, regardless to which altars they are sought. The biblical remedies for these needs are clear and effective in changing the way we view our lives and transform the way we think. All of these together address the individual's problem.

Part 2

Repairing the Breach

The first phase of counseling those who are *addicted* is primarily for the individual and his recovery. It is important to do this, because the root issues must be dealt with to achieve success. Figuratively, if you strike at the roots, you will affect the trunk, the limbs, the branches, and leaves. No man lives to himself, and people involved in the false worship of addiction not only cause damage to their own lives and health, they affect others. The second phase of counseling addresses the issues of harm cause to others because of addictive behaviors. It is focused upon restoration and renewal.

It happened that one individual, who was doing very well with recovery, desired to return to his wife and family and take his role as the man, husband, and father that God wanted him to be. In effect, it didn't go well. He told me he was very excited and couldn't wait to get home to tell his wife and kids that daddy was back and he was all better! To his great surprise he was not met with a red carpet and open arms. He said his wife swore at him and threw an ashtray straight at his head, saying, "Get out, and never come back!" To his dismay, he had come to the realization that he had left a long trail of abuse, betrayal, deceit, and damage behind him. He had left this trail for a number of years, and the tremendous person struggle he had in overcoming his self-worshipping addiction seemed small in the face of this giant.

The second phase then requires the direct intervention of the counselor into the family and other relationships to help facilitate the restoration of the individual to his or her rightful role in the family. Because the roles are different, the counseling is also different; there must be individual programs to address each role and situation. Biblically, the roles of the husband and father, wife and mother, son and daughter, and even church member, are clearly defined. Though the roles are different, many of the same issues are involved, such as, reentering the family, trust and betrayal, responsibility, respect, obedience, leadership, submission and control. For this writing, the focus shall be on the issues faced by the husband and father, because it is the principle leadership role in the family relationship.

The first issue that must be faced is "repairing the breach," or how the husband and father can reenter his family.

Repairing the Breach

One of the most difficult problems the United States had in establishing diplomacy with Japan after the Second World War was accepting them as an ally and forgetting them as an enemy. After all, they declared war upon us and attacked us with ruthless, deadly, and undeserved fury. The aggressive action taken by Japan was despicable and villainous. In order for us to accept her as a part of the community of nations required three things: total surrender, the dismantling of their forces, and occupation.

The husband and father, who has failed to lead his family in a way that is pleasing in the sight and will of God, has in effect declared an unjust war on the family. Regardless of the severity of the attack, or whether drug or alcohol was involved, or adultery, violence, gambling, or a hundred other offenses caused the betrayal, he has fired upon the wall that protects his family and broke it down. He has done this because he has failed to provide his family with the godly leadership it needs. In order to repair the damage that has been inflicted upon the family, he must meet requirements very much like Japan did.

In this second part, we will look at the problems of the family today and learn about the issues of restoring the right leadership position back to the husband and father.

First, let's go back to the issue we had with Japan. Remember, the United States required three things of Japan in order to establish a peaceful relationship: surrender, laying down her arms, and allowing occupation. If a man has betrayed his family, he must first stop firing on them, surrender unconditionally, and allow his family pur-veyance over his life. To do this, he must first be willing to repair the damage he has caused and count the cost of the rebuilding process.

Restoring the family is much like rebuilding the wall of protec-tion that a good leader keeps around his family. It is a wall of security, provision, protection, trust, and love. In the Scripture, Nehemiah tells about the rebuilding of the wall around Jerusalem after the Babylonian captivity. There is also the repairing of the temple in the time of Josiah, king of Judah. These stories can help us to understand by a figure the troubles we will have rebuilding the wall of protection around our families.

To begin with, we can see an example set for our necessary tak-ing in Psalm 60: "O God, thou has cast us off, thou has scattered us, thou has been displeased; O turn thyself to us again. Thou hast made the earth to tremble; thou hast broken it: heal the breaches thereof; for it shaketh. Thou hast showed us thy people hard things: thou hast made us to drink the wine of astonishment" (Psalm 60:1–3).

Like the psalmist, the father must acknowledge that the break-ing down of his family's walls and the holes that have been shot into it are by his own foolishness and his own fault. Secondly, he must acknowledge that the ruination of the family is likely a judgment of God against him for his failure to obey Him. When he gets to the bottom line, which is what he needs to see, he will come to the real-ization that he is responsible for leadership—to God and to his fam-ily. The first lesson in the Bible to man is that man will be required of God to be responsible for all of his actions.[12] God made man to be responsible and to be a leader. Of all of the cases of family difficulty I have heard, I can say that the greatest, overwhelming percentage of them is due to bad leadership on the part of the husband and father.

Repairing the breach may be a painful experience, correction usually is. It may also be costly. King Jehoash found that out in the second book of Kings: "And Jehoash said to the priests, All the money of the dedicated things that is brought into the house of the LORD, even the money that every man is set at, and all the money that

---

[12] Genesis 3:9–12, 17–19.

cometh into any man's heart to bring into the house of the LORD, let the priests take it to them, every man of his acquaintance: and let them repair the breaches of the house, wheresoever any breach shall be found" (2 Kings 12:4–5).

Much of the time, in particularly cases where there are problems of substance abuse, gambling, or compulsive shopping, the household finances suffers. Bills can go without being paid, credit problems spring up, and more. Serious reparation of the family can mean having to bite the financial bullet. Depending on the type of damage done, it may take years to correct. Sometimes it is necessary to seek financial counseling as well, to help ease the burden. We will address financial problems specifically later on. Improper handling of household finances alone constitutes bad leadership. You may be good everywhere else, but financial troubles can be an enormous burden on the family. Of course, in these times, there is no such thing as job security and many people lose their jobs. Though this can strike a serious blow to your finances, it doesn't indicate poor leadership.

The next two examples of our counting the cost are found in the great wall-building story of Nehemiah. This is not counting the cost financially, but in the acknowledgment of sin.

> And it came to pass, when I heard these words, that I sat down and wept, and mourned certain days, and fasted, and prayed before the God of heaven, and said, I beseech thee, O LORD God of heaven, the great and terrible God, that keepeth covenant and mercy form them that love him and observe his commandments: Let thine ear now be attentive, and thine eyes open, that thou mayest hear the prayer of they servant, which I pray before thee now, day and night, for the children of Israel they servants, and confess the sins of the children of Israel, which we have sinned against thee: both I and my father's house have sinned. We have dealt very corruptly against thee, and have not kept the commandments, nor

the statutes, nor the judgments, which thou hast commandedst thy servant Moses, saying, if ye transgress, I will scatter you abroad among the nations: but if ye turn unto me, and keep my commandments, and do them; though there were of you cast out unto the uttermost of heaven, yet will I gather them from thence, and will bring them unto the place that I have chosen to set my name there. Now these are thy servants and thy people, whom thou hast redeemed by thy great power, and by thy strong hand. O Lord, I beseech thee, let now thine ear be attentive to the prayer of thy servant, and to the prayer of thy servants, who desire to fear thy name: and prosper, I pray thee, thy servant this day, and grant him mercy in the sight of this man. (Nehemiah 1:4–11)

That is a rather long prayer, and I wanted to include the entirety of it so that we can see the two examples shown here by Nehemiah. First, he shows a mourning over the destruction of the city and the wall, and secondly, a sincere act of repentance. There are four questions that the husband and father must answer before he can expect to reenter his family: *Is your family everything that God has designed it to be? Is your house in order? If not, are you aware of the damage? Are you mourning over the mess that you have made?*

God's design for the family is not a big house, with two cars in the garage, perfectly respectful and obedient children, and a wife that wears a dress while vacuuming. Life is not like the TV shows of the fifties, like *Ozzie and Harriet* or *Leave It to Beaver.*

It should be obvious what the extent of the damage is, unless a person is in complete denial or so self-absorbed they don't see it. Hopefully, at this point, the offender has made a significant turn-around in their life with the salvation of Christ and the work of the Spirit. This should produce the mourning that Nehemiah speaks of and fervent desire to make things right.

When Nehemiah heard the news of the condition of Jerusalem, he wept and mourned, fasted and prayed. In his prayer, he acknowledged that his sin and the sin of all Jerusalem were to blame for the judgment that had come upon them.

"And it came to pass, when I heard these words, that I sat down and wept, and mourned certain days, and fasted, and prayed before the God of heaven."

The first step to restoration of the family is an acknowledgment of responsibility and a deep regret and sorrow. Nehemiah also repented of his sin and brought it before God.

"Which I pray before thee now, day and night, for the children of Israel thy servants, and confess the sins of the children of Israel, which we have sinned against thee: both I and my father's house have sinned. We have dealt very corruptly against thee, and have not kept thy commandments, nor the statutes, nor the judgments, which thou has commanded they servant Moses."

Repentance, true repentance, is first of all agreement with God. He is God, and you are not. It must begin with the acknowledgment of who God is. As Nehemiah prayed, "I beseech thee, O LORD God of heaven, the great and terrible God, that keepeth covenant and mercy for them that love him and observe his commandments."

Repentance also includes a deep regret for the acts that have been committed and a desire to make it right. Most importantly, however, repentance comes with the understanding that we alone, by our own strength, are incapable of making things right, and so we must turn from ourselves and turn toward God, seeking His divine intercession and submitting to His authority and control. This is not the bending or breaking of a person's will to be obedient to a greater authority than them, but is merely recognizing reality. God is real. The Lord Jesus Christ is real and is in the position of absolute authority—and His authority is directed by love and understanding of what is best.

Depending on the duration, frequency, and intensity of the abuse to a man's family, the reentry may take an extended period of time. In some cases, as I mentioned before, the families may have come to a point of separation that cannot be practically bridged. The wife may have divorced the husband or decided not to deal with him anymore. It is important for a man to be restored to his family; it is equally important for a family to be willing to accept the husband and father back. In any case, restoration must be moderated. In such situations, a counselor or pastor must act as the "go between" for the man and his family, until reentry is achieved. Including the family in the process that is directed to the husband and having them observe the changes that are taking place to prepare him for restoration may expedite the reentry. It may provide convincing evidence of change that is necessary to soften the heart and allay the fears of the spouse and family. It is also a great opportunity to reach unbelievers with the gospel.

During these counseling sessions, the conditions for reentry *(surrender, disarm, and occupation)* give the spouse and family power, when they have been previously powerless. The ability to have some control over the process of restoration will facilitate an agreement to set it in motion. Once this is established, it is necessary to monitor the progress, give ear to complaints, and work out differences. The wife may feel she has some power to control the situation, but will need support from a source she knows her husband will attend to.

In the best situation, the husband adheres to the demands placed upon him for restoration, the wife and family come to know Christ as Savior if they were previously unsaved, and the family begins to heal, becoming the family that God desires them to be.

Trust and Betrayal

One of the most difficult things to countenance in any relationship based upon trust is a betrayal of that trust. For a marriage, those few words that we say standing before the preacher are a covenant of a trust relationship. Words like, *forsaking all others* and *for better, for worse,* though spoken with the utmost sincerity at the altar, seem distant and trivial as the humdrum of everyday life passes on. How these words come back with stinging clarity, when our covenant companion has betrayed that which we have been so comfortable in! There is an old saying, "Hell hath no fury like a woman scorned." Rightly so, for a betrayal caused by the pursuing of a more pleasurable relationship than the one you enjoyed with your spouse is hateful. It is telling that person that you have shared the most intimate part of your life with that you are rejecting them for someone or something else.

In his book, *Point Man,* Steve Farrar brings back to memory the days when "real men don't" (followed by something meant to be humorous) was popular. One phrase, "Real men don't eat quiche!" was the most well-known at that time. Farrar adds, *"Real men don't commit adultery."* Certainly, having a sexual relationship with another person outside of marriage is the cruelest and most belittling of betrayals. It should be considered the most unspeakable horror to happen to a marriage. However, *any* relationship that takes the husband away from his spouse because it is more pleasurable than her is adulterous. Whether it is drugs, alcohol, gambling, sports, the guys, work, the pursuit of riches, or even ministry, it constitutes a rejection of the spouse for something that pleases more or what he thinks is more important than her. Renewing a trust relationship after betrayal may be long and may require counseling for all parties, but as sure as God lives and reigns, there is hope.

The first step in restoring a trust relationship is to prove trustworthiness. I heard a story once told by, I believe, Chuck Swindoll. My apologies for not recalling the exact details of the story as he so wonderfully told it. He was talking about a bright young attorney, having just graduated at the top of his class from a most respected university. The attorney was being shown the ropes of his new job in an important law firm, surrounded by the senior members of the firm, sitting around a long, mahogany table. At the end of the table was the firm's senior partner, and he said, "You will start here doing mostly leg work for other members, and when you are trusted, you can do *pro bono* work. After that, when you are trusted, you may begin working as a team member on some cases. After that, when you are trusted, you will be assigned cases of your own." The young man whispered to the partner next to him, "How can I gain your trust?" to which the partner answered, "Try being trustworthy."

Trust must be earned; it must be proven. In the case of betrayal, trust must be earned again in small bits, over an extended period of time. How long that is depends on the willingness of the betrayed person to trust again. Trust requires vulnerability—the trusting partners lower all their shields and place themselves once again in the *line of fire*.

An important aspect of rebuilding trust is forgiveness. Many people do not really understand what it means to forgive someone. It is certainly not the *I-forgive-you-but-I will-never-forget* kind. That is not forgiveness. Forgiveness is the act of restoring a person to the position or relationship that was enjoyed prior to the offense.

There is a story about forgiveness. A man had this great desire to have a classic muscle car. It had to be the exact right car, with the right color, engine, trim, and the whole package. He saved for years, every penny he could spare, in the hope that he would someday find his dream car. After a long time and much searching, he found it! It was more costly than he had wanted, but it was available and he really wanted it. So he bought it. No one was allowed to touch his beauty, and he spent hours detailing and polishing it to perfection. It was a thing to behold. His brother, who also loved cars, came to see it. He begged his brother to let him drive it, but he said, "Absolutely *not!*" His brother kept pleading with him, saying that he only wanted to drive it once around the block. He promised he wouldn't get a scratch on it. Finally, he wore him down, and with a great deal of anxiety, the older brother said he would let him drive it only around the block once. He warned him sternly not to let anything happen to it, because he would never be able to get another one. The younger brother immediately jumped into the driver's seat, fired it up, and slowly and cautiously backed the car out of the driveway on to the street. Off he went and disappeared out of sight. Standing at the end of the driveway, the owner stood, impatiently waiting for the return of the car. Some time went by, and he thought that his brother should certainly have made it around the block. An hour went by, then two. After three hours, he got a telephone call. It was the police. There was an accident, and his car was totaled. His brother was okay, but he was taken to the hospital for some minor injuries. He rushed to the hospital and found his brother, sitting, with an ice pack on his head. He walked up to his little brother, so angry he couldn't even speak. His brother looked up and burst into tears. "I am so sorry," he said. "I don't know what happened, I just lost control." The older brother just stood there for quite a while and then went and hugged his brother. "It is okay, I forgive you. I am just glad you are all right."

True forgiveness restores the offender to the place they were before the offense and bears the loss. The man who owned the car accepted the loss of his prize to restore his brother. Now, there are many who would say, "*That is impossible!*" It is definitely not easy, but in Christ, nothing is impossible.

Trust and forgiveness are two sides of the same coin, though they are distinct from one another. After an offense is made, you can't have forgiveness without trust, and though forgiveness is not earned, trust must be. Forgiveness restores a person to the position they held before, regardless of past behaviors, but trust restores a relationship after proven changes in behavior.

This brings us back to the model of Japan and the United States. In order for Japan to gain trust, it had to meet stern conditions. These conditions were surrender, disarmament, and occupation. Let's transfer these conditions to the subject of addictive behaviors.

Surrender

In order for trust to be reestablished, it must be born of fertile soil. Trust is a building process that begins with repentance, forgiveness, and reconciliation. When a person receives Christ as Lord and Savior, he first came to the understanding that he was guilty of the offence that separated him from God. He repented of his sin and turned away from it, seeking forgiveness. The same principles apply to reconciliation in the family. The betrayer must admit his wrongdoing, show genuine remorse for his actions, and demonstrate a change in his thinking and action. This takes humility and the willingness to suffer rebuke and reproach for the sake of the family. The Lord demonstrated His humility and willingness to bear reproach for the sake of reconciling man from sin. Paul wrote, "Let this mind be in you, which was also in Christ Jesus: who, being in the form of God, thought it not robbery to be equal with God: but made himself of no reputation, and took upon him the form of a servant, and was made in the likeness of men: and being found in fashion as a man, he humbled himself, and became obedient unto death, even the death of the cross" (Philippians 2:7–8 NKJV).

The writer of Hebrews tells us, "But we see Jesus, who was make a little lower than the angels for the suffering of death, crowned with glory and honour; that he by the grace of God should taste death for every man. For it became him, for who are all things, and by whom are all things, in bringing many sons unto glory, to make the captain of their salvation perfect through sufferings" (Hebrews 2:9–10).

The husband also, as a follower of Christ, needs to surrender to the will of the Father, humbling himself and bearing reproach that there may be reconciliation of the family to God's purpose and will. It is our understanding of Christ's sacrifice that breaks our hearts for Him. He was serious about our reconciliation to the Father. The cross was serious business. The family needs to see that same seriousness, commitment, and dedication in the husband for the sake of the family.

Disarmament

Disarmament means a laying down of the weapons that cause injury and offence and a promise never to take them up again. For a husband seeking restoration with his family, this means that he must lay down all of those old habits and behaviors that signified conflict—those that were associated or akin to those direct assaults on the family. Repentance means to turn away from those behaviors and turn toward the will of God. So disarmament, in this case, is similar to repentance. In the case of addictive behaviors, used as an extreme, there are many behaviors that typify as system of abuse. Anger, moodiness, refusal to account for time or money spent, loss of interest in marriage and family, are all symptoms of something terribly wrong. Secret associations or "bad friends," along with distancing from the family and true friends, are also strong indicators. These behaviors tell the family that dad hasn't changed and is still a threat. The apostle Paul spoke about changing behavior in many of his letters. If the husband truly claims to be a "new" person in Christ Jesus, then that must be demonstrated by his actions and attitudes.

Paul wrote:

> Let us behave properly as in the day, not in carousing and drunkenness, not in sexual promiscuity and sensuality, not in strife and jealousy. But put on the Lord Jesus Christ, and make not provision for the flesh, in regard to its lusts. (Romans 13:13–14 NASB)

> That ye put off concerning the former conversation the old man, which is corrupt according to the deceitful lusts; and be renewed in the spirit of your mind; and that ye put on the new man, which after God is created in righteousness and true holiness. Wherefore putting away lying, speak every man truth with his neighbor: for we are members one of another. Be ye angry, and sin

not: let not the sun go down upon your wrath: neither give place to the devil. Let him that stole steal no more: but rather let him labor, working with his own hands the thing which is good, that he may have to give to him that needeth.

Let no corrupt communications proceed out of your mouth, but that which is good to the use of edifying, that it may minister grace unto the hearers. And grieve not the Holy Spirit of God, whereby ye are sealed unto the day of redemption

Let all bitterness, and wrath, and evil speaking, be put away from you, with all malice: and be ye kind to one another, tender-hearted, forgiving one another, even as God for Christ's sake hath forgiven you. (Ephesians 4:22–32)

That is a lot to chew on, and those scriptures should be continually used as the restoration process goes on to encourage and guide. It is clear to see, even from our own experience, that the behavior Paul speaks of clearly demonstrates change. Even the best Christian husbands and fathers need to be mindful of these wonderful exhortations. Now, no one is yet perfect, or has *arrived,* as it is said in some circles, and I trust that you won't find one either, this side of heaven. But disarmament means that the husband is serious about his renewed relationship, that the spirit of God is working in him and he is not resisting it.

Occupation

After the Second World War, one of the things we imposed on Japan was the occupation of their country with a military presence. This showed good faith on the part of the Japanese and allowed an opportunity to make them immediately accountable for any actions that would violate that faith.

The husband must also allow his sovereignty to be occupied by his wife and family. It may not be possible or even reasonable to be accompanied by a family member everywhere and every hour of the day, but there must be accountability for what he is doing, with whom, and when. Communication is required, and there is sufficient technology to meet that need, without excuse. Even if a husband has never betrayed the trust of his wife, he honors her by sharing every part of his day with her. If he is going to be a little late, he calls. If he has any change of plans out of the ordinary, he calls. If he is having a good day or a bad day, he calls.

It is important to understand that the relationship men enter into with their wives is more than mere companionship. It is more than friendship. It is more than love. It is an *association*. For example, if you were to enter into a business with another person as an associate, it would be that person's right to know everything you did in respect to the business. To make any purchases, or sales, or investments without the knowledge and approval of your associate would be a serious violation of the association and would not be tolerated. Your wife is your associate in the business of life. There is nothing that happens to you in your life that does not pertain to her. You are to conduct yourself as if your wife were present with you at all times. This is allowing yourself to be occupied, allowing your wife and family the privilege of knowing all that you are doing. In a relationship that has suffered a betrayal, the husband must allow total accountability—no freedom of action outside of the spouse's purview.

These actions, initially enforced to build a new, trusting relationship, should not have a determined termination. At first, they are employed to reestablish trust, but it is difficult to determine when that is achieved. The safe way to go is to continue them indefinitely. Somewhere, in the future, the motive for the actions changes. The reestablishment of trust will eventually come, and the husband continues his association with his wife by applying the same principles of surrender, disarmament, and occupation. The motive changes from one of proving trustworthiness, to duty to his associate, to finally honor, consideration, and love. The trust relationship of marriage is entered into with love and honor. The betrayal of that trust shows that love, hone, and consideration have departed. The three princi-ples of restoration must be enforced until the reason they are applied is again love, honor, and consideration.

Stand and Deliver

Being a husband and father is a great responsibility; everybody knows that. I am not so certain that everyone knows what *responsibility* is. I imagine if you took a poll of a thousand men, you would get a near one hundred percent response that they feel they are doing what is required of them for their wives and families. We all have varying opinions as to what is right and responsible. Unfortunately, many families are struggling, or in ruin, because the man of the house does not know or accept his responsibility.

The American Heritage Dictionary defines responsibility as: 1) legally or ethically accountable for the care of welfare of another; 2) involving personal accountability or ability to act without guidance or superior authority; 3) capable of being trusted or depended upon: reliable; 4) based upon or characterized by good judgment or sound thinking.[13]

Based upon these definitions, how do we, as biblical counselors, help men coming out of a lifestyle where it was all about them, to measure up to what is being responsible? Working with each of these definitions, we can help them understand the depth of the meaning of responsibility. The first definition has three words that sting in the ears of those involved in self-worship. They are: *legal, ethical,* and *another.* These words represent demands that are placed on us.

The first word, *legal,* speaks of the demands that our system of government places upon us. Responsibility is not only recognized and demanded of by the nation that we live in, it is enforced. I know many that have come out of the haze of drugs and alcohol to discover

---

[13] American Heritage Dictionary. 1982, 1985. Boston. Houghton Mifflin Co.

that the state government holds them liable for thousands of dollars of unpaid child support and unhappily find that defaulting on the governmental demands may lead to incarceration.

The second word, *ethical*, speaks of the demands that society places upon us. In spite of the seemingly obvious nosedive that morality has taken in our country, society as a whole still holds a high standard for the taking care of our families and the responsibilities of the male head of the family. It is odd that in many state prisons, inmates may be thieves, murderers, arsonists, and cheats, but if a man has abused or neglected his family or made children their prey, the other inmates hate him. In some instances, the life of an inmate that has abused his own children, or other children is decidedly marked and in danger.

The third word, *another*, speaks of the demands that people we have established a relationship with place upon us. It is also the demand of God that He places upon us for the care of our neighbor. The saying "No man is an island" is true. It is said that we commonly affect over one hundred people in the course of an ordinary day. Of course, if you live in the middle of the Mojave Desert, this number may be less. The commandment of God that we should *love our neighbor as ourselves,* drives our responsibility to others to a much deeper level. When the Pharisee questioned Jesus as to who his neighbor was, Jesus told the parable of the Good Samaritan, found in the gospel of Luke 10:26–37. The idea is that our worst enemy, the one we hate the most, is our neighbor, and we are responsible to God for his care. A responsible person thinks and cares for others. Responsibility is an acknowledgment that we must serve others, rather than expect others to serve us. We can improve leadership by understanding God's principles of responsibility.

The first principle is that we are accountable for the welfare of another. Paul writes to us in his first letter to Timothy: "But if any provide not for his own, and especially for those of his own house, he hath denied the faith, and is worse than an infidel" (1 Timothy 5:8).

The word *infidel* is very strong. It is not just a person who is an unbeliever, but a person who has denied the faith—an atheist and blasphemer. *Infidel* comes from the Latin as *faithless,* with the implication of a deliberate act of the will. Paul says, a person that does not see to the needs of his family is worse than an infidel. In some translations, the word infidel is rendered as "dog."

What do the Scriptures give us to understand our responsibilities of providing for our families?

Let us begin by understanding the different levels of provision that are necessary for having a healthy and happy life. Firstly, there is physical provision. Parts of physical provision are food, shelter, protection, comfort, and security. Jesus asked the multitudes, "Or what man is there of you, whom if his son ask bread, will be give him a stone? Or if he ask a fish, will he give him a serpent? If ye then, being evil, know how to give good gifts unto your children, how much more shall your Father which is in heaven give good things to them that ask him?" (Matthew 7:9–11).

In the parable of the prodigal son, Jesus gives us an understanding of a good father's care:

> Now his elder son was in the field: and as he came and drew nigh to the house, he heard music and dancing…and he was angry, and would not go in: therefore his father came out, and entreated him.
>
> And he answering said to his father, Lo, these many years do I serve thee, neither transgressed I at any time thy commandment: and yet thou never gavest me a kid, that I might make merry with my friends: But as soon as this thy son was come, which hath devoured thy living with harlots, thou hast killed for him the fatted calf.
>
> And he said unto him, Son, thou art ever with me, and all that I have is thine. It was meet that we should make merry, and be glad: for this thy brother was dead, and is alive again; and was lost, and is found. (Luke 15:25, 28–32)

It is not enough to provide for the physical needs of your wife and children, but also to secure the generations to follow. "A good man leaves an inheritance to his children's children: and the wealth of the sinner is laid up for the just" (Proverbs 13:22).

Another way we provide for our family, especially our wives, is to know their desires, their likes and dislikes, and how to make them happy. "Husbands, likewise, dwell with them with understanding, giving honor to the wife, as to the weaker vessel, and as being heirs together of the grace of life, that your prayers may not be hindered" (1 Peter 3:7 NKJV).

The "weaker vessel" is not to be meant as the wife being inferior, but rather that she is to be viewed as precious and fragile, like a valuable vase.

It is not enough that you provide for all of the physical needs of your wife. You must also take care of her emotional, intellectual, and spiritual needs. To dwell with them according to knowledge, as Peter put it, means to know everything about your wife. That takes quite a commitment. In order for us to know our wives and fulfill this standard, we must be *interested* in them, if not captivated by them. Your wife's greatest need is security, and your devotion and commitment to learn about her and please her will help provide that.

A simple case in point would be, suppose your wife is a little insecure about your fidelity. Whether there is cause or not, you need to make her feel secure about it. If she doesn't like you looking at pretty girls, you can bet she will be watching you. Now I understand that there are a lot of pretty girls in the world, and you can rest assured that our enemy will bring them in your view. A good solution is to look at your wife. Remember how you cast your eye upon her the first time? Do you remember how you couldn't keep your eyes off of her? Bingo.

Another way we must provide for our wives is intellectually. Women, at least many women, love to talk. Believe it or not, your wife would rather talk to you than anyone else. For some couples, the husband is away from the home for most of the day working. The wife may be home all day, perhaps dealing with small children, or she may have her own place in the working world. If she is a stay-at-home mom, she probably does not get a lot of intellectual grati-fication during this period. She can't wait for her Prince Charming to get home so she can have an adult conversation with someone other than the dog. If she works, her day is filled with challenges and frustrations, triumphs and setbacks, and she needs to share her day with you. So it would be to your benefit to prepare yourself on the way home. Leave the problems of the workplace there. Whatever had transpired during the day is behind you, and all of your thoughts should be on your place of refuge and your best friend. She has been waiting all day for the opportunity to talk with you; you should be waiting all day to hear what she has to say.

Now, there are quite a few guys that would say, "Hey, what about me? Don't I get to have my needs met too?" Well, you have to be the man. God created man first, to lead, and we must. If we are doing what we are supposed to do, God will see that all of our needs are met. Don't worry about it. If you are doing all you can for the welfare and happiness of your wife, she will respond in like manner.

It is also necessary for you to provide spiritual leadership for your wife and family. Paul makes this very clear: "The women are to keep silent in the churches; for they are not permitted to speak, but are to subject themselves, just as the Law also says. If they desire to learn anything, let them ask their own husbands at home; for it is improper for a woman to speak in church" (1 Corinthians 14:34–35 NASB).

Paul addressed a situation of confusion in the Corinthian church. In those days, and in that culture, some women were priestesses of the pagan gods that were worshipped. They often spoke outlandish things and performed shocking acts. They would stand and shout or shriek, or begin speaking in an unknown tongue; they would let their hair fly and would bare their breasts, signifying that they were under the influence of a god as an oracle. Some of this unseemly behavior had presented itself in the church. In his strong statement to remedy this, Paul give the men charge for taking the role of spiritual lead-ership in the church and in the home. This charge also includes the instruction of the children.

"And these words which I command you today shall be in your heart. You shall teach them diligently to your children, and shall talk of them when you sit in your house, when you walk by the way, when you lie down, and when your rise up" (Deuteronomy 6:6–7 NKJV).

The Scriptures also speak of our responsibility to provide for our children emotionally and intellectually. "Train up a child in the way he should go: and when he is old, he will not depart from it" (Proverbs 22:6).

What this verse is saying to us, is that training your child is more than just teaching them how to be morally correct. The implication here is that we are to be mindful of the gifts and abilities, along with the desires that God has given our children, and to direct their lives accordingly. In order for us to do that, we must *know* our children well. It is your responsibility to discover the abilities of your children, to not only know and do what God created you to do, but to discover what God has made them to do. This is a rare thing indeed. Most people never find out what God purposed for them to do in this world, to build His Kingdom. We desperately seek to find out who we are and what we are supposed to do, and we strive to find, in this world, what that is. If we seek to find the meaning and purpose of our life in this world, we will miss it entirely. If we trust and seek to find the meaning of life in Christ, we will find it. We are to find out what our children, who were created by God for His purpose, were made to do, and to encourage them to find and do that.

Every mom and dad wants their kid to be successful, to live a happy life with a great career, so they can be comfortable and happy in this world. In other words, every parent wants their kid to be a doctor or at very least, the president of the United States. It is natural that the parent would desire success for their children. It is not natural for a parent to decide what that child shall be when they grow up. Many parents frustrate their children by trying to force them into a mold that they have designed. Paul also warns us of that: "And ye fathers, provoke not your children to wrath; but bring them up in the nurture and admonition of the Lord" (Ephesians 6:4).

The second definition of responsibility is to involve personal accountability to act without the guidance of a superior authority. This means that a person is dependable to make the right choices without another person present to act as a deterrent. This also speaks of being able to make up your mind, decide what you should do for the sake of your family and doing it. Indecisiveness is a terrible weakness that effects the godly foundation of the family. No one said that making decisions would be easy, or that you will always be right. We learn from our mistakes. True leadership is not measured by how often we are correct in our decisions, but in our taking accountability for the decisions we make. We must understand that this definition, which says, "Our ability to act without guidance of superior authority," is speaking of the authority in the world. There are no responsible people in jail. Every single inmate in jail cannot act without the direct supervision of a person in authority. The same goes for children in a schoolroom or little children in the home. They are not able to act responsibly. They cannot maintain a personal accountability, which means to choose to do what is right or wrong, without guidance. We are responsible when we respect the laws that we are governed by and live obedient to them. Paul wrote, "Render therefore to all their dues: tribute to whom tribute is due; custom to whom custom; fear to whom fear; honor to whom honor" (Romans 13:7).

They key to this definition then is *personal accountability*. This is also called integrity. Someone once said that integrity is what you do when no one is watching.

The problem with personal accountability in the life of a person who has come out of addiction is that the altars at which a person worships himself are usually very private.

It goes without saying that personal accountability is the weakest point for the self-worshipper. The reason for this is that the sin of addiction is all and only about the self. The idea of personal accountability for the benefit of others is unimaginable. Yet this is what must be conveyed to the man or woman seeking restoration to the family. How this is conveyed is through the occupation of the family into his or her life. The family is a present deterrent for improper choices, if allowed occupation. The husband and father must maintain contact with his wife frequently to insure that he is being accountable for his actions. As time goes on and the trust relationship is reestablished, the man becomes more *personally accountable,* and he gains enough trust with his wife to be on his own.

More importantly, the man is not to think that he is free from the guidance and superior authority of God. That is not a mark of responsibility, but irresponsibility. We are to continually seek God's favor and guidance. We are to follow hard after the will of God. A truly responsible person understand that he, without the guidance and aid of God actively in this life, will fail in the greatest areas of life.

The third definition is an extension of the second, in that a man is considered responsible when his personal accountability proves to be reliable over time. Reliability is tested with frequency of use. A flashlight that works six times out of ten tries is not one we will take camping with us. Reliability is connected with dependability. The flashlight that works ten times out of ten tries we will depend on to work for us. Dependability is subject to reliability, so it is also a demand for reliability. In the case of a husband and father taking the enormous responsibility as head of the family, it is with the knowledge that the family is dependent upon him. Their dependence upon him demands him to be reliable.

The fourth definition speaks of a man making decisions that take into account the impact that decision has on himself, his wife and family, and others. Sound judgment does not act selfishly and deprive the wife and family of their need. The husband and father must take all into consideration before he makes a decision and bases that decision on what is best for the family. This is sound judgment, and good, responsible leadership. Soundness of mind is also a gift of the Spirit.

There are many gifts of the Spirit, and the apostle Paul speaks of the first gifts: "For God has not given us a spirit of fear, but of power and of love and of a sound mind" (2 Timothy 1:7 NKJV).

When a person receives Christ as Lord and Savior and feeds upon the whole counsel of God in the Scripture, they will learn how to make sound judgment. In the verse above, power speaks of courage and boldness. God gives us the ability to courageously lead our families for His purpose in the face of this wicked world. Here are some more verses about courage:

> Have I not commanded you? Be strong and of good courage; for the LORD your God is with you wherever you go. (Joshua 1:9 NKJV)

> Finally, my brothers, be strong in the Lord, and in the power of His might. (Ephesians 6:10 NKJV)

The love spoken of in Paul's letter to Timothy is the love of Christ, which passes knowledge and is implanted in the heart of the believer. Jesus commands us to love with His love in the gospel of John: "This is My commandment, that you love one another as I have loved you. Greater love has no one than this, than to lay down one's life for his friends" (John 15:12–13 NKJV).

The soundness of mind is our ability to reason and judge according to the will of God, as stated in the Bible, "Commit your works to the LORD, and your thoughts will be established" (Proverbs 16:3 NKJV).

In order for a man to lead his family responsibly, he must commit his works to the Lord, submit himself to the teaching of the Spirit, and feed on His Word. Soundness of mind is what happens when God knocks some sense into us. He has opened our eyes to the truth of His Word and the wonders of His mighty counsel.

Respect

"R-E-S-P-E-C-T, find out what it means to me!" Aretha Franklin belted that out in the early '70s to a generation of kids that grew to be the adults and leaders of our nation and world and has since passed the torch onto their children today. Oddly enough, many of us never found out what it meant to her or what it means to our loved ones and us at all! Respect and trust are very much alike, in that we all desire it, feel we deserve it, and yet are unwilling to freely give it to anyone else. As Christians, we are commanded by the Word of God to give respect to others, where it is due, no matter whether we feel that person is undeserving of it. Paul wrote, "Render therefore to all their dues: tribute to whom tribute is due; custom to whom custom; fear to whom fear; and honor to whom honor" (Romans 13:7).

Paul continues in his argument with the understanding that respect comes from love: "For the commandments, 'You shall not commit adultery, You shall not murder, You shall not steal, You shall not bear false witness, You shall not covet," and if there is any other commandment, are all summed up in this saying, namely, "You shall love your neighbor as yourself.' Love does no harm to a neighbor; therefore love is the fulfillment of the law" (Romans 13:9–10).

So what is respect, anyway? One of the dictionary definitions is a *polite expression of consideration.*[14] I don't think we need to go much further than that. Paul again conveys God's will for us in his letter to the Philippians: "Look not every man on his own things, but every man also on the things of others" (Philippians 2:4).

Another definition is to show deferential regard for, or esteem. Again, we go to Philippians: "Let nothing be done through strife or vainglory; but in lowliness of mind let each esteem other better than themselves" (Philippians 2:3).

A key to understanding the type of respect we desire for ourselves is in the respect we show to others. One of the failures of leadership is demanding respect, without knowing what proper respect is and not being deserving of it. When respect is commanded and not deserved, it has to be forced. The forcing of respect produces much, but none of it is respect. What it does produce is oppression, fear, resentment, and ultimately rebellion. Many times, parents demand respect from their children and have the nerve to be angry and surprised when their children rebel. One of the surest ways to prevent that is to respect (show polite consideration and esteem for) the wife and kids.

---

[14] American Heritage Dictionary. © 1982, 1985. Boston. Houghton Mifflin Co.

Another key to understanding and obtaining respect is by being respectable. Respectability is purely attitude in action. It is one of those things that *gets what it gives*. It is much like friendship as it is described in the Proverbs: "There are 'friends' who destroy each other, but a real friend sticks closer than a brother" (Proverbs 18:24 NLT).

In order for a person to be trusted, they must prove themselves trustworthy. For a person to be respected, they must prove themselves respectable. Respectability is modeled by the presence of three attitudes: capability, consideration, and consistency.

Respectability comes from the assurance that you are capable of performing to a standard or in a manner that is reliable, signifying by your action that you know what you are doing, and demonstrate that with confidence. Respectability comes with the ability to lead confidently and to make decisions that are right and benefit the family. It is important not to confuse confidence with arrogance. An arrogant man may make right decisions, but his arrogance is demonstrated by his excluding counsel from others or input from his family. An arrogant man thinks he knows what his wife and family need without having to hear what they say. They are know-it-all, and nobody likes them, really. A confident man is concerned with and values the ideas of his family, and after considering all, makes a decision. There are a number of verses that speak on this. Here are a few:

> Where there is no counsel, the people fall: but in the multitude of counselors there is safety. (Proverbs 11:14)

> He who gives an answer before he hears, it is folly and shame to him. (Proverbs 18:15 NASB)

> The mind of the prudent acquires knowledge, and the ear of the wise seeks knowledge. (Proverbs 18:15 NASB)

Responsibility is demonstrated by a willingness to take instruction. Some other verses that really point to the capabilities are found in Proverbs, chapter 31. This is about the capability of the wife, but the principles are exactly the same; in fact, they are equal, which we will discuss in a little bit.

> She perceives that her merchandise is good, and he lamp does not go out by night.
> She extends her hand to the poor, Yes, she reaches out her hands to the needy.
> She is not afraid of snow for her household, for all her household is clothed with scarlet.
> Strength and honor are her clothing; she shall rejoice in time to come. (Proverbs 31:18, 20, 21, 25 NKJV)

Wow, that is respectability shown by a capable, confident person. What is the outcome of such devotion and character? "Her children rise up, and call her blessed; her husband also, and he praises her" (Proverbs 31:28 NKJV).

Isn't that what being respected is? If your wife and children rise up and praise you, honor you, and call you blessed, that is the greatest show of respect humanly possible.

Consideration is the second model of respectability in our text. Consideration is a deliberate, thoughtful act that is directed for the benefit of others. It is a positive attitude that exemplifies the value of others to you. It is the husband that listens intently to the problems and counsel of his wife and children.

Understanding our value is one of the four great needs of our lives. We must feel that we are of value and that we are important. For our families, and especially our wives, they must feel that they are of value to us and that they belong as an active member of the family. It would be shameful for a husband to treat his greatest love and partner in this world with such disdain.

The writer of Hebrews addresses the church, but it also has an application for the family members: "Let us hold fast the confession of our hope without wavering, for He who promised is faithful. And let us consider one another in order to stir up love and good works" (Hebrews 10:23–24 NKJV).

Oftentimes, in a situation where the husband and father is struggling with addictive behaviors and is so consumed with his own thing, the children feel isolated, because their desires, opinions, and input are not considered. Though children are young and have not experienced much in this world, they still need the consideration of being listened to and shown that they have value. It is the duty of the father to instruct his children in the way that they should go, without frustrating them. It is wise to show the children under your authority, that you are also under the authority of God, and must subject yourself to His great love and instruction. Paul wrote, "Fathers, do not provoke your children to anger; but bring them up in the discipline and instruction of the Lord" (Ephesians 6:4 NASB).

The Bible also speaks how we are to be considerate in love with our wives: "Husbands, love your wives, even as Christ also loved the church, and gave Himself for it" (Ephesians 5:25).

So here is the deal, if you do not consider your wife and children and demonstrate their value to you, you are simply not worthy of respect and are more like a wicked despot. That is certainly not what our Lord modeled for us.

Our last model for responsibility is consistency. Consistency can be equated to steadfastness. It is difficult to respect the leadership of someone who changes with every breath of wind. Consistency of course is not to be confused with stubbornness or hard-heartedness. Consistency is dependability, reliability. It is an anchor that holds your family under your leadership. Of all the models for respectability, consistency is the strongest. There are many ways by which we can model consistency in our lives and leadership. There is consistency in action, consistency in faith, and consistency in example.

Consistency in action is how we react to certain events in our lives in a manner that is expected and typical of the character we model. For example, John is a model husband and father. He is kind, good-natured, loving, and considerate to his wife and family. He is confident in his leadership and care for his family. Unexpectedly, he receives notice that he is no longer needed at his place of employment. He immediately goes to unemployment and begins to look for another job. Time goes on, and the bills begin to pile up. John becomes moody, angry, and impatient with his wife and children. He does not want to go to another city to find employment, for that would mean having to sell his house and move his family to a strange location. Things get pretty tough for John and his family for a while, but he finally finds a job in a company nearby. The job is within his field, but the pay and benefits are less than they were used to. In spite of the difficult circumstances, John held firm to his family, his leadership, and his faith. There were times of frustration and anger, but never in a way that was inconsistent with John's character and devotion to his family. His determination to see the problem through gave his family security and confidence. This is respectability.

Consistency in faith will sustain a person and a family through the worst storm. Perhaps Job is the best example of this faith in Scripture, though there are others that would certainly give him a run for his money.

> Then Job arose, and rent his mantle, and shaved his head, and fell down upon the ground, and worshipped, and said, "Naked came I out of my mother's womb, and naked shall I return thither: the LORD gave, and the LORD hath taken away; blessed is the name of the LORD." (Job 1:20–22)

> In all this Job sinned not, nor charged God foolishly. Then said his wife unto him, "Dost thou still retain thine integrity? Curse God, and die." But he said unto her, "Thou speakest as one of the foolish women speaketh. What? Shall we

receive good at the hand of God, and shall we not receive evil?" In all this did not Job sin with his lips. (Job 2:9–10)

But what of those that do not have such consistency of faith? How shall we respect them? Jesus told a parable about those who were inconsistent in faith: "He also that received seed among the thorns is he that heareth the word; and the care of this world, and the deceitfulness of riches, choke the word, and he becometh unfruitful" (Matthew 13:22).

The last form of consistency is by example. What I mean is, are you living by the same standard by which you demand others to live by? There is an old saying, *"Do as I say, not as I do."* This is the definition of hypocrisy. Parents, do you warn your children about the evil of drugs and alcohol, yet have liquor in your house? Do you warn your children never to smoke, yet you yourself puff away? Husbands, do you command your wives not to spend foolishly, and then come home with a new and very expensive toy?

Living according to a double standard will ruin all hope of respectability. There is another old saying which says, "Don't ask anyone to do something that you wouldn't do." Here is a better one: "Don't ask anyone to do anything that you are not already doing." That is a simple principle of leadership. Our Lord set that example for us: "You call Me Teacher and Lord, and you say well, for so I am. If I then, your Lord and Teacher, have washed your feet, you also ought to wash one another's feet" (John 13:13–14 NKJV).

Respect is due when it is deserved. It must be, like trust, earned. It is deserved when it is demonstrated in love by consideration, capability, and consistency.

Obedience School

And Samuel said, Hath the LORD as great delight in burnt offerings and sacrifices, as in obeying the voice of the LORD? Behold, to obey is better than sacrifice, and to hearken that the fat of rams.

For rebellion is as the sin of witchcraft, and stubbornness is as iniquity and idolatry. (1 Samuel 15:22–23a)

One of the most important things we learn from childhood is to obey. My parents were kinda big on it. For much of my young life, I thought my parents wanted me to obey just to spoil my fun and to make their life easier. After I had children of my own, I found that obedience was much more. Obedience is an act of love. It is the mark of an established relationship. Obedience is how we are protected from harm, pain, discomfort, and unhappiness, when it is obvious we cannot see the danger. As children, our parents demanded obedience to protect us and help us to understand God's rightful authority. When we are obedient to our parents, it is because we love them and respect them. Our obedience to God is a testimony to the lost world of His loving authority over our lives and our families. As I said in the last chapter, it is important for our children to know that though they are under the authority of the father, he too is under the authority of God and His Word. The writer of Hebrews noted, "Now faith is the substance of things hoped for, the evidence of things not seen" (Hebrews 11:1).

Obedience can be described in a similar fashion: "Obedience is the substance of things believed, the evidence of your faith."

Walking in faith is a visible testimony of knowing what to expect at the end, for that is what hope is—an expected end. Obedience is a visible testimony of a true relationship, and it defines the nature of that relationship. When we are obedient to God, it shows the world that we have a relationship with Him and that we are subject to Him in that relationship.

For many of us, our idea of being obedient to God is to go to church on Sunday and pray before each meal. They are important, to be sure, but I am afraid we are way short of the mark, if that is all we think it is.

The idea of obedience, the loving obedience of a child for his parent, or for a servant to his employer, or a citizen to their king, is a familiar one. Paul speaks of it in his letter to the Ephesian church:

> Children, obey your parents in the Lord, for this is right. (Ephesians 6:1 NKJV)

> Bondservants, be obedient to those who are your masters according to the flesh, with fear and trembling, in sincerity of heart, as to Christ. (Ephesians 6:5 NKJV)

Another good example is Samuel's rebuke of Saul: "Has the LORD as great delight in burnt offerings and sacrifices, as in obeying the voice of the LORD? Behold, to obey is better than sacrifice, and to heed that the fat of rams" (1 Samuel 15:22 NKJV).

As I said, obedience is the mark of a true relationship. Our obedience to God is a natural response to the understanding of God's authority over us and our lives. This authority can only be likened to that of a king's authority over his servant. When we understand that relationship, we are free to do His will without the encumbrance of our own selfish aims and desires. Perhaps, in all of this exercise, as I said in the beginning, the most important thing we can learn is that God is God and you are not. Understanding the way that authority works solves a multitude of problems. One of the things that Jesus said is about trusting God for all we need and not to be anxious. "But seek ye first the Kingdom of God, and His righteousness; and all these things shall be added unto you" (Matthew 6:33).

For the sake of our understanding the freedom we can enjoy in obedience to the authority of God, let us change the word "kingdom" to "kingship." We are to diligently see the *kingship* of God; that is, His rightful rule and authority over every area of our lives. The kingship of God is greater than any other authority in this world, because of the ownership of His creation.

A question I like to ask kids seeking their identity and way in this world is "Before you were born, did you choose your parents, your sex, your race, your intelligence, your looks, likes, dislikes, your talents or abilities, the place of your birth, the time of your birth, or the *why* of your birth?

As I said previously, we didn't choose how many fingers or toes we would have, or hair, or anything else. To be perfectly honest, we have very little to do with whom and what we are. We do not exist because of our will. We aren't an accident either. We are a creation of God—for His purpose, for His pleasure, and for the working of His will in this place and at this time. You don't own you, God does.

That should pretty much clear up the authority business, shouldn't it? And if not, there are a couple more things to take a serious not of:

> For not one of us lives for himself, and not one dies for himself; for if we live, we live for the Lord, or if we die, we die for the Lord; therefore whether we live or die, we are the Lord's. For to this end Christ died and lived again that he might be Lord both of the dead and of the living.
>
> But you, why do you judge your brother? Or you again, why do you regard your brother with contempt? For we will all stand before the judgment seat of God. For it is written,

"As I live, says the LORD, every knee shall bow to Me, and every tongue shall give praise to God."
So then each one of us will give an account of himself to God. (Romans 14:7–12 NASB)

Whether we acknowledge it or not, God has that authority. Whether we like it or not, He is our King and will hold us accountable for all we do. If we do acknowledge it and seek His authority over our lives, He is more than Ruler or King. He is a tender, loving Father that desires to bless us with the very best of an abundant life. He is our shield and great reward, deliverer and provider, comforter and healer. For these, and a thousand other reasons, we owe our obedience to Him.

How then are we to be obedient to God? In what manner do we show obedience?

First, we are to be obedient as children. Children respond to the voice of their parent when they are directing them, though the child does not know why the direction is given. Children are obedient though the outcome of their obedience is not made clear right away. A child is obedient because they have faith that their parent is looking out for their best interest, and act on trust. As children of God, we are to be obedient in the things that do not have a perceivable outcome or that is not revealed to us immediately, if at all. One of the areas in which this applies is prayer. Our prayer life is necessary to us, as it is how we communicate the thoughts of our hearts to the Lord. Certainly, He knows our hearts, desires, and needs before we speak a single word, but He wants us to bring them to Him. A problem we have with prayer is that too often our prayers are superficial. What I mean is that we pray for protection, for the salvation of our children, for wisdom, money, health, healing, etc. Now those are all good things, to be sure, but in your heart there is a little back room, with a heavy door shut with a rusted lock. Inside that room there is a tarp and under that there is a chest, covered with chains and locks. Inside the chest there is a little, black safe, with a combination lock. Inside that safe is our deepest regret, or greatest fear and shame, our worst pain and suffering, our worst abuses, and the sins we don't even wish to remember. But that is exactly what God wants us to bring to Him. We carry those things around us quietly, privately, and they are like a huge boulder on our back, crushing us into the ground. He wants to set us free, but we refuse to bring that bondage to the cross. Jesus said, "Come to Me, all you who labor and are heavy laden, and I will give you rest. Take My yoke upon you and learn from Me, for I am gentle and lowly in heart, and you will find rest for your souls. For My yoke is easy and My burden is light" (Matthew 11:28–29 NKJV).

We labor so hard in this world trying desperately to be something we are not, to accomplish enough good to earn God's favor. We can never be good enough, and our struggle is vain. We are heavily burdened with the contents of our little, black safe, and find no place to get rest. Jesus said, "Bring that stuff to Me, and I will give you rest."

Another area of obedience is in Bible study. The Lord beckons us in that verse above to learn of Him, and how can we do that without filling our souls with His Word? Like I said in the first part, the Word of God is the water that feeds the tender plant. Deprive the plant of water and it shrivels and dies. We need to be hungry to learn, like children. Children want to learn all about the wonderful world we live in. It is known that most of all we learn in our entire lives is learned in the first five years. Children constantly ask questions and soak up as much as they can handle. Oddly, after children reach a certain age, their desire to learn new things begins to fade as they acquire an attitude of "I know all I need to know." Well, that is a testament to the pride of mankind. Sadly, a lot of adult Christians fall into this category when it comes to learning about their Savior. The Bible is the number one best-seller of all time and yet is the least read book in the world. By the way, how much dust has settled on your Bible? I pray that the Lord grant us a renewed desire to read His Scripture.

Also, we need to be obedient as stewards. A steward is a slave who has been given charge of all of his master's property and goods. As we have already learned regarding our relationship with God as our King, we must act then as good stewards, toward what He has entrusted us with. What is it that God does not own? Surely, He owns you and me and everything else in His creation. It is written in the prophet Haggai: "The silver is mine, and the gold is mine, says the LORD of hosts" (Haggai 2:10)

Also, in the Psalms: "For every beast of the field is mine, and the cattle upon a thousand hills. I know all the fowls of the mountains: and the wild beasts of the field are mine" (Psalms 50:10–11).

Again, the apostle Paul writes, "For whether we live, we live unto the Lord; and whether we die, we die unto the Lord: whether we live therefore, or die, we are the Lord's" (Romans 14:8).

God has entrusted you, and as stewards, with the keeping and care of His property. This means that we need to be obedient with what He has entrusted us with. We have been entrusted with the wealth that He has blessed us with, with the car and ministry to His other children, and to those who are not yet His children. So then, a good part of our obedience to God is wrapped up in how we handle His property, His gold and silver, and how we treat His people.

I remember hearing a story about a guy that visited England, and on one of his tours, he visited the beautiful estate of one of the dukes. It was an ancient house of massive proportions surrounded by the most beautifully kept gardens ever seen. At a point in the tour, the master gardener was present, and one of the people on the tour said, "The duke must be very pleased with the way that you keep his gardens." The gardener answered, "Well, the duke lives in London and hasn't been here for many years." Surprised, the person then asked, "Then why do you labor so hard to keep them so perfect?" He answered with a smile, "He might come back today."

That is obedience; that is love. I like this story because when I heard it, I thought, "This is exactly the attitude we as Christians should have. We are to be busy in His work, for His glory, driven by His love, wholeheartedly fervent, because He may come back today!"

Also, we are to be proper stewards with how we handle the gold and silver He has entrusted to us. You may have seen that bumper sticker that reads, "Honk if you love Jesus!" There is another one out there that is much better. It reads, "Tithe if you love Jesus, anyone can honk their horn!" So the question is, are you tithing to your local church? Are you giving regularly with the substance that God has blessed you with?

Oddly enough, there are many, if not most, Christians that love the Lord in everything but their purse strings. In Malachi, the Lord said, "Will a man rob God? Yet ye have robbed me. But you say, Wherein have we robbed thee? In tithes and offerings. Ye are cursed with a curse: for ye have robbed me, even this whole nation" (Malachi 3:8–9).

Money is always a tender subject with people. If you do not trust the Lord with your finances, you are missing a tremendous blessing. In this same line, we are to minister to others. We are commanded throughout the Scriptures to minister to each other and to take care of each other, bearing one another's burdens. If we are to be obedient as stewards, we must minister to others. Luke wrote, "Neither was there any among them that lacked: for as many as were possessors of lands or houses sold them, and brought the prices of the things that were sold, and laid them down at the apostles' feet: and distribution was made unto every man according as he had need" (Acts 4:34–35).

Paul wrote, "And let us not be weary in well doing: for in due season we shall reap, if we faint not. As we have therefore opportunity, let us do good unto all men, especially unto them who are of the household of faith" (Galatians 6:9–10).

Lastly, we must be obedient as heirs of the Kingdom of God. The responsibilities of this privilege are in our witness and testimony and in our godly conduct in this wicked world. We are ambassadors of Christ in this world, representing the Kingdom we belong to and in which we will eternally dwell. Again, Paul speaks on this:

> Now all things are of God, who has reconciled us to Himself through Jesus Christ, and has given us the ministry of reconciliation, that is, that God was in Christ reconciling the world to Himself, not imputing their trespasses to them, and has committed to us the word of reconciliation. Now then, we are ambassadors for Christ, as though

God were pleading though us: we implore you on Christ's behalf, be reconciled to God. For this He mad Him who knew no sin to be sin for us, that we might become the righteousness of God to Him. (2 Corinthians 5:18–21 NKJV)

We have been saved to be with God in heaven for all eternity, but He has left us here to do the work He has given us to do, while we still have time. The Scriptures teaches us that there is a judgment coming and no one knows the hour or the day that it will happen. Knowing this should give us a sense of urgency to do the work we are commanded. Peter puts this in perspective: "Therefore, since all things will be dissolved, what manner of persons ought you to be in holy conduct and godliness, looking for and hastening the coming of the day of God, because of which the heavens will be dissolved, being on fire, and the elements will melt with fervent heat?" (2 Peter 3:11–12).

If we are to be obedient then and obedient to our Savior and King, we are to be obedient, diligent, and cheerful in our prayer and Bible study, in our tithes and offerings, and in our witness and testimony, which are all our godly conduct in this world. We have so much to be thankful for, let us show it in simple obedience.

Submission and Control

Submission and control are two opposing subjects, but they are naturally born together in our daily lives, so we will look at them together as a singular subject. The object of this whole ministry, with emphasis on the second part—the restoration of the husband and father to the role that God desires is proper leadership for the man, and nothing expresses leadership more than submission and control. The man that wants to lead his family in a godly manner needs to learn self-control and submission.

Submission

The definition of submission, according to the world, is weakness. For men, it is a hateful thing and detestable. All of our lives, boys are told to be strong, don't give in or give up. A real man doesn't quit! If you show weakness, the world will walk all over you! So submission is viewed by many as unmanliness, at least by their delusion of what a man should be. Strangely, how many of these same men that profess those opinions break into a cold sweat if they oversleep in the morning and are late for work. Whether they like it or not, submission is a part of life. They must submit to the will of their employer, or department head, or boss. We all have to submit to the authorities that are placed above us, whether it is parents, teachers, employers, law enforcement, and ultimately, God. The jails are full of men and women who have a problem with authority. Submission and obedience are two links in the same chain—one is the sign of the other.

Submission is not a bad thing, and it is certainly not unmanly. It is a common, necessary part of our life in society. As believers and disciples of the Lord Jesus Christ, we have learned that the ideal example for all men to follow is the Lord Himself, and His example was total submission to His Father. His submission was not weakness at all, as we understand that surrendering to the will of the Father meant the ordeal of the cross. The apostle Paul gives us this understanding:

> Let this mind be in you which was also in Christ Jesus, who, being in the form of God, did not consider it robbery to be equal with God, but made Himself of no reputation, taking the form of a bondservant, and coming in the likeness of men. And being found in appearance as a man, He humbled Himself and became obedient to the point of death, even the death of the cross.* (Philippians 2:5–8 NKJV)

Also, His submission to the Father's will, though it would mean that death, is in the gospel of Luke: "And He was withdrawn form them about a stone's throw, and He knelt down and prayed, saying, 'Father, if it is Your will, take this cup away from Me; nevertheless, not My will, but Yours, be done'" (Luke 22:41–42 NKJV).

Submission, for the sake of the welfare of the family, is what a real man does, regardless of how difficult it may be, trusting in and submitting to the will of the Lord. That is sound, godly leadership. Good leadership requires submission. The best leaders in the world value and listen to the input from others and show regard for their welfare. One of the dictionary definitions of "submit" is *to commit (something) to the consideration or judgment of another.*[15] A person that is truly confident in their leadership is not afraid to share, delegate, or even surrender authority to his wife or family member. A confident leader does not require absolute control over everyone and everything in his life, but understands that as a weakness, and ultimately, impossibility. It is important to understand that leadership is your responsibility before God, who gives it according to His will,

---

[15] *American Heritage Dictionary.* © 1982. Boston. Houghton Mifflin.

and that submission to and obedience to something that is not God's design and, in His will, results in failure of leadership and a loss of blessing.

There are a couple of places in Scripture that mark this failure:

> Then Saul said to Samuel, "I have sinned; I have indeed transgressed the command of the LORD and your words, because I feared the people and listened to their voice." (1 Samuel 15:24 NASB)

> Then to Adam He said, "Because you have listened to the voice of your wife, and have eaten from the tree about which I commanded you saying, 'You shall not eat from it; cursed is the ground because of you.'" (Genesis 3:17a NASB)

Now, it is not bad to listen to your wife, unless it contradicts the role that God has given you or is in opposition to the commands and will of God. Leadership is authority, but it is also *under* authority, the authority of the One who is greater, who gives leadership to you. God spoke to Abraham concerning Sarah: "And the thing was very grievous in Abraham's sight because of his son. And God said unto Abraham, Let in not be grievous in thy sight because of the lad, and because of thy bondwoman; in all that Sarah hath said unto thee, hearken unto her voice; for in Isaac shall thy seed be called" (Genesis 21:11–12).

In this way, submission is to be careful consideration, with the goal of leading the family according to God's order and benefit.

Again, the apostle Paul gives us this truth: "Therefore do not be unwise, but understand what the will of the Lord is...Submitting yourselves one to another in the fear of God" (Ephesians 5:17, 20 NKJV).

I have, over many years, spent a good deal of time counseling married folks, and I find that generally, if the wife is happy, the husband will be also. However, if the wife is not happy, it affects the entire household, and much of the time we have to look at the leadership of the husband as the root cause. The Bible tells us that man was created first and that he was given the responsibility of leadership. The

RONALD J. MORSE, PHD

woman was created for the man to be a perfect complement to him, not less than him, but created to respond to his leadership. Wives respond to the leadership of their husband, and if that leadership is bad, it won't be pretty. I like to tell guys, "Look, you only have one job on this earth regarding the things of the flesh—that is, to make your wives happy."

It makes complete sense to do whatever it takes to make your wife happy and secure. It is not an easy task to be everything that your wife needs. Many times, it requires you to put your dreams, your desires, and your plans aside, but that is all right. God knows your desires and your plans and the sacrifices you make for your family. It isn't all about you. The world sees this as weakness, but it takes a lot of strength to do it all and be it all for your family, as much as God gives you the ability.

Getting back for a moment to the warning of Paul in Ephesians, it is important to understand that this section of Scripture is focused on spiritual warfare. As the leader of your family, it is your job to keep a keen eye out for the traps of the enemy and to protect yourself and family from them. The devil hates you and your family and will do whatever he can, fair and unfair, to trip you up and destroy what God desires for you. The enemy cannot destroy us, but he sure can make us ineffective for Christ in the world. If he can worm his way into the family, he can cause a lot of damage. A husband that cannot submit himself to his wife and children, for the sake of the family, has already driven a wedge and has opened the door for the enemy to come in and easily wreak havoc.

Control

When we think of control, we naturally think of exercising authority over our family in a way that will make our lives comfortable and easy, without much regard to what they must do to make it so. This may not be our conscious intention, but it is the way of the world, and frankly, which requires the least amount of effort on your part. It is the easy way, the lazy way, and seeks your comfort at the expense of the family. This too is a failure of leadership. Rather than delegate authority, we assign tasks and load expectations. Because it is a natural thing for man to do, meaning the *natural man who is only concerned about the self* and something that is not done with a great deal of thought or deliberation, it is also a failure of control—of control of the self.

The Bible speaks about self-control quite a bit. Paul speaks of those that have no self-control as a symptom of the last days.

> But know this, that in the last days perilous times will come: for men will be lovers of themselves, lovers of money, boasters, proud, blasphemers, disobedient to parents, unthankful, unholy, unloving, unforgiving, slanderers, without self-control, brutal, despisers of good, traitors, headstrong, haughty, lovers of pleasure rather than lovers of God, having a form of godliness but denying its power. And from such people turn away! (2 Timothy 3:1–5 NKJV)

A person that has no self-control is one that vacillates and changes with the slightest shift in the wind. They are unpredictable, unsteady, and unreliable. Consistency is one of the most necessary qualities of leadership, and consistency requires self-control.

If you look at the verses from 2 Timothy above, you can see that there are a lot of nasty behaviors there. Consider this, if you will, incontinence or lack of control is the reason for all of the rest. Now consider what the apostle Paul says about himself:

> Do you not know that those who run in a race all run, but one receives the prize? Run in such a way that you may obtain it. And everyone who competes for the prize is temperate in all things. Now they do it to obtain a perishable crown, but we for an imperishable crown. Therefore I run thus: not with uncertainty. Thus I fight: not as one who beats the air. But I discipline my body

and bring it into subjection, lest, when I have preached to others, I myself should become disqualified. (1 Corinthians 9:24–27 NKJV)

Apparently, that whole section of his letter to the Corinthians is dedicated to matters of conduct and control. Self-control and discipline are the meager qualities of life, for without them, our lives are of little value to the world. The strength of human will is feeble in regard to the self and how well we know it, that try by our own strength to follow Christ. We have one certain control issue in our life: to choose who we will serve. Every day we awaken to thousands of choices presented before us, and to each we must choose with discipline and control. For many of those choices, the weighing decision is whom we will serve—ourselves or God.

Years ago, there was a book titled *In His Steps* by Charles Sheldon, which tells the story of a group of people that decide to question every action by "What would Jesus do?" This popular book started a craze of *WWJD* bracelets, necklaces, bumper stickers, Bible covers, and too many other things to mention. Its popularity came from the recognition of the simple choice we have to make—our way or God's way. One thing is certain, if we decide to go our way, God will let us and after we fall on our faces, He will lift us up. It we decide to go God's way, He will strengthen us and give us the ability and courage to see it through. We have already covered this in the section in part 1, "Working out the Knots." God's way may not always be the smoothest, but it is the safest and ultimately the best.

Paul refers to control as temperance. When a knife is tempered, it is able to withstand great heat, pressure, and abuse, and still maintain flexibility, strength, and sharpness. Being temperate in our walk with Christ means that through Him, we can withstand the troubles, disappointments, and trials of this life without being knocked of course. God will test your mettle every day, because He wants us to learn how to control the self. The ultimate control of the self is denying it. Jesus said, "If any man will come after me, let him deny himself, and take up his cross, and follow me" (Matthew 16:24).

Well, this does not mean that we are to kill ourselves, but rather to recognize who the rightful authority of our life is and to follow Him. To deny the self means to seek God's will and not our own.

In the first section of part 2, "Repairing the Breach," we explored how to restore the rightful leadership position of the husband and father. We have looked at the foundational issues of trust, responsibility, respect, obedience, and finally submission and control. Though all of these are important issues, the most important keys to restoring proper leadership by far are self-control and submission. Only by close association with our Lord and His Word, can these qualities be learned.

Dad's New Religion

One of the greatest difficulties in life is trying to explain to the people who have known you for many years that you have had a life-changing experience. Jesus said, "A prophet is not without honor, except in his own country." When Jesus stood in the synagogue of his hometown of Nazareth and read the prophetic verses from Isaiah, declaring that the prophecy had been fulfilled that day in their hearing, they all marveled and questioned each other, saying, "Is this not the son of Joseph the carpenter, and of Mary?"

Well, at least we are not trying to get people to understand that we are the Messiah! At times, however, it seems to be that tough.

For many, the idea that some great criminal, that has committed heinous acts upon defenseless others, has found God and is no longer the person he used to be, is preposterous. Imagine how difficult it must be for a wife and family that have tolerated the actions of an abusive husband and father to believe that a complete metamorphosis has occurred!

What may compound the problem is the basis for the change itself. The monster of the household has received Jesus Christ as Lord and Savior, coming by faith to an entirely different way of living and thinking. Unbelievers ordinarily scoff religion, and claims of having experienced something that is completely foreign to the rest of the family may arouse some strange reactions. It would do the husband well to be prepared for the various responses that will come from his family and friends.

There are three things he must learn and demonstrate to be a good witness for his faith in Jesus Christ our Lord. Bringing the good news to family and friends involves *talking the talk, walking the walk, and staying the course.* They are presented in declaration, different dad, and durability. It is also dealing with a family that is already founded in Christ, dealing with a family that is not, and lastly, with angry or spiteful attitudes in spouses and children.

Declaration: Talking the Talk

When a man desires to be restored to the rightful leadership position God intends for him, it cannot be done without some serious knee bending. Receiving Christ as Lord and Savior is the paramount issue in a person's life and is the predetermining factor for family restoration. It should only seem natural after having experienced the unspeakable joy of salvation that you would want to share it with the people that you love. Unfortunately, many get cold feet when it comes to witnessing to their families. Familiarity and past history can be like buckets of ice water dumped on our little fires of zeal. It is hard to witness to your family for two reasons: they can be intimidating and you don't know much about what you are talking about. As a point of fact, the greatest reason Christians do not share their faith with anyone is that they feel they are not qualified to do so. Well, just what do I mean by *qualified?*

For the sake of our understanding, we will use two extreme examples of qualification. First, we will use the apostle Paul. Now if anyone was qualified to preach Christ with authority, it was he. He was trained his entire life to be a master of the Hebrew law. He was a Pharisee, of the strictest order of Pharisees, and was probably being groomed for a position in the Sanhedrin, the ruling body of elders for the state of Israel. He could argue the law and the Scriptures with the best of them.

> I am verily a man which am a Jew, born in Tarsus, a city in Cilicia, yet brought up in this city at the feet of Gamaliel, and taught according to the perfect manner of the law of the fathers, and was zealous toward God, as ye are all this day. (Acts 22:3)

> Though I might also have confidence in the flesh.
> If any other man thinks that he has whereof he
> might trust in the flesh, I more: circumcised the
> eighth day, of the stock of Israel, of the tribe of
> Benjamin, an Hebrew of the Hebrews; as touch-
> ing the law, a Pharisee; concerning zeal, persecut-
> ing the church; touching the righteousness which
> is of the law, blameless. (Philippians 3:4–6)

Of all of the apostles, I cannot believe that anyone understood the relevance to the fulfillment of the law in Christ Jesus more than Paul. Yet Paul considered himself a poor witness for his Lord. In Ephesians, he asks believers to pray for him that he may preach the word boldly. " And for me, that utterance may be given to me, that I may open my mouth boldly to make known the mystery of the gospel, for which I am an ambassador in chains; that in it I may speak boldly, as I ought to speak" (Ephesians 6:19–20 NKJV).

The other extreme is the man born blind, who is mentioned in the gospel of John. He faced excommunication from the temple and from the ritual sacrifices, which, by Jewish understanding, would condemn him and destroy his soul. Yet he stands before the most learned men of the council and gives a bold witness of his faith in Christ, with no more knowledge than that he had been blind, but now sees. John wrote:

> He answered and said, "Whether he be a sin-
> ner or no, I know not: one thing I know, that,
> whereas I was blind, now I see."
>
> Then they said to him again, "What did he
> do to thee? How opened he thine eyes?"
>
> He answered them, "I have told you already,
> and ye did not hear: wherefore would ye hear it
> again? Will ye also be his disciples?"
>
> Then they reviled him, and said, "Thou
> art his disciple; but we are Moses' disciples. We
> know that God spake unto Moses: as for this fel-
> low, we know not from whence he is."

The man answered and said unto them,
"Why herein is a marvelous thing, that ye know
not from whence he is, and yet he hath opened
mine eyes. Now we know that God heareth not
sinners: but if any be a worshipper of God, and
doeth his will, him he heareth. Since the world
began was it not heard that any man opened
the eyes of one that was born blind. If this man
were not of God, he could do nothing." (John
9:25–33)

I wanted to include the entire conversation this poor man had
with the ruling elders of Israel to show his boldness and presence of
mind, even in the intimidating face of the doctors of the law, who
had the power to cast him out.

Here then are two extremes: the apostle Paul, who was the most
qualified, asking for boldness, and the blind man that knew nothing other than that he had been healed, speaking boldly before his
judges. Somewhere between these two witnesses, we will find ourselves. Though we may face controversy and persecution, we can't use
unqualified as an excuse for not sharing our faith. Paul, in one of the
great statements of his faith, said, "For I am not ashamed of the gospel of Christ: for it is the power of God unto salvation to every one
that believeth; to the Jew first, and also to the Greek" (Romans 1:16).

It is absolutely vital, in hope of restoring and improving the family, that they understand the reason for this change. They may not
accept it at first, but if it is spoken in love and supported by a testimony
of a new life, they may also come to faith. Is there anything greater to
desire for a family than that? So it is essential to tell the family what you
believe, why you believe it, and what has happened to you.

Different Dad: Walking the Walk

This is the testimony of dad's life that supports what he is saying
about his new faith.

Imagine that your life as an effective servant of Christ is like a house. The foundation of the house is the Lord Jesus Christ, and your house must be built upon that rock, if it is to stand. The walls of the house are the conduct of your life. The roof of the house is the spoken witness of your faith. Can you imagine a house without a roof, or a foundation with a roof but with no walls?

As believers, we are encouraged by the Scripture to live a life that is pleasing to God. We are commanded to share our faith with others, in fact commissioned to take our witness to the farthest ends of the earth.

We understand what *talking the talk* is, but what about *walking the walk?*

Walking the walk is the manner of conduct that reflects a new life in Christ. It demonstrates the placing of trust for all of the situations of your life in Him and governs the reactions to trials and troubles we will face. For myself, the first evidence of a new life in Christ was a dramatically altered vocabulary. I spent a good deal of my adult life in the service of our country as a soldier. Anyone who shares that experience can attest to the fact that much of the language used by our peers is "colorful." After coming to Christ in my mid-thirties, the habitual use of such coloration was abated. I no longer felt the need or the desire to use such language. Also, I began to react differently to situations that normally caused frustration and anger. I began to react with more patience, seeking answers from God's Word and through prayer. Believe me, I am still working on it, but now that it has been thirty years on, I am making a little progress. I can honestly say that the application of God's Word to your life will give you understanding for the proper responses to life's challenges, and the indwelling spirit of God will change your life.

It doesn't come so much with individual effort or *trying to be a better person,* but rather submitting yourself to the work of the Spirit. In theological terms, this is called sanctification—a lifelong process of God working in you to make you more like His own dear Son. He gives us eyes to see, ears to hear, and a new heart. That is quite a tune-up. Once we receive the Spirit, the work begins, and we are to allow that work to happen. The problem with spiritual growth, which is the process of sanctification, is that though God is working to change us, we resist it. It is the struggle between our old nature and the new one. This area of Christian living is so vital, because it is the proof that the authority over your life is no longer you. Paul wrote:

> This I say, therefore, and testify in the Lord, that you should no longer walk as the rest of the Gentiles walk, in the futility of their mind, having their understanding darkened, being alienated from the life of God, because of the ignorance that is in them, because of the blindness of their heart...but you have not so learned Christ, if indeed you have been taught by Him, as the truth that is in Jesus: that you put off, concerning your former conduct, the old man which grows corrupt according to the deceitful lusts, and be renewed in the spirit of your mind, and that you put on the new man which was created according to God, in true righteousness and holiness. (Ephesians 4:17–24 [selected] NKJV)

Friends, the world is watching. They are watching to see you act exactly like everyone else who does not know Christ. They want to see you fall. They want to see you not show faith in the Lord that saved you. They want this, because it will be evident to them that your faith is just as empty as every other so-called religion in the world. They do not want to know what you are saying is the truth, because that means they are condemned in their sin. People don't want to know about hell or eternal punishment for the lives they believe they are enjoying. To be perfectly honest, who would? The preaching of Jesus is a rock of offense. If unbelievers hear the truth of God and then see the evidence of Christ in you, they will at least understand that you believe what you say *is* true and that they are in peril. If you act the same as the world, then they will figure that you don't believe all that stuff because you act no differently and conclude that it is not true.

For the sake of a man trying to restore his position in the family, there is going to be a lot of distrust from them and they need to see the evidence of change. They are watching you even more closely, not because they want you to fail, but to succeed, to be sure that what you are saying is true. It does not mean that you are to pretend to be perfect, or anything anywhere near it. But an inconsistent testimony can erode trust and communicate hypocrisy. This is not what you want.

Durability: Staying the Course

As I just mentioned and have mentioned before, consistency is necessary to regain trust. It is also the strongest witness of Christ in our life. The apostle Paul said:

> Remember that Jesus Christ, of the seed of David, was raised from the dead according to my gospel, for which I suffer troubles as an evildoer, even to the point of chains; but the word of God is not chained. Therefore I endure all things for the sake of the elect, that they may obtain the salvation which is in Christ Jesus with eternal glory. (2 Timothy 2:8–10)

> I have fought a good fight, I have finished my course, I have kept the faith. (2 Timothy 4:7)

Paul spoke a lot about enduring—about staying the course. Understandably, there will be shortcomings and setbacks, but the mark of a true Christian is getting back up after he stumbles. Now what I mean by setbacks does not include returning to the altars of self-worship, where there is destruction, for that is a sign to the family that you have not changed and have picked up arms against them. We all fall short, we all fail at some point from being the men and women that God means for us to be, but if our faith is genuine, so is repentance and restoration. The Christian life is not an easy one, but it is a joyful one. We will still face trial and disappointment, pain and suffering. The Bible says it rains on both the just and the unjust. When the storms come, we do not run back to the gutters of our former life but trust in the Lord. Sometimes He calms the storm, but most of the time He calms us in the midst of the storm. There is always a divine purpose in the storms of life, though it may take a long time to see it—long after it has passed. Paul encouraged the believers in Rome who were suffering persecution: "And we know that all things work together for good to those who love God, to those who are called according to His purpose" Romans 8:28)

The durability of your faith, the trusting of the Lord, the zeal and desire to learn the Scripture, the fellowship of the saints and obedience to the Lord, and keeping in prayer will impact your family greater than you can possibly imagine. Devotion to a new life in Christ and godly leadership will produce an entirely new dynamic for the family, but it may not come quickly. Long years of abuse may only be erased by long years of faithfulness, and the family may take a long time to renew their trust. Your desire should be to win your family to Christ, but it will only come in His time, not yours. You will not win your family to Christ by demanding that they attend church with you or by beating them over the head with your Bible. If the Lord brings your family to faith it will come with a faithful testimony of words, actions, and durability.

Staying the Course: The Banner over Me Is Love

In the last chapter, we learned about the importance of being a bold witness for our Lord Jesus Christ. We learned about the three things necessary for us to be effective in the world for Him. I used the model of a house as an image of our witness, with the foundation being in Jesus Christ, the walls of the house being the testimony or conduct of our lives, and the roof of the house as our verbal witness to others about the Lord.

We also learned that one of the most powerful tools for reaching others for Christ was durability. We must stay the course.

In 1814, Francis Scott Key wrote the "Star Spangled Banner," our national anthem. The inspiration for this song came in the midst of the battle that raged on Fort McHenry through the night. The fort was under siege and was continuously bombarded by British cannons. Combat is the most confusing chaos in human experience, even in the daylight. In the dark, it was difficult to know how the battle was faring, so the battle-weary soldiers looked to see if their banner was still flying by the light of the rockets and bomb bursts. All of their hope depended upon it. If, in the greatest tumult, they could still see that they were prevailing, it would rally their courage and fighting spirit. If, in the most trying circumstances for your family they see that you are holding strong and standing for your faith, they too will be encouraged and strengthened. Again, Paul wrote, "You therefore must endure hardship as a good soldier of Jesus Christ. No one engaged in warfare entangles himself with the affairs of this life, that he may please him who enlisted him as a soldier" (2 Timothy 2:3–4 NKJV).

The Christian walk is war, and though our enemy is spiritual and not always visible, the wounds and suffering are physical. The test of a battle-worthy soldier is his continuing in battle, campaign after campaign, until the conflict is over. The test for a Christian is holding to the faith and not allowing the setbacks and defeats to sway him from the path. The apostles stayed with Jesus all the days of His ministry, even though many others turned away because of some of the hard things He said. For them, there was no other way to go. They would stick with Him because they believed in and trusted Him. John wrote:

> From that time many of His disciples went back and walked with Him no more. Then Jesus said to the twelve, "Do you also want to go away?"
>
> But Simon Peter answered Him, "Lord, to whom shall we go? You have the words of eternal life. Also we have come to believe and know that You are the Christ, the Son of the living God. (John 6:66–69 NKJV)

Paul wrote to the Ephesians that our warfare is spiritual, not carnal. He told them to arm themselves and to stand, for the enemy is powerful but the victory is ours.

"Therefore take up the whole armor of God, that you may be able to withstand in the evil day, and having done all, to stand" (Ephesians 6:13 NKJV).

For the next few pages, we will look at some of the most common problems and challenges to overcome, as you seek to bring the family back together under God's design and authority. Overcoming the personal struggles you faced with self-worship may seem small compared to these, but as sure as God has given victory over our foolishness, He will bless the family. The difficulties we will face as Christians are many, but there are a few that are as tough as dealing with wives and children that do not know or reject Christ.

How should we deal with the hope of restoration in families that are already saved, with those that are not, or may also be resentful?

The Saved Family

Let's start with one that should be a little easier. The very best condition we can have existing in our family today is one where the husband and father is employing proper godly leadership principle in an environment where the wife and children are also walking in obedience in Christ. If you have come from a position of ungodly leadership and are seeking to change that through Christ, the believing family is fertile soil for that. Abuse and ungodly leadership of the husband may cause the family to come to the cross of Christ. I don't know how many times I have seen families shattered by the abuse of a self-worshipping husband, whether it involved drugs, infidelity, or any of the other altars of such worship, find refuge, solace, hope, and security in Christ.

This does not mean that because your family shares the same faith and are going to church, that you can just step in and assume authority. All of the issues about trust, responsibility, obedience, respect, submission, and control, have to be well-established before that authority will be accepted. Restoration is a process that takes time. It is likened to being restored to health after an illness or injury. Hopefully, however, your wife and children will desire to help you go through that process and will be encouraging, knowing that the outcome is what they have been praying for.

In dealing with the unbelieving family, there are three principles of godly conduct that need to be set that will work toward your first priority—getting your family to know Christ. These principles are also applicable to the family that already knows the Lord, in that they will grow more in their faith and service to Him.

The Unsaved Family

It is hard enough to walk in Christ in newness of life, with all of the temptations that exist in this world and all of the fiery darts of the wicked one being aimed directly at you. It is even tougher having to deal with a family that is skeptical, if not antagonistic, toward your newly found and professed faith. This is where you will need a lot of counseling and support from a pastor or counselor. You will be like a babe in the woods. The Lord, however, did not promise us an easy road. John recorded what the Lord spoke about trouble:

"These things I have spoken unto you, that in me ye might have peace. In the world ye shall have tribulation: but be of good cheer; I have overcome the world" (John 16:33).

We cannot stop *all* of the trouble we will have to face in this world, but there is much we can do to alleviate some of the trouble in our families. Little is much when the Lord is in it.

Three principles we can employ that will help us to lead our families to the Lord if they are still unconvinced are: 1) personal commitment, 2) patience, and 3) prayer.

The first principle, personal commitment, is about your determination to walk in obedience to Christ regardless of what the circumstances of your life and that of your family are. There are also three things within this principle that we must work at. We must be committed to the following of our Lord, and to growing in our faith. That is a personal commitment. We must be obedient in setting an example for our families by being a member of, attending the services of, and involvement in the ministry of a local, Bible-believing, Bible-teaching church. We must be committed to learning more about our faith and applying those things to our lives. Paul said, "Be diligent to present yourself approved to God, a worker who does not need to be ashamed, rightly dividing the word of truth" (2 Timothy 2:15 NKJV).

We must also be diligent in the teaching of our wives and children of the Word of God. It is commanded in the Old Testament book of Deuteronomy to Israel, and thereby to us as well:

> And you must commit yourselves wholeheartedly to these commandments I am giving you today. Repeat them again and again to your children. Talk about them, when you are home and when you are away on a journey, when you are lying down and when you are getting up again. Tie them to your hands as a reminder, and wear them on your forehead. Write them on the doorposts of your house and on your gates. (Deuteronomy 6:6–7 NIV)

Understand though that we are not to bash our families over the head with our Bibles. This means that we are not to place demands or expectations on our families that we cannot keep ourselves. This is a great failure in many Christian leaders. The example of Christ shows us that He never forced or pushed anyone into obedience, but rather led through example, persuaded with love, and encouraged with the truth. Peter scolded the elders who tried to convince the Gentiles that they needed to follow all the laws of Moses to be saved. "Now therefore, why do you test God by putting a yoke on the neck of the disciples which neither our fathers nor we were able to bear? But we believe that through the grace of the Lord Jesus Christ we shall be saved in the same manner as they" (Acts 15:10–11 NKJV).

Perhaps we need to look at the word *diligently*, with the stress on the latter syllables—dili*gently*.

We must also be content with whatever the Lord has blessed us with. True contentment comes when we realize that all we have struggled to gain in this world is but rubbish if we gain Christ. Everything is temporary in this world and is subject to the decay and corruption of it. I had a sports car once that I rebuilt from the ground up to total restoration. It looked like it just came out of the box. What killed me was that I continually had to replace parts that were naturally falling apart, without even using them. It is important for us to focus on the eternal and not on the temporal. We should also come to the understanding that God owns everything and blesses us with His provision as He sees fit. He owns you, and He owns your family. They are His, entrusted to you for their care.

Being content with the state that God has blessed us with allows us the freedom to focus on greater things, like the spiritual welfare of our family.

The second principle of leadership is patience. One thing I, with all sincerity, will do is to warn you not to ask God for patience. I did, and it was a terrible experience! The first thing the Lord showed me was that I had none and that I was not capable of getting any. He did this by immediately testing me in every form imaginable. It was quite overwhelming, I assure you.

The Bible teaches us the trials build patience. The dictionary defines patience as a capacity for calm endurance. It also defines it as capable of bearing affliction with calmness, understanding, and being constant. These are great definitions, if we consider the situation we may be in with an unbelieving spouse or children. We all want our families to immediately receive Christ as Savior, but that may not be the case. If not, then we will, with all endurance, remain constant in the faith, bearing the afflictions of having to deal with loved ones that cannot understand the hope and peace of life in Christ, and encourage them daily with witness and conduct. Paul spoke of this in his letter to the Corinthians: "For how do you know, O wife, whether you will save your husband? Or how do you know, O husband, whether you will save your wife?" (1 Corinthians 7:16 NKJV).

The last principle is prayer. Prayer is communicating our needs, our troubles, our desires, and our thanks to God in heaven. He already knows everything that is in our hearts, but He wants to hear us. This is not for Him; it is for us! Prayer is therapeutic. It has been found that people that pray on a regular basis are the least likely to suffer from stress-related illness, heart attacks, and digestive problems. People that pray and attend church services regularly on the average live fifteen to twenty years longer than those that don't. More important than all of these facts remains the wonderful truth that God answers prayer. When we pray for others to be saved, this glorifies God, and He honors those that desire to glorify the Father.

The great American preacher D.L. Moody prayed for his brother's salvation for over twenty years. Shortly after Mr. Moody went home to be with the Lord, his brother received Christ. We must never think that our prayers are unheard or that God is not responding to them. Sometimes we must be constant and faithful in prayer, knowing that God will answer according to His perfect will.

Resentful Children

Often, the toughest crowds to work are kids. Children have strong, independent wills and, depending on their age, may have difficulty forgiving a father or mother that has treated them or their other parent in a way that was harmful. Teens can be especially resentful of a parent that has robbed them of what they believe to be an idyllic childhood. The principles we have discussed need to be amplified a hundred fold when we are dealing with resentful kids. The very best weapons we have in our arsenal for winning our kids back are honesty, love, patience, and prayer. It may be necessary to submit to family counseling, where many of these difficulties can be worked out. There are a number of resources for the parent that desires to help their kids through this struggle. Some of them are:

Shepherding a Child's Heart by Ted Tripp, 1995, Shepherd Press

How to Really Love Your Children by Dr. Ross Campbell, 1996, Inspirational Press

How to Help Angry Kids by Lou Priolo, 1996, S.E.L.F. Publications

Teach Them Diligently by Lou Priolo, 2000, Timeless Text

There is more about this when we deal with not just resentful but spiteful children. Keep going. In the next chapter, we will look at this.

Spiteful Children

In the last chapter, we learned about dealing with the saved family and the unsaved family. We also took a brief look at dealing with resentful children. I would like to devote this chapter to the topic of spiteful children, because it is one of great difficulty, ever for the family where godly leadership principles are and have been in place.

All children will, at one time or another, become rebellious or exhibit behaviors that are rebellious. Part of this is due to the sin nature, which we have received from Adam. Part of this is due to the natural tendencies of adolescents to exert independence from their parents, which is typical behavior that is a part of growing up. This is not what we will address here. The spiteful rebellion of children caused by a deep resentment or mistrust toward a parent for past offences or bad leadership is what the object of our focus will be.

Spite is defined as a malicious, ill will prompting an urge to hurt or humiliate. Spite then, is a deliberate action and attitude that results in someone being hurt.

Let's look at this problem by trying to answer three basic questions:

1. What causes a child to be spiteful and rebellious?
2. How is spitefulness manifested in our children?
3. How can we remedy this problem and heal our family?

What causes a person, especially a child, to be spiteful? The Bible tells us that basically, all people are capable of such an attitude and that it is even our nature to be that way. Jeremiah wrote, "The heart is deceitful above all things, and desperately wicked: who can know it?" (Jeremiah 17:9).

After God had destroyed the world by flood, He remembered Noah and the aroma of his sacrifice came before Him. "And the LORD smelled a sweet savour; and the LORD said in his heart, I will not again curse the ground any more for man's sake; for the imagination of man's heart is evil from his youth: neither will I again smite any more every living thing, as I have done" (Genesis 8:21).

Man, by his own nature, seeks retaliation. It is not a survival instinct in a sense that an animal will fight to protect itself and its young by inflicting injury. Retribution is only found in man, who does so to assert his idea of justice. Man will repay as he has been given. If someone does good to us, we desire to do good in return. If someone does evil against us, we seek to repay with evil. The problem with this sort of justice is that man is not just. If someone does evil against us our desire is to do greater evil against him or her. *If you punch me in the eye, I will break your arm!* Violence always escalates. That is why God gave Moses the laws of retribution that demanded an "eye for an eye, tooth for a tooth."

So it is with spiteful children. Spite is open rebellion and is not something that happens overnight. It is a feud that burns and hurts for a long time. Spitefulness is, as we have learned previously about anger, a determined state of mind. It defines the offence, plots and assesses a "just" retribution, and exercises it in order to satisfy this need to get back. It takes a long time to establish. It burns and grows in a person's heart until the need for action is achieved. So the child that becomes spiteful has already established a long history of anger.

Lou Priolo writes there are five steps to rebellion.[16] They are:

1. a wounded spirit
2. bitterness
3. anger
4. stubbornness
5. rebellion

---

[16] Priolo, Lou. *How to Help Angry Kids.* pp 6–9. © 1996. Alabama City. SELF Publishing.

I agree with much he has to say, but I would like to define it a bit more. First, what is a *wounded spirit?* The wounded spirit of a child is one that has been hurt more than once. It is caused by repeated misuse and hurtful attitudes. A child's spirit is resilient, and their love is strong. It takes repeated assaults to affect a child this way. Also, it is important to look at how this may otherwise be affected. Children at a very early stage do not know how to express anger, and any perceived offence to the child, whether it is legitimate or not, can make the child angry. We are intellectual, logical beings from birth, and we are able to make assumptions and draw conclusions, even in youth. A child perceives that something is not right is perhaps frightened by a behavior of a parent or does not get what they feel they need at that moment. They react with anger, but the child is unable to correctly process anger or express it, and the parent attempts to soothe or shut down their display. The anger in the child's noggin is not resolved. A pattern emerges where the child's anger is continually shut down because they are not able to explain or seek resolution. The child learns to internalize that anger, to let it simmer. Here, in this case, the repeated abuse is only in the understanding of the child—the parent has no idea that there is an offence. This can wound the spirit, so to speak, and breaks the ground where the seed of rebellion takes root.

Secondly, I believe *anger* comes before *bitterness.* Anger is a strong, emotional response to an unfavorable condition that is expressed in varying degrees and manners of violence. Bitterness is a deep-seated anger that is not lessened by expression. Bitterness becomes habitual anger and a willful attitude of anger. Until this point, all of the actions and attitudes are not caused by a deliberate act of the will. Bitterness is the turning point. After this comes *stubbornness* or an unforgiving spirit. This eventually becomes open *rebellion* or a vengeful spirit.

How is spitefulness manifested in children? We have discovered that spitefulness is the resultant product of a process of habitual, unresolved anger. Spitefulness is a deliberate act and is sin. It may be expressed in different ways.

Adolescents naturally search for their identity, and if they have not yet found it in Christ, they will seek for it in the world. This is dangerous, but a young person seeking to find out who they are and where they belong is not necessarily rebellion. It is sometimes difficult to distinguish between the two. Our natural inclination, as we have been created to be social beings, is to find out *who we are* and *where do we belong* in society or where we will find *acceptance*. By the time a kid reaches middle school, you can clearly see the need growing. By high school, the search for identity and acceptance becomes almost desperate. Go to any high school in America and you can clearly distinguish one "tribe" from another. There are nerds, and jocks, preppies, skaters, goths, druggies, and others. Children will gravitate to any of those tribes to seek acceptance, and if one tribe shuns them, perhaps another won't. In teens, changes in hairstyles, clothing, friends, and activities may constitute nothing more than this search. It is explained away as a temporary "phase" the child goes through, and that is because most will grow out of it in adulthood. Rebellion, however, may also be manifested in changes in appearance or behavior, but the goal is directly aimed at humiliating or hurting the parent. Rebellion is a deliberate attitude that seeks vengeance; it is malicious. Extreme changes, such as piercing, tattooing, and modes of dress that are socially offensive, are ways in which a child may express a rebellious attitude. Because rebellion is deliberate, the child will seek out that which they know will offend the parents or things that they hate and gravitate to them. The child can't physically hurt the parents, so they hurt themselves in order to hurt the parents by proxy.

I remember asking a teen once who was sporting a multicolored Mohawk, dressed in torn or rather slashed black clothing, and had about five pounds of varied hardware pierced through his face, why he dressed that way. He said that he just wanted to be different. The funny thing was that he was in a group of about ten kids that looked just like him. I said, "You certainly are making a statement, and that is, I hate my parents."

When I said that, a look of hurtful surprise came over his face for a second, and I figured I hit it on the head. A moment later, he shook it off, laughed, and they all went their way.

If you are a strong religious family and your child is rebellious, he may involve himself in all manner of behavior that would offend you. He may break the law or involve himself in self-destructive behaviors like alcohol, smoking, drugs, or even homosexuality. He may involve himself in other religions, cults, or satanic worship. Whatever the child feels may hurt or humiliate, that is what they will do. It may be no more than a messy room, but it may be as much as verbal abuse, outright disobedience, or at the last, physical reprisal.

However manifested, rebellion has had a long time to develop, and it may take a long time to correct.

How can we remedy the problem? As the leader of the family it is your responsibility to bring about an atmosphere conducive to change. Rebellion is sin, but there also must have been sin to produce it. The first thing that needs to be done to remedy rebellion is to be accountable for the sin. We must take a hard look at ourselves and determine what we have done in our lives that would cause the wounding of the spirit of our children. This takes humility and courage. We must address our sin and confess it before addressing the child's sinful reaction of rebellion.

Parents are responsible for creating an environment that is the seedbed and permit of sin. The child is responsible for his own sin, no matter who caused it or continues it.

The prophet Ezekiel declared, "The soul who sins shall die. The son shall not bear the guilt of the father, nor the father bear the guilt of the son. The righteousness of the righteous shall be upon himself, and the wickedness of the wicked shall be upon himself" (Ezekiel 18:20 NKJV).

Before we approach the rebellious youth with the confronting of his sin, it would be wise and best to acknowledge our own.

Again, there are three steps that can help bring restoration to the family. First, confess your sin before your children and point out that your sin caused them to fall into the sin of rebellion. This should be done in the presence of and the full support and forgiveness of your spouse. It is necessary to show that the husband-and-wife team is united and inseparable, especially if the anger of the child is caused by the perceived mistreatment of one spouse to the other.

Secondly, model behavior that gives no cause for retaliation and ceases the sin cycle. Give no more excuse for the child to sin. One of the best models we can set for children is the godly design for the order of the family. The family is the husband and wife. Children are never a guarantee but a blessing from God. The presence of children in the family is not what constitutes the family. The union of the husband and wife into one *is* the family. Children need to see that the parents are one and that the relationship is one that is unbreakable, with mutual love and respect. In this, the apostle Paul gives God's requirement: "Husbands, love your wives, even as Christ also loved the church, and gave himself for it" (Ephesians 5:25).

The apostle Peter also spoke on the responsibility of the husband toward the wife: "Husbands, likewise, dwell with them with understanding, giving honor to the wife, as to the weaker vessel, and as being heirs together of the grace of life, that your prayers may not be hindered" (1 Peter 3:7 NKJV).

The husband and wife must display their relationship as singular, with no signs of division. Children, even at a young age, learn to play the parents against each other in order to get what they want. This divide-and-conquer strategy is dangerous, as it is an outside influence (the child) driving a wedge between the parents. In the matter of disciplining a wayward child, it is vital that the husband lays down the law, as he is the authority of the family, with his spouse standing by his side. I tell ladies that they should stand holding their husband's hand and looking at him, not the child, with approval. This completely disarms the power of the child and shows him or her that the family unit of the dad and mom is one and strong. In the case of a rebellious child or teen, or even an adult child, the solidifying factor of the marital relationship offers an opportunity to get to the root of their rebellion and expose their sinful behavior and hopefully produce reconciliation and healing.

Recently, there was a great movie about the life of Bart Millard, the lead singer of the Christian band Mercy Me, titled *I Can Only Imagine*. This was based on the hit song of the same title and told of his difficult relationship with an abusive father and how, through

Christ, that relationship was reconciled and healed. It was a true story and a great example of the power of Christ for healing in the lives of broken families.

The Bible also gives us many directives for the raising of our children, and it is never too late or too soon to start.

"Train up a child in the way he should go: and when he is old, he will not depart from it" (Proverbs 22:6).

As I said before, this verse means that we are to find the gifts, talents, and abilities of our children that the Lord has given them for His purpose. We are to train them to develop them that they may be useful servants of God and their lives will be full and joyful. The opposite of that was Paul's warning to fathers about driving, rather than training their children: "And you, fathers, do not provoke your children to wrath, but bring them up in the training and admonition of the Lord" (Ephesians 6:4 NKJV).

The admonition of the Lord is the firm direction that God gives to us to obey, that our lives will be blessed, safe, and fruitful. We are to warn our children of the foolishness of falling into the traps that the world sets to destroy us. A loving parent will protect his children from choosing things that will harm them. It is said that there is no greater teacher than experience, and if the father is dealing with a rebellious child due to their failure as a responsible parent, the change in the father's heart and life into obedience and sanity is powerful. Humble confession and the asking for forgiveness, with the heartfelt advice to *not do what I have done before,* can make a difference. When that has been honestly done, the child can easily distinguish what is the good and bad way to do things and what the results are.

In some versions, the *training* of the Lord is translated as *nurture.* The nurture of the Lord is the tender, loving care and concern for your child. It is the open expression of your affection for them. Spend time with your children. Make them feel loved and important. Talk to them and listen to them. Most importantly, share your faith with them, in a loving way. Pray for them.

Dr. Charles Stanley said that the greatest influence in his young life was that every night his mother would kneel by his bedside and pray for him.

It shouldn't matter how old the child is, even through teens. If you pray for your children, it will affect them greater than you can imagine and they will never forget it.

Lastly, work through the child's sin, beginning at the wounding of the spirit and anger, to the place where the decision was made by the child to retaliate. The child may have been right to be angry because of the hurts that were done to them, but they have no right to vengeance. Paul wrote about vengeance, "Beloved, do not avenge yourselves, but rather give place to wrath: for it is written, 'Vengeance is Mine, I will repay,' says the Lord" (Romans 12:19 NKJV).

It may be best to get some outside help. A trained biblical counselor can be a neutral go-between for a parent and child, that can help the child discover the root of their behavior and help them to understand and overcome it. It will not disregard the cause for the anger or hurt, but will show that rebellion is not the answer to overcoming or alleviating the pain. Forgiveness is the determined attitude that erases the terrible burden of a vengeful spirit. Here are a few verses on the matter:

> Be not overcome of evil, but overcome evil with good. (Romans 12:21)

> For if you forgive men their trespasses, your heavenly Father will also forgive you. (Matthew 6:14 NKJV)

> Then Peter came to Him and said, "Lord, how often shall my brother sin against me, and I forgive him? Up to seven times?" Jesus said to him, "I do not say to you, up to seven times, but up to seventy times seven." (Matthew 18:21–22 NKJV)

It is important to know that rebellion is deliberate and malicious. This is sin and, as any other, must be met with firm, loving discipline and correction. Samuel denounced King Saul with a stern rebuke: "For rebellion is as the sin of witchcraft, and stubbornness as iniquity and idolatry" (1 Samuel 15:23).

Though the child may feel justified in his rebellion, it is unjust and unholy. It has gone beyond any actions or feelings that have caused it and has become will worship. It is idolatry, the idolatry and folly of self-worship.

With much prayer, biblical obedience, and love, the rebellious child will eventually cease from his sin and family unity will be restored. Children will respond to love, for they desire love and peace. If proper leadership and love are demonstrated, they will respond. Love breaks down walls. Love heals.

Finances

Financial problems account for a great number of failed relationships today. Many families are broken up over financial difficulties, which are caused by irresponsible self-worship that wastes that resource away. It is hard enough on a family when the expected leader and protector of the family is engaged in behaviors that shake its foundation. When those behaviors also impact the ability of the family to afford basic necessities and the needed resources for paying bills, keeping the rent or mortgage paid, or the lights on and the cupboard filled, it is an attack on the wellbeing of the family. It is selfish and cruel, and many families are shattered by this behavior. For the man working to get his life and family back on track, there may be significant challenges in this area. The path back from prodigal to responsibility and growth is a long, rocky one.

The Bible speaks much about money and our stewardship. Two of the most well-known verses are:

> For the love of money is the root of all evil: which while some coveted after, they have erred from the faith, and pierced themselves through with many sorrows. (1 Timothy 6:10)

> No man can serve two masters: for either he will hate the one, and love the other; or else he will hold to the one, and despise the other. You cannot serve God and mammon. (Matthew 6:24)

Perhaps because these verses are so well-known and do not speak well of our money management, many people believe that the pursuit of wealth is carnal and that money itself is a bad thing. Money is only a means of exchange for goods and services. It is something we all need in order to live in this world. Money is neither good nor bad, it is just a tool to be used. The problem with wealth is the *love* of money. One of the richest men in the world was once asked, "You have more money than you could ever spend, how much more do you need?" His response was, "Just one more dollar." That is a craving, a lust that can never be filled—it is never enough. The desire to acquire wealth just for the sake of having *enough*, which is never enough, is just an altar where a person worships himself.

So these two verses alone will provide us with a misconception of money and how we are to use it. It is important to explore the whole counsel of God to understand how we are to be accountable for our finances and to manage them properly and, yes, biblically. There are also other misconceptions about finance that derive from isolated views. The first is that "if I give, I will receive abundantly." Some have a tendency to *name it and claim it*, when it is in regard to things that we feel may benefit us. We are not so willing to name and claim the many promises about suffering, trial, and tribulation. Though Abraham, Job, and Solomon were immensely wealthy, God does not promise financial prosperity for all believers. It may be His will that you barely make ends meet. It is not important that God does or does not give us bountifully in regard to money; it is important to be good stewards of what He has blessed us with.

How then do families get into financial difficulty? The first is that people are rarely content with what they are blessed with. This means simply that people live above their means to support it. Everyone wants that nice house, or new car, or whatever. Keeping up with the Joneses puts a lot of pressure on the family. Why do we want to look like we are doing well to the neighbors or the world? What makes us want to present a picture that we are better off than we really are? That can be explained in two ways. One, it is because we view success and ultimately our human worth based upon what the world judges is so. Two, it is because the thing that drives that is covetousness. The Bible speaks of this as a great sin. The tenth commandment says, "You shall not covet your neighbor's house; you shall not covet your neighbor's wife, nor his male servant, nor his female servant, nor his ox, nor his donkey, nor anything that is your neighbors" (Exodus 20:17 NKJV).

To covet meant to excessively desire the possessions of another. This is the most ghastly and pitiful expression of self-worship. The apostle Paul ranks covetousness with the most unspeakable sins.

> But fornication and all uncleanness or covetousness, let it not even be named among you, as is fitting for saints. (Ephesians 5:3 NKJV)

> For this you know, that no fornicator, unclean person, nor covetous man, who is an idolater, has any inheritance in the kingdom of Christ and God. (Ephesians 5:5 NKJV)

Now it is not wrong to desire nice things for yourself and your family. It is not wrong to strive for a better life. It is wrong to obtain those things that you cannot afford for the sake of making a false appearance of wealth. It is wrong to be consumed with acquiring more and more wealth to gain a sense of security or ease. Luke wrote regarding this: "For which of you, intending to build a tower, does not sit down first and count the cost, whether he has enough to finish it—lest, after he has laid the foundation, and is not able to finish, all who see it begin to mock him, saying, ;This man began to build and was not able to finish'" (Luke 14:28–29 NKJV).

We live in a generation of *"I want it, and I want it now."* I mean really, is that the expression of a disciplined adult or the ranting of a spoiled child? Let us not be children in our understanding. Paul said, "When I was a child, I spoke as a child, I understood as a child, I though as a child: but when I became a man, I put away childish things" (1 Corinthians 13:11 NKJV).

The second reason people run into financial difficulty is foolish spending. Foolish spending is a discipline problem. In this day of easy credit and multiple charge cards, if we are not wise in how we spend our money and maintain close accountability, we can very quickly find ourselves in trouble. Let me give you an example.

Bill and Jackie are both employed and are paid reasonably well. They are planning their wedding, which is a smart thing to do, but are faced with having to pay for both the wedding and the reception. Sensibly, they understand that it would not be to their benefit to run up a huge debt for the sake of a grand wedding, but plan a wedding that fits comfortably in their budget. Weddings are difficult. It is hard to have to tell family and friends that you would love to have them attend your wedding, but cannot afford to do so. They may be saddened or hurt, but they will get over it. If your family loves you, they will understand. They will also appreciate your honesty and good sense.

It is hard enough to learn how to deal with the many changes being married can bring. Adding a heavy debt to the mix is not wise.

Bob and Maryann are also planning a wedding. They are in the same boat as Bill and Jackie. They have elected to have a grand affair, with all the trimmings, and invite no less than one hundred and fifty people. The wedding is beautiful; the reception is great. Bob and Maryann spend a wonderful week together on a tropical island and return to start their new lives together with a thirty-five-thousand-dollar debt hanging over their heads. Everybody that went to their wedding, both family and friends, will remember this day for years to come, with only thoughts of love. They, however, do not have to pay for it. Though both Bob and Maryann have relatively good, middle-class incomes, it may be hard for them to get a new car or a mortgage on their dream home for ten years or more because of this debt. If they decide to have children, this debt will haunt them. For a big splash that is over in one day, the may have to put other matters on hold for a number of years.

Another problem that is huge today is the one of college student loan debt. College tuition and expenses have skyrocketed and thousands of young people, hoping that their degree with give them a job that pays well, rack up thousands of dollars in debt. Many, after not being able to get *that job,* default on their loans. Bankruptcy does not alleviate their debt and responsibility. Kids getting out of high school sign off on these huge loans feeling that they have no other choice. College is their only hope to make enough money to live well and then retire as early as possible—just what their parents have been urging and counseling them to do. Entering into such debt is a huge decision and responsibility, and it can affect and deter a person's ability to enter into marriage, buy a house, and have children for years.

And then, there is the credit card. Credit spending is *soooo* easy, and many people place items on their cards with every intention of paying it off right away. Actually, very few people have the discipline to follow through with their intentions. Multiple credit cards multiply the problem—enough said. Another problem with credit cards is the bombardment of credit applications received in the mail. I admit that is not as big a problem for me as it was years ago. I have one credit card and I never use it. Credit companies *know* your history, and if you have a number of cards, they will try to get you to add theirs to your stack. Many, if not most, of them make great offers that expire quickly, like lower interest rates or debt consolidation. Then, before you know it the interest is very high.

The temptation to use the plastic to get what you want when you want it, even though you don't have the money on hand, gets a lot of people into a spiraling out of control trouble. The idea that you can buy something on credit and pay for it a little at a time over an extended period sounds good. When you actually compute the cost of such spending, you end up paying a lot more for the item than you dreamed. The most common problem with credit spending is that people run up huge debts and are only able to pay the *minimum charge,* which literally extends the life of that debt into decades and ruins your ability to control your finances.

Foolish spending is simply a problem of misplaced priorities. We need to be adult and wise in our spending, discerning between what we really need and what we merely want.

The third reason people run into financial difficulty is poor planning. Without a plan of action, there is chaos, especially in the role of finances. A good case in point happens around the middle of April every year. This is the time when we must be accountable to Uncle Sam and our state tax collectors. How your income tax return looks is a good judge of whether you are planning and working your finances well. That does not mean that you are taking advantage of every opportunity to avoid paying your rightful taxes, but that you are taking advantage of every opportunity to prepare your return correctly. One of the ways to help judge whether you are in good control of your tax accountability is how much you get back or how much you owe on your return. The best way to end up is that you don't owe or get back very much. That means that you have it figured pretty close. If you are getting a huge amount back, you are letting the government hold too much of your money that you can be using for other things. On the other hand, if you owe tons of money, you aren't withholding enough.

Now I know that there are a lot of people that like to get that big check from the government. Some say it is because they would not be able to save that money through the year. Some look forward to it and then blow it on a big vacation like a cruise or a big dollar item that they want. If they saved up for it, they might get more than they would in interest than letting the government blow it on whatever they want; although, these days the interest is really very low. Still, it is a good discipline to save up to buy things and patiently wait until you have the cash to do it. That is how it was done before credit cards came into existence. It took planning, patience, determination, and discipline. With that came the enormous satisfaction of accomplishing a difficult goal.

How then do we deal with our finances? It is often very easy to point the finger at what the problem is but hard to find a good, workable solution. For those of us that may have already found ourselves in money troubles, there is hope, but it will take diligent care, stern discipline, and time. The best advice I can give is to seek and find the counsel of a good, professional financial planner. They can show ways in which you can work out a long-term goal for debt settlement and financial health.

The best way to solve or prevent the problems that we have just looked at is to establish a financial plan that fits your income. Like I said, the best way to do that is through professional help. It is always to your benefit to work on a budget. A budget is nothing more than taking account of all of the money you earn over a specified period of time and determining how that money will be spent. This should be done with the advice and consent of the spouse, and it may be wise to include the children so they can know about the limitations your income holds.

If you are going to allow credit spending, there are some pretty simple rules to follow. First, have only one card, preferably one that requires full payment of debt every billing cycle. If you have ten credit cards, you need to choose one, then cut the others into tiny bits with a nice sharp pair of scissors and throw them away. Secondly, do not buy anything on the card without the advised consent of your spouse. Have a no-use-without-thorough-discussion rule apply to that card. Thirdly, do not buy anything on your card that is consumable, such as gasoline or food. Many banks offer debit cards, which comes right out of your checking account. This is a great convenience, as long as you record or carefully manage how much you use it.

Do not buy impulsively. If you need to purchase something, do your homework: shop for the best price, wait for the sale. Here is a story about dear friends, Bob and Sally.

Bob and Sally decided they needed to purchase some furniture for their dining room. They saved for some time and were then prepared to spend it on table and chairs. Now Sally is the best, shrewdest, and most tireless shopper in the world. There is no end to the length she will go to get exactly what she wants at the very best price. On their quest for furniture, they went through catalogs and showrooms, looking at what they liked and could afford. They compared different styles, manufacturers, and quality. They visited every furniture store in the entire county where they live at least three times each. Sally had a notebook filled with vast amounts of information they received, and when they had exhausted every area of possibility, they sat down and discussed it. At long last they had decided on manufacturer, style, color, and so on. The last thing they did was call the manufacturer and ordered the dining room set direct. That alone saved them hundreds of dollars, though they had to wait a few weeks for the furniture to arrive. It was hard work, but they also had a lot of fun and it was well worth the trouble.

My wife and I plan every major purchase very much the same way. You can plan for major purchases and budget savings toward that goal. In our house, we don't use the credit card at all. It is kept "for emergency use only." If something pops us, like the refrigerator dies or some other emergency, if we cannot pay for it directly out of our savings, we talk about it. If we agree it is absolutely necessary, because of an immediate need, we do it. Though our income is sufficient, we are neither poor nor rich, by any means, we live on a budget, plan well, and save. We are content to live with the blessings God has given us. We have one credit card, and she carries it. I have one, but I am not allowed to use it.

There is also another principle of finance that we have in our home. It is a principle of honor and love. The principle is simply this: the husband honors the wife with all of the fruits of his labor, for her control, and she honors the husband by doing the very best with what he has provided. Now, in this day and time, that is a little old-fashioned. Many families have both spouses working and have two incomes. The principle is still the same, regardless of who the provider is and who manages the finances. If you are the manager, it is your responsibility to honor the labors of those who contribute all of their earnings to you. If you both have incomes it goes in one pot. The household and family income is *all* from both. In that way you honor each other. It is a commitment made to everyone in the family without *self-consideration*.

If there is a serious financial problem, like accumulated debt perhaps caused by selfish ambition or waste, it can take a long time to fix. Expert guidance can help make a plan to see this through, and for a person who desires to bring his family under the blessings of God, commitment and discipline are essential. Live within your means.

Remember that it is the Lord God who provides all that we have and we should honor that blessing with regular tithes and offerings. Trust in Him to bless you and be content with what He has. You may not get everything that you want, but He promises to give you all that you need.

Being good stewards of His blessings is also being able to know the traps and pitfalls of bad money management and avoid them. God will give us the wisdom to control our finances if we obey His Word and be faithful in the small things.

Other Applications

The model I used for the recovered self-worshipper being restored the family was the husband and father. The perspective and application was directed, for the purpose of this writing, to the male head of the household. Though it was directed as such, the same principles may be adopted for counseling other family members with some variation. The other necessary applications would be directed to the wife and mother, the son or daughter, or even to a fallen church member being restored to fellowship with his or her church. For the remainder of this chapter, we will look briefly at how the principles and issues may be modified to be applicable to other family members.

Wives and Mothers

The unique position and role of the wife and mother has always been regarded as a sacred thing in our society. The image of the mother has always been one of purity and goodness; an image protected and preserved at any cost. For this reason, many of the abusive behaviors that are due to the matriarchy are overlooked or secreted away. The families of abusive wives and mothers would rather face the pain and difficulty of living with an *addict* than face the shame of exposing her. The two most horrifying words that can ever be used as a label are "unfit mother." This is a legal term, which is in actuality a sentence upon a woman. In New York State, women are given an extraordinary amount of leeway in regard to the custody of children. Every possible avenue is explored and exploited to give opportunity for the mother to set her course right.

My late wife and I were foster parents in Monroe County of New York many years ago. We were amazed at the number of opportunities and advantages that were offered by the Department of Social Services to mothers, that they might have their children restored to them. It is truly a wonderful thing. Sadly, there are many cases where, after months of wasted opportunities and intervention by social services, the mothers cannot gain enough control of their lives to justify and enable restoration.

Many times, the family will offer the mother as many opportunities to be restored as the government does—perhaps even more. They will be willing to overlook setbacks and failures and less likely to report them when they occur. This makes the job of the counselor more difficult in monitoring the progress and process of restoration.

The same principles that are used for the husband and father must be applied to the wife and mother. The principles of surrender, disarmament, and occupation are equally applicable in each case. Though the role of the mother may cause some variation in the details, it is important to understand that in the Christian marriage, husband and wife are coregent and equal. What is good for the goose is also good for the gander, as the saying goes. Paul wrote, "There is neither Jew nor Greek, there is neither bond nor free, there is neither male nor female: for you are all one in Christ Jesus" (Galatians 3:28).

There is, or should be, no distinction between male and female in respect to recovery from addictive behaviors or restoration of the family. It is true that God created man first and that the individual roles assigned to man and woman are different according to the will of God, but difference does not mean inequality. In fact, equality between the sexes only exists in the Christian worldview. The status and equality experienced by American women is not found in many other cultures.

The same issues of trust and betrayal, faithfulness, submission and control, etc., are applicable to any member of a family.

The restoration of the wife and mother to her proper biblical role is complicated by our present cultural norms, as I said. Not all moms are stay-at-home, baby-raising, soccer moms. Many wives and mothers spend as much or more time away from the household as the husband and father. Many are in the workplace by either necessity or choice. It is not my intent to judge whether or not a mom stays at home, homeschools her kids, or sings in the choir. Though the traditions of some Christian groups celebrate this and hold that this is the proper role for women, it is not really a biblical perspective. The role of the wife and mother is to be a companion to her husband, a model for her children, and most importantly, a faithful servant of her Lord. It is a role of responsibility, honor, and respect. So whether mom works or not is not an issue of restoration to a biblical role. It is so important to assert this when counseling, particularly when the couple is being counseled together, to dispel any notions of forcing a woman to conform to a particular "Christian model" of a wife and mother. It is not un-Christian to disagree with that model.

One of the difficult issues of restoring a wife and mother to her proper biblical role is the issue of forgiveness. This is a difficult issue on any perspective, but because so much emphasis is placed upon the image of the American mother, when that image is stained, the sheer weight of our cultural mores causes a persistent, bitter attitude in many family members. For some odd reason there is an understanding that even if the father is a drunk, womanizer, or whatever, the core unit of the family can survive because of the strength of mom. However, if it is the mom that is the drunk or is promiscuous or unfaithful, it seems to be more devastating to the family. Because of this *cultural* inequality, the crimes committed against the family by the mother are more shameful and less forgivable. Though in essence, the offences committed are no worse than that of the father, cultural attitudes force us down another avenue of counseling.

The issue of forgiveness is paramount to the restoration of the wife and mother and requires careful and perhaps extended counseling for the entire family. Older children may have a difficult time forgiving the mother because of the image that has been destroyed. They will look at the mom as "damaged goods" and may be overly harsh or critical in their judgment. It cannot be too strongly emphasized that though she is *the mom,* she is also a person, subject to the same failings and temptations as anyone else. Though her standing and position is elevated in the home, the family, and the community, she is no better that any other poor sinner trying to make their way.

Because they are persons with the same frailties, feelings, misjudgments, and capabilities as the rest of us, they should not be judged any differently.

The difficult issues of trust, betrayal, and forgiveness are not insurmountable. Even the terrible stigma and devastation of adultery is not impossible to overcome.

When I spoke of the different avenues of counseling, it is in respect to a choice that must and can only be made by the spouse. The issue is the one of adultery. Biblically, adultery is the only justifiable cause for divorce. If a person abuses the family relationship through truancy, drug or alcohol use, or the many other abuses that are associated with addictive behaviors, they are hardly grounds for divorce. These are problems that can be worked out. The seemingly insurmountable problem of sexual infidelity is different because adultery strikes at the very heart of the family relationship. For this reason, the road to recovery for the family has a fork in it. The one fork is biblically supported divorce, with the family trying to pick up the pieces of what remains. The other is the road of biblically supported forgiveness. Both are difficult avenues to follow. We find ourselves standing at the crossroads of the yellow brick road, as Dorothy in *The Wizard of Oz,* not knowing which path to follow. We, as she, were instructed only to follow the one road (in our case, the yellow brick road is sound biblical counsel). Both paths will eventually lead to the Emerald City, but choosing the best way is hard. Sadly, many choose the same way Dorothy did—by taking the counsel of a person with no brains. It is not a decision that can be made by anyone but the person that must walk down that path. As counselors, we can only suggest what the consequences will be for each path. We shouldn't recommend which one to take, unless we want to end up looking too much like the scarecrow.

If the offending spouse, having recovered from his or her self-worship by receiving Christ as Savior, sincerely seeks restoration with the family, for the sake of the repentant offender counsel can be made to the spouse and family to encourage them to forgive and restore. The best example I can think of is in Paul's letter to the Corinthians, when a man who had committed acts worthy of having fellowship broken with the church repented, desiring to be brought back into fellowship. Paul encouraged the church to restore him for his sake: "This punishment which was inflicted by the majority is sufficient for such a man, so that, on the contrary, you ought rather to forgive and comfort him, lest perhaps such a one be swallowed up with too much sorrow" (2 Corinthians 2:6–7 NKJV).

If the husband, in this case, chooses biblical divorce, it must be respected. The counselor will be faced with helping the recovered wife deal with the consequences of her addictive behaviors and abuses (losing her family through divorce) and perhaps to help the family deal with divorce as well. If forgiveness and restoration are chosen, then the road to wellness will probably involve counseling the whole family.

Sons and Daughters

For sons and daughters that have been separated from their families because of their addictive abuses, the greatest issue that faces them in their desire to be reconciled to the family is a sense of powerlessness. Children that have rebelled against the authority of the parents often do so because they have never been able to voice their hurts honestly with them without a lot of emotion and frustration. The parents are the authority, and what they say goes. For the child, strict obedience is required and the point of view of the child is not regarded. Rebellion and addictive behaviors are both about the self and may even feed off of each other. That does not mean that all cases of addictive behaviors are related to issues of rebellion against the parent. They are rebellion against God. Whatever the cause, the fact that there exists a break in the family by a child's abusive activities shows a lack of communication and inclusion. The break in that relationship often begins long before it reaches the point of rebellion and addictive behavior.

Having been a teenager involved in illicit activity and living a life completely separated from the knowledge of my parents and then having the payback of parenting teens of my own has given me some insight on the problem of communication. It is incredibly easy for a teenager and his or her parents to drift away from each other to the point that their lives are separate from the other, though they live in the same house. Teenagers will naturally become more independent, which is a good thing, to help them prepare for life outside of parental control as adults. For the parents, the absolute authority they had over the infant and young child is rarely challenged, and the parents slip into a sort of parental cruise control. While they are comfortable in their parenting style, time rushes past them and the child, who was once easy to take care of, grows into and independently minded, hormone-driven semi-adult who begins to resent an authoritarian relationship with the parents.

Secondly, there is probably no time in life as challenging as the teen years. Many look back and say, "Ah, things were so great when I was a teen; they were the best years of my life." Ask a teenager if he or she is enjoying the *best years of their life*. You will more than likely get a far different response than one steeped in nostalgia. In fact, for most teens, it is the worst time of their life. They are torn between childhood and adulthood, desperately trying to find out who they are and where and how they will fit in with their peers. The teen years are the open cocoon of a life that is metamorphosing from infancy to adulthood. The changes in the life of an individual are drastic and are made even more so by external pressures. There are physical changes that can cause varying degrees of pressure, such as acne, early maturation, or late maturation, awkwardness, dental realignment, etc. Every aspect of a person's developing life, whether it is physical, social, emotional, or even intellectual, is under the hypercritical eye of the peer group.

Teens have an acute desire to become something that they find an attractive, acceptable model, but are presented with an unmistakable reality that they will probably not fit that model. The teen years are a desperate search for identity, acceptability, and value. When you add all of the pressures together, it is easy to see how many teens are introduced to and quickly adopt selfish addictive behaviors.

Although we are, by our own fallen nature, inclined toward addictive behaviors, many of the more dangerous or risky addictive behaviors are commonly entered into as a means to find acceptance or initiation into a particular group. The attraction for risky or counter cultural activities creates excitement and a little fear. *Taking the dare* in these behaviors, particularly in drugs and alcohol use, gains acceptability in the group. The three main social drives are: acceptability, being "cool"; entertainment, being "risky"; or escape, being "comforted." Sadly, the long-term results are just the opposite. Instead of acceptance, there is rejection. Instead of entertainment, there is isolation. Instead of comfort, there is dependency and fear. For a developing teenager, these behaviors are dangerous, both physically and psychologically. Physically, the brain is not fully formed until around the age of twenty-three, and the use of drugs and alcohol can not only delay this development but may impair it permanently. Psychologically, the end result of these behaviors is defeat and a loss of sense of value or worth. This is a no-win situation, and those who are ensnared by it realize it but feel trapped. This only increases that sense of powerlessness.

It may be hard to convey this to a family that has been abused by a rebellious teen, because their experience with the teen has been one of deceit, aggression, manipulation, and isolation. For the family, these trademarks of the abuser appear as power. It is common for the parents to feel that they are the ones who are powerless in the situation. They feel powerless because their son or daughter has taken a destructive path that they feel strongly against but are unable to effect any change. They don't know what to do or where to turn. The only authority they have left over the teen is to banish them. That is the common response, and it is one that defeats both parents and teen and builds a wall against reconciliation. The parents say, "Honey, you know that we love you, but we can't deal with this anymore, you have to go."

In far too many counseling situations involving abusive children and family, this is the common problem. Power and authority must be restored to the parents, and a sense of individual control must be restored to the teen.

For the parents, the issues of trust and accessibility put forward in the case of *husband and father* equally apply. Surrender, disarmament, and occupation gives the parents the power and authority needed to make them feel secure in reestablishing a relationship with their son or daughter, who is seeking to be restored.

For the child, they must learn that power can be exercised in a new and unique way. Power does not have to be exercised by aggression or strife to verify its presence. Power can best be exercised by choice and restraint. A person that violently opposes authority for the sake of demonstrating power does not have power. True power comes in the ability to make reasonable choices for the betterment of self, of others, and of relationships.

This may mean accepting correction or discipline or just being teachable. Jesus manifested His power and authority in humility and meekness. He did not have to subject Himself to humanity, to the frailty of human life, but He chose to do it for the sake of man.

Jesus exercised great power in meekness. It is important to understand the significant difference between true meekness and what the world perceives as meekness. Meekness is not weakness, as it is often perceived. In fact, meekness requires strength, fortitude, character, and power. Meekness is perfectly demonstrated in Jesus's willing submission to His Father's will, knowing fully what that meant. It meant rejection, humiliation, torture, and the death of the cross. His prayer in the garden was pure strength: "And He was withdrawn from them about a stone's throw, and He knelt down and prayed, saying, 'Father, if it is Your will, take this cup from Me; nevertheless not My will, but Yours, be done'" (Luke 12:41–42).

Jesus knew exactly what He had to face and endure for the will of His Father. He understood the need for His obedience to His Father's will and authority, for the sake of the salvation of mankind, and He chose to be obedient, submitting Himself to the Father. This is the greatest exercise of individual power ever recorded or experienced.

For the teen or young adult who has received Christ as Lord and Savior, recovered from his or her addictive self-worship and abuses to the point where they desire reconciliation with the family, it is vital to insure that the necessary steps imposed on him or her do not construe defeat. Surrender, disarmament, and occupation are mutually agreed upon as terms for reconciliation. The ability to agree to terms is an exercise of power through choice. The child has a say in his or her behavior, in the individual responsibility to himself or herself, and to the parents.

For the parents, the security of the agreement allows the opportunity to establish a good relationship with the son or daughter through communication and respect, not commandment and expectation.

And so It Goes

It is impossible to deny the incredible transformation a person goes through when Jesus Christ becomes the focus of their life. Whether it is a husband and father, wife and mother, or son or daughter, the testimony of a life rescued from self-worship and addictive behaviors is powerful. The only tried and true solution to the problem is a personal relationship with Jesus Christ. There is no human power or will that is able to break the chains of addiction—no heart strong enough to turn away from its selfish desire, no one righteous enough to transform themselves into the person God wants them to be. As it is written:

> Who can bring a clean thing out of an unclean? Not one. (Job 14:4)

> There is none righteous, no, not one; there is none who understands; there is none who seeks after God. (Romans 3:10–11)

> I am the vine, you are the branches; he that abides in Me and I in him, he bears much fruit, for apart from Me you can do nothing. (John 15:5 NASB)

We know that what is impossible for man is possible for God and that Jesus Christ will set us free and give us strength to walk in newness of life. We can only make shipwreck of our lives, but the Lord can save us, make us new, and give us abundant life.

As the apostle Paul wrote: "I can do all things through Christ who strengthens me" (Philippians 4:13 NKJV).

Appendix: Addressing Counseling Problems

The Nature of the Beast

For many of us, the incredibly complex world of addiction and addictive behavior is something that seems quite foreign to our understanding. The associated behaviors that make up the egocentric universe are extreme to a degree beyond our comprehension and capability. Because of this, it is difficult to establish and maintain a good working relationship with people coming out of addiction. Ordinary matters such as trust, communication, responsibility, obedience, and consistency (matters so basic to Christian fellowship) are for the self-worshipping addict objects to be avoided or worked around. These are challenges and problems for the addict to dodge and slip past in order to maintain his or her lifestyle. They become remarkably skilled at it and are masters of manipulation.

Just as any other sinner, coming to salvation and a new life in Christ is still far from perfection; those coming from a lifestyle of addiction and self-worship are too. We may have walked and matured in Christ for many years but would still blush at the thought that we may have *arrived*. This is rightfully so, for there is no one who is beyond sin but the dead. After receiving Christ as Savior we all bring the latent behaviors from our past with us. It is odd that when we become believers, God gives us a new nature, a nature of obedience, but He doesn't take the old nature, the *old man*, as Paul put it, away. We are freed from the penalty of our sin and from the power of sin over us, but we can still commit sin and do. This is why we need to be disciple, why sanctification is a process. The funny part is this, that

235

RONALD J. MORSE, PHD

all lost sinners need Christ and all Christians need counseling. Can you think of anyone who has reached a point where there is nothing left to learn or that the Spirit no longer has need of conviction?

We understand that in ourselves, though we do our best, we are not yet perfect. Because of this we still need grace—lots and lots of grace. If we are still in such need of grace, what about the person who has come from a life of self-worship, sin, and blasphemy?

Some old behaviors die hard, and those associated with this egocentric life, recognizing or respecting no authority greater than the self, can be real die-hard. We are not asking someone to just drop a bad habit, but to alter every facet of his or her life—to think, live, and act in a manner that is opposite to his or her well-established manner! Truly, only the Holy Spirit can do such work.

Grace upon Grace

One of the frustrating parts of ministry, where we try to encourage others to live a more productive life in Christ, is that they rarely meet *our* expectations. That is, we spend a great deal of time and energy counseling and instructing others so their lives will be blessed and happier, and they do not respond to the counseling as we wish they would. Part of our frustration comes from knowing what the Scriptures say about sin, such as *John 5:14 and 8:11*. The command "Go, and sin no more" seems very clear. It is just as clear as Genesis 17:1 where God commands Abram to "Walk before Me, and be thou perfect." In respect to the commandment to Abram, we know that he was not perfect the rest of his days. It is reasonable to assume that the man healed from palsy and the adulteress also lived imperfect lives. It is also reasonable to say that from that point in each of those three lives, the lives of each was drastically altered. Though they did both live perfect lives, they most certainly lived *better* lives. All believers who set on a new life course in Christ will see their lives get better. Some will resist the work of the Spirit, fighting against the conforming into the image of the Son, and will suffer because of it. We all resist God's conforming in one way or another; that is just our old nature. It is a nature we struggle with all of our lives. What is important is that God is continually gracious to us whether we allow His conforming work or fight Him tooth and nail.

As God is so ever gracious to us, we must also be gracious to those we are trying to help and disciple. There *are* going to be setbacks and failures. It may take going through the counseling program several times, with a lot of support and encouragement for some to make it. There will be some that may go for quite a while doing great and suddenly fall. These things happen, and not everyone will respond the same way. It's OK. The ministry is not for us—it is for them. We do not profit or benefit from the ministry, with the exception of the incredible satisfaction and joy in seeing a ruined life made new.

This of course brings us to the subject of discipline. It is ineffective and inappropriate to exercise disciplinary authority over those who are being counseled from an addictive lifestyle. It is appropriate, however, to exercise proper church discipline on a member of the church when their repeated behaviors can be construed as defiance to the counseling program. It is a fuzzy area, one that needs to be administered with much grace and more prayer. As a counselor and member of a church ministry, you are subject to the authority of the pastor. It is part of his responsibility to monitor the conduct of church members that desire to remain in fellowship with the church body. Deliberate sin and defiance of counsel should be a matter of concern for the pastor. He cannot allow sin to go without being addressed. If there is a member under your counseling that is exhibiting such behavior, the pastor must be brought in to discuss disciplinary measures. Everything must be done in proper order, in accordance with scriptural principles, such as those found in Matthew 18:15–17. It is appropriate for a counselor to admonish, exhort, or rebuke a counselee in the manner of their conduct; that is part of the counseling experience. If the counselee receives the rebuke, repents, and genuinely shows a cooperative attitude, then the matter is settled. Secular agencies that deal with drug and alcohol abusers use the term "compliance." If there is "noncompliance," meaning the behaviors are not changed and there is no evidence of repentance, then the pastor must be brought in.

Oddly enough, when the matter falls into the realm of the church and church leadership, you as a counselor then become an advocate or the counselee. The counselee must understand that you are on his or her side and that you are genuinely concerned for their spiritual welfare. It would be disastrous for that person if you were to sever a relationship you both worked hard to establish. This does not mean that you oppose the pastor of church discipline, but that you *counsel through* the discipline, never releasing or giving up on the counselee. Accepting responsibility for our actions is the first part of learning to be a responsible person. The counselee must know that you are trying to help them learn to be responsible. At some point, they will probably get with the program. It is impossible to determine exactly when that will happen; it is different for every person. Of course, there will be those who decide to break fellowship and go their own way. Those we must let go, but do keep the phone lines open. The apostle John aptly describes them: "They went out from us, but they were not of us; for if they had been of us, they would have continued with us; but they went out that they might be manifest, that none of them were of us" (1 John 2:19).

According to Matthew 18:17, rebellious persons that would not repent were to be considered as unbelievers. Well, what do we do with unbelievers? We give them the gospel and hopefully lead them to the Lord.

Preventive Measures

Obviously, the counseling experience will not be the same for everyone. Many, if not most, individuals coming into the ministry will do very well from the start. After all, participating in the ministry is voluntary. People enter the ministry looking for help, for answers, and because they are tired of the life of failure, denial, and pain.

There are tools we may employ that will help to make that necessary connection with the counselee—tools and methods that can break down walls and build bridges. As with any other major construction project, it requires commitment, time, and effort.

There are four tools that I use that work very well for me and have proven to work in even some of the more resistant cases. They are the four *A's* of addiction counseling:

1. acceptability
2. accessibility
3. accountability
4. adaptability

Acceptability. One of the first things that would instantly disqualify a counselor from effectiveness is an attitude of authority. People coming out of a lifestyle of self-worship have a history of hating and rebelling against any authority that would impose on what they want to do. In many cases, this rebellion begins at an early age and is directed against the parents. Imagine, if you will, a twenty-seven-year-old man who has come for counseling and restoration. Since the age of twelve, he has rebelled against the authority of his parents, his teachers, his friends, and his employers. Is it more than coincidence that many guys that are caught in drug or alcohol abuses are self-employed? They are roofers, carpenters, masons, or some other handicraft. They do their best to make their way using their skills, without having to answer to a boss. Now, this young man comes to the saving knowledge of Jesus Christ and desires counseling to help him deal with the necessary life changes that come as a part of leaving a life of self-worship and defeat, to a life of victory in Christ. As a newborn babe in Christ, he is still carrying the many years of distrust of authority and a tendency to *duck and cover.* There is also another hurdle to overcome, which is that he may be twenty-seven, but developmentally only about twelve or thirteen.

Let's look at one of the many cases I have encountered with this experience:

This twenty-seven-year-old (we will call him Scott) had been using hard drugs since he was twelve. His family situation was that he had no father present in his life and, at that tender age of twelve, began his rebellion. He had spent years caught in the trap of severe drug abuse. At twenty-seven, he came to know Christ in jail and began his long journey of recovery. After his release, he became a member of my church and eventually, my family. I remember, having him over for a meal one day that he was sitting on the floor with my youngest daughter and they were playing video games and eating candy. The game was *Donkey Kong,* I believe. They were having a great time, with a lot of laughing and so on. What I found amazing was that though he was a fully grown man, he interacted with my daughter as though he was the same age as her. Now, she was only about ten at the time. I did a lot of research and talked to a lot of very qualified people and discovered that when he began using those hard drugs, he ceased to develop intellectually, emotionally, and socially. He was still a *twelve-year-old kid* in a grown man's body. He talked like a twelve-year-old, displayed a lack of emotional control, like a pre-teen, and reacted to situations the same way. As we continued in counseling I explained this to him, and he understood. It took years for him to *catch up,* so to speak, and even in his late thirties, he was still like a late teenager. He may never fully develop, but he is certainly doing much better. Today, he is married with a couple of beautiful children that he absolutely adores and still following Christ.

In order for a relationship to be established where trust on the part of the counselee is earned, and also on the part of the counselor, it must be based on mutual acceptance. The counselor accepts the counselee as a person who has come for help. For our part, we must take a little risk. We accept the counselee as not only a person in trouble, but as a brother in Christ and a friend. We must be careful not to present a lot of expectations or demands. We have what they want, but they are somewhat reluctant to take it. We offer friendship, fellowship, and information that is vital to their recovery and understanding the nature of their problem. This we give freely without making demands. They must choose to receive it and become involved in active participation. As the relationship develops, they will come to the conclusion that they need what you are giving out so freely. They will eventually become more comfortable in the relationship and, by their own determination, submit themselves to a relationship where you have some authority. Their transformation is from a life that is all about them, where they have the absolute authority, make all the rules, and do not trust or regard others. This change is gradual and, for some, may mean leaving the counseling ministry and returning perhaps three or four times. As they learn to walk in faith and trust in Jesus Christ, they will also learn to submit to His authority and also to accept the authority of others. You can be sure that your acceptability to them will be tested regularly and frequently until they decide it is safe to trust you.

Accessibility. It never surprises me to find that people that are in an extremely egocentric lifestyle, that are also living in *survival mode,* are so needy and dependent. When a person decides to battle the dragon of the self and live free in Christ, they are often overwhelmed by their own weakness. There is nothing as frightening as trying to gain control over your life, when there is something else that controls you. In addictive behaviors, there are generally two controlling factors. The first is chemical dependency, which we have looked at previously. Chemical dependency is terrible but not insurmountable. Within a few days you can be detoxified from nearly every known substance. A heavy smoker that quits cold turkey is absolutely miserable for about ten to twelve days. After that, the urges and cravings subside. Chemical dependency is not the greatest obstacle; it is psychological dependency that makes it so difficult. What frightens people in recovery the most is that the dragon they are battling with is their own mind. Years ago, there was a comic strip called *Pogo* and Pogo with his friends were standing a looking at their reflection in a pool of water. They were all dressed for some type of battle, with helmets, shields, and weapons. The caption read, "We have met the enemy, and he is us."

The battle over the old man, the self, rages at peculiar times. Moments of struggle, temptation, and weakness often come when a person is alone or has empty time on their hands. It is at these times that they need to reach out for help. We, or someone else that is trusted, are that help. We must be accessible (within reason of course) to comfort, counsel, or intervene when called upon. Though it has happened rarely (thank God), I have had to go out in the wee hours to talk and pray with someone over a cup of coffee. Most of the time, a few minutes on the phone can make the difference between victory and failure.

Being accessible does not mean that we have to sit by the phone in case someone calls. It may mean having to provide occasional extraordinary care, but that should be both occasional and extraordinary. Accessibility is an attitude of openness. A counselee should feel comfortable about talking to you and not feel embarrassed to call on you. We, for the most part, are not professionals that are paid exorbitant fees for solving problems and cut you off when the time is up. The relationship between counselor and counselee exceeds the normal bounds of "professional use only." We get down in the gutters and pull them out. It is a relationship of brother or sister in the Lord. We don't help them because it is our job, or even ministry; we help them because we love them.

Accountability. In a nutshell, accountability is the ability to show that you do what you say. When a person is accountable to another in a relationship, they are open, honest, and willing to lay the cards on the table. It is absolutely necessary for a counselee to be accountable to his or her counselor. There is no room for intrigue. The most effective relationship a counselor has with a counselee is one that is based on mutual trust and respect. Accountability is most effective when it is also mutually exercised. However, things that are required from a counselee for accountability are different than those required of the counselor.

The counselor may realistically impose a number of activities that are mutually agreed upon for the counselee that range from accounting for time, whereabouts, and associations, to verifying communications between them and even for paychecks and family involvement. It is vital that they know that they are coming from a position of untrustworthiness to being trusted. This must be earned, and if the person is sincere about their restoration, they will agree. As trust is built and time in the ministry shows that the counselee is doing well, it is important to lighten up on the reins a bit, as a sign that trust *is* being established. In one instance, a man grudgingly agreed to my request that he called me three times a day to let me know how he was doing. After a few days, we agreed to one call a day, then every other day, until contact was made during sessions or once a week. He eventually looked forward to calling, just to let me know how good things were going or if he was struggling.

Accountability also works the other way, and there are two areas in which a counselee may hold and counselor accountable. The first, and most important is what secular agencies and professionals commonly call counselor-client privilege. That privilege is that the counselors receive sensitive, personal, and private information that should never be disclosed to anyone else without the expressed consent of the counselee. I had, through the Rochester Drug Treatment Court, worked with several secular agencies. Their greatest fear in working with faith-based groups was the sensitivity of that privilege. They are bonded by law and license to hold that privilege, but are unaware of whether faith-based counselors are as well. We are also held to that standard, but also a much higher authority binds us and the relationship that we have in trust must never be broken. As any true friend would hold the confidence of another with fierce guardedness, so must we hold private what is given privately.

The second area of accountability is faithfulness to commitments. If we make a commitment to be somewhere or to do something that is important to the counselee, we must be faithful to those commitments. If you make an arrangement with someone to have them call you at a specific time, it is essential that you are there to answer the phone and engage in conversation. One of the greatest drawbacks I have encountered with some groups, where they employ sponsors for individuals, is the unreliability of the sponsors. Lots of times, when I deal with people that have been to these groups previously and have had terrible times with their sponsors, they are reluctant to give their trust in an accountability relationship because they have been burned. It is hard to establish trust in those cases.

Adaptability. Counseling is a unique ministry and there is very little in it that is carved in stone. The Word of God is our basis and standard for the ministry, and that is unchangeable. However, what works in the application of those standards for one may not work for another. Every individual has needs and problems that are unique to him or her alone. In teaching the eight initial sessions of the CLEAN ministry, I have had more people get stuck in session three than anywhere else. The application or the actual working through the session may be different, having to be tailor-made for some to get it. This doesn't mean that the information is changed, but that the application of that information into life. These are people who have come out of a totally self-absorbed life, into a new life in Christ. Learning how to deal with temptation and conditioned responses can be challenging.

There will always be difficulty in a ministry of this type. There will be failures and challenges. The very best counsel in the world is useless if it is not followed. If a person comes into the ministry as a sincere believer in Christ as Savior, it will work. It may not work the first or even second time, but it will work. This is because the power and effectiveness for the ministry does not come from anywhere but the Holy Spirit. If we do our best, for our part, to be acceptable, accessible, accountable, and adaptable, we will not get in the way of the Spirit, who does the work of recovery. For only a new life in Christ and the indwelling Spirit can change a person from what he was into what God wants him to be.

References

Anderson, Neil T. 1996. *Freedom from Addiction*. Ventura. Regal Books.

Campbell, Ross. 1996. *How to Really Love Your Child*. Wheaton. Inspirational Books.

Collins, Gary R. 1988. *Christian Counseling*. Dallas. Word Publishing.

Farrar, Steven. 1990. *Point Man: How a Man Can Lead His Family*. Colorado Springs. Multnomah Books.

Priolo, Lou. 1996. *How to Help Angry Kids*. Alabama City. S.E.L.F. Publications.

Priolo, Lou. 2000. *Teach Them Diligently*. Timeless Text.

Tripp, Ted. 1995. *Shepherding a Child's Heart*. Wapwallopen. Shepherd Press.

Welch, Edward T. 1995. *Addictive Behavior*. Grand Rapids. Baker Books.

Zodhiates, Spiros. 1994. *The Complete Word Study of the Old and New Testaments*. Chattanooga. AMG International.

The American Heritage Dictionary. 1982, 1985. Boston. Houghton Mifflin Co.

ESV Holy Bible, English Standard Version. 2003. Crossway. Wheaton.

NASB New American Standard Bible. 1996. Anaheim. The Lockman Foundation.

NKJV Holy Bible, New King James Version. 1994. Nashville. Thomas Nelson.

NLT Holy Bible, New Living Translation. 1996. Carol Stream. Tyndale House.

All Biblical references unless otherwise noted are from the Holy Bible, King James Version.

Zacharias, Ravi. RZIM.org

About the Author

Ron has been in ministry for thirty years and has served as a full-time pastor for seventeen years in Rochester, New York, and also as a biblical counselor for twenty-five years. He has an earned PhD in psychology and Christian counseling from Louisiana Baptist University and currently serves as a chaplain with the Good News Jail and Prison Ministry, where he served in Rochester, New York, and currently in the Aiken County Detention Center. Ron lives in Aiken, South Carolina, with his wife, Cindy. They have five children and seven grandchildren.

CPSIA information can be obtained
at www.ICGtesting.com
Printed in the USA
LVHW032243040223
738685LV00021B/280